Conundrums of Humanity

# The Raoul Wallenberg Institute Human Rights Library

VOLUME 28

# Conundrums of Humanity

## The Quest for Global Justice

*by*

Jonathan Power

MARTINUS
NIJHOFF
PUBLISHERS

LEIDEN · BOSTON
2007

Printed on acid-free paper.

A C.I.P. record for this book is available from the Library of Congress.

и⌐

ISBN 978 90 04 15513 8

© 2007 by Koninklijke Brill NV, Leiden, The Netherlands.

Koninklijke Brill NV incorporates the imprints Brill, Hotei Publishers, IDC Publishers, Martinus Nijhoff Publishers and VSP.

http://www.brill.nl

Typeset by jules guldenmund layout & text, The Hague

PRINTED AND BOUND IN THE NETHERLANDS.

For Jeany

# Table of Contents

# Foreword

Long before meeting Jonathan Power, I knew his name from opinion page columns on foreign affairs in the *International Herald Tribune* and from his most recent book, *Like Water on Stone, A History of Amnesty International*. (London: Allen Lane, The Penguin Press, 2001). These writings made me and many others in the human rights movement aware of his strong interest and deep insights into human rights issues.

In the present book, *Conundrums of Humanity*, Jonathan Power covers a wide range of topics by posing eleven thoughtful and provocative questions that are facing the international community. Some of these questions and his answers to them directly address human rights, and all of them have pertinent human rights aspects that are highly relevant at a time when international organizations, for good reason, are wanting to mainstream human rights throughout their varied activities.

It is a pleasure and a privilege to invite Jonathan Power to publish this book in the Human Rights Library (blue series) of the Raoul Wallenberg Institute of Human Rights and Humanitarian Law (RWI). Over a period of ten years, some 30 volumes have appeared in this and other RWI series under the imprint of Martinus Nijhoff Publishers (www.rwi.lu.se/publications). This volume is different from many of the previous ones whose authors and editors have for the most part presented academic texts. This book is a distinguished journalist's well-informed "take" on the world we now inhabitat, written in a light, accessible but rigorously analytical style, one that academics could usefully emulate!

*Conundrums of Humanity*, with an experienced foreign correspondent and columnist identifying several challenges that will certainly influence the realization of human rights, is therefore a welcome and valuable addition to our publication list. The author's forward-looking, realistic and ultimately optimistic assessment is an encouragement to us all.

Gudmundur Alfredsson,
Director, Raoul Wallenberg Institute for
Human Rights and Humanitarian Law,
University Of Lund, Sweden.

ڧ  ڧى

# Acknowledgements

First a thank you to Professor Gudmundur Alfredsson for inviting me to contribute to the writings of the Wallenberg Institute for Human Rights and Humanitarian Law at the University of Lund, Sweden; and to the Palme Foundation and the Sveriges Författarfond for giving me some seed money to get started on the book. Second, a thank you to my editors, who over many years at the *International Herald Tribune*, *Encounter* magazine, *Prospect* magazine (where I am a contributing editor), the *Los Angeles Times,* the *Arab News* of Saudi Arabia, the *Nation* of Kenya and the *Statesman* of India, have given me licence to gradually explore and unfurl my ideas.

After 40 years as a foreign correspondent and columnist the eleven, rather difficult, questions, posed in this book are the ones that have most seized me. If I come up with positive answers it is because I remain optimistic that if we had informed thinking and good leadership in the world no problem is inherently unsolvable and the world could become, without exhausting ourselves with effort, a much more attractive place to live, with much less serious conflict, abuse and poverty.

These were my own instincts even as a schoolboy; as I have said to my schoolmate, Paul McCartney, there must have been something special in the air in Liverpool in those days, for the songs of the Beatles, while often melancholic (and I am one of the world's great melancholics!) like *Yesterday* and *Eleanor Rigby*, are also infused with optimism and a sense of the goodness and compassion of mankind. Think of *Sergeant Pepper's Lonely Hearts Club Band, When I'm Sixty-four, Back in the USSR* or *Hey Jude!*

But there have been many influences, many mentors, in my post-school life. I single out, Trevor Huddleston, Andy Young, Olusegun Obasanjo, Barbara Ward, James Grant, Mahbub ul Haq, Sartaj Aziz, Melvin Lasky and Murray Weiss as the most important ones. All of them have planted the seeds that have grown into this book, a five-year undertaking, that I just wish they had all lived to see.

Finally I thank my family for all their support over the arduous years it took me to write this book.

Jonathan Power

# Introduction: Rights for All?

We live in extraordinary times. Change has never been so rapid. Economic opportunity has never been so varied or so world-embracing. Political processes have never been so open or so informed. Communication in all its forms, from transport to the internet, gives billions of people the chance to know what was only until recently the prerogative of the few. Yet throughout the world there is a malaise settling on the mind of mankind. For some people it is the very insecurity of fast change that troubles them. For others it is the loss of personal or institutional power and for some it is the massive and rapid accumulation of wealth. For many it is the fear of being left behind and for an overwhelming majority, despite all the progress made in extending and bettering the living of life, it is the fear that man's devilish capacity for violence and destruction is hell bent on destroying all the benign attributes of progress.

Old problems, the existence of world-wide colonial systems, the ideological and military struggle between East and West and the rigid economic demarcation lines between North and South may now be bygones but new problems set to overwhelm us are in abundance – the drug business, terrorism, the traffic in nuclear materials, the spread of new diseases, growing poverty, the laundering of illicit wealth, the growth in ethnic conflict, the "clash of civilizations", and the disintegration of a number of countries that cannot adequately deal with the strains of modern day life. All these issues beset us and often befuddle us as they explode before we have ready the institutions and the resources to confront and control them. Add to them the problems that have been with us all along but which have now mushroomed to enormous proportions – population growth, over-consumption and the impairment of our delicate life-sustaining habitat – and it becomes obvious we do not have time on our side.

The visible and most dramatic change of our age is in the destructiveness of military power. At the very time delegates were meeting in San Francisco to draft the Charter of the United Nations only 1,000 miles away in New Mexico scientists were perfecting the atomic bomb. It is a cloud that has hung over civilisation ever since. In those almost seventy years nuclear weapons have only been used twice – on Japan – but trillions of dollars have been spent on developing massive nuclear arsenals. Although never used they have become the currency of power, to which many countries still aspire. Although the Cold War, the major flashpoint for over 40 years, is over, nuclear weapons in abundance still exist, as do biological and chemical weapons of mass destruction. And the chance that some country will use them at some time remains very real.

Between 1945 and 2002 there were 167 wars, all fought with conventional weapons, which themselves have become ever more sophisticated and deadly. Arms exporting has become a major business for industrial countries, and the five permanent members of the Security Council sell most of them. The frequency of war, the tensions born of confrontation and change and, not least, the rapid spread of sophisticated weapons have helped breed in many parts of the world a culture of violence. War has a brutalizing effect, particularly on children and young people.

The legacy of war is often an arsenal of weapons and a low threshold for violence. In newer nations, undergoing rapid change, violence has become all pervasive, whether it be the urban violence of the US, Brazil and South Africa, the criminal gangs of the former Soviet Union, the ethnic pogroms of central Africa or the terrorist movements of the Middle East.

The world over people lock their doors – security is a fundamental instinct of the human species. Yet where does security end and destructiveness begin? Until the advent of the nuclear bomb the question, though poised, was usually brushed aside by those in power. No longer. World War II made it clear to even the most unlearned that the search for security could not be left to every nation state to pursue its interests without regard for another. The racheting up of war-making machines without any international discipline could only lead to World War III and that war, if fought with nuclear weapons, could well lead to the end of civilization.

The writers of the UN Charter attempted to devise a system that would maintain peace without resort to war. Although the successes of the UN have been limited – it did not avert the nuclear arms race between the superpowers – it did provide a forum for resolving severe moments of superpower tension, such as the Cuban missile crisis. And it did, by its embrace of sovereignty and the inviolability of national boundaries, appear to have markedly diminished the likelihood of one country invading another. Now, 60 years on, we have to seek how to improve the UN's ability to keep the peace, to consider whether it is merely a question of changing mechanisms but of changing attitudes too.

Even though the Cold War is over we live with its inheritance – nuclear, biological and chemical weapons of mass destruction, ballistic missiles, long-range aircraft, inflated military budgets and an over influential military-industrial-academic complex. As more and more countries gain the economic means to build modern military establishments and feel the need to assert their sovereignty, irrespective of any real immediate threat, the less chance there is that the older established military powers will seriously consider disarming. Yet as long as they put such a premium on a strong military few new-comers are going to listen to their advice on how better to apportion their scarce resources.

People have the right to be as secure as states and it is one of the tragedies of modern day life that the objectives and priorities of states undermine the se-curity of individuals. Likewise, the security of our planet as a whole, an intact working organism, can be put at risk by the selfish and narrow short-termism of both states and peoples. When we discuss security we must not only count guns but exhaust pipes. We must not only measure missile trajectories and troop movements but also the depth of traditional aquifers and the density of our forests and plant life. The Conventions on Biodiversity and on the Aboli-tion of Torture stand side by side on the same platform of human well-being as the Conventions on Chemical Weapons and Biological Weapons. All add to our security.

Avoiding conflict is far better than having to deal with it once it has erupted. It is far cheaper too, both in lives lost and money spent. Common sense would suggest we put more store in it. Our practice, however, tells us how bad we have been at it. We have to start looking at underlying trends that if left un-doctored can lead to political, social, economic and environmental stress that in the end erupts into murderous violence or serious famine. Governments, however, working under severe budgetary constraints, are loath to look far ahead. But they have to learn that a decision to prevaricate and delay can often catch up with them, in our fast-moving world, remarkably quickly.

Too often governments are media-led. The fickle and fast-moving eye of tel-evision can demand attention one minute, only to ignore the issue the next. This is reporting dangerously close to entertainment. The danger is cumula-tive. As we are fed a random diet of suffering, based on misleading criteria of what is most important, we lose over time not only our discernment but our confidence in out ability to make intelligent priorities.

Governments probably cannot legislate to change the techniques of televi-sion. Television, over time, has to acquire its own wisdom. But neither are gov-ernments in hock to media simplifications. They have to take the high ground and lead public opinion. They have the resources to pre-empt crises as well as to alleviate them. They need to give far higher priority to looking down the road ahead.

In economic terms we live in a transformed world. In one generation, from 1950 on, per capita income increased in most of Europe as much as it had dur-ing the previous century and half. Many Third World countries have moved from rags to riches in a single lifetime. In most of the former communist coun-tries a capitalist revolution is in full swing.

Enormous progress has been made, even in the poorest parts of the world, in improving the quality of life. People live longer, infant mortality rates have fallen and disease is less rampant. Nevertheless, for ever larger numbers of people, progress has not been sufficient to pull them out of poverty. While, in proportionate terms, it may appear that the worst of poverty for most people (even counting in the new numbers of the population explosion) has been conquered, it still leaves well over a billion people living on the margins of existence.

The progress that has been made has certainly been uneven. In the western world there have been major shocks such as the severing of the dollar-gold link, the dramatic rise in oil prices and the on-rush of fast technological change. In Latin America during the 1980s and 1990s, there was the impact of rising interest payments and the debt trap that sent economies into decline from which a number have still not fully recovered. In Eastern Europe there was the ending of the state run economy and the complicated and painful transition to market forces. For westerners this meant increasing unemployment, for a number of Third World countries it meant a "lost decade" of development and for ex-communists it meant a dramatic rise in mortality and criminality.

These changes, military and economic, cannot but throw into relief the social and environmental constraints of our planet. Resources are not infinite and society does not stand still. We bend the world to our will, for both good and ill, not least by the rate at which we populate it. More than twice as many people inhabit the earth today as they did at the end of World War II. Thanks to our inventiveness, a Malthusian crisis has been avoided, although for some regions it may be only a crisis deferred, not avoided. Over-rapid population growth is a terrible burden for the poorest countries and for the most crowded cities.

The pressure on resources mounts in tandem with population, indeed even faster as economic progress produces ever more demanding levels of consumption. We pollute more. We over-graze and over-fish more. We shrink the forests and drain the earth's fertility. In too many places we take out far more than we put back in.

No greater force now exists on earth, other than nuclear weaponry, than the collective might of industrialized economic endeavour. It has moved in half a century from being a localised phenomenon to one that now reaches almost everywhere. Governments, if not exactly helpless before this mighty tide of wealth creation, are in danger of being marginalised by it unless they are clear both about their own priorities and the institutional structures they build to monitor it, guide it, police it and, when necessary, in the interests of the poor and impoverished, to change its direction or to soften its cutting edges.

Economic activity, willy nilly, throws us together. We are linked in our now intense, new found economic life by a continuous umbilical cord which feeds on the womb of individual economic enterprise, nourishing ideas, resources and finance to create a massive explosion in wealth and well-being.

Yet our economic system has a flaw. It seems incapable of relieving destitution, at least for the billion at the bottom of the human pile. Twenty percent of humanity has no safe water or sanitation, are illiterate and underfed. For them life is too often nasty, brutal and short.

The economic life force of accumulation, investment, job creation and increasing reward surges on, changing the life styles of most of the world with unprecedented speed. Tied together by trade, television and the computer revolution, everything moving from market to market, from screen to screen, from bank to bank with an alacrity that the generation of 1945 could never in their wildest imaginations have conceived. Yet we are still bound by the institutions they created. No wonder that our forms of economic governance appear so dated and that the harmonisation that has been initiated between different political societies to tie economies closer together seems so often inadequate for the world we live in. The challenges are immense: to smooth in eastern Europe the rapid transition from communism to capitalism, to incorporate thirty new countries into global and regional institutions and to adapt their economies to global trading rules, to absorb the impact of the surge in economic strength of large parts of the Third World, without ignoring the tribulations of those still in the early stages of development and, not least, to deal with the "old age" of the original industrialized countries with their apparently intractable problems of high unemployment, growing welfare payments and increased immigration.

The world as a whole is opening out, but the danger is that the countries already rich may be closing in, refusing to give the leadership that continues the process of removing the barriers to the free movement of goods, capital and people, while at the same time reinvigorating and expanding the mandate and responsibilities of existing international economic institutions and creating the necessary new ones.

At the present there is too much human waste – the unemployed, their despairing families and their devastated communities in the rich world, the undereducated, hungry, ill and overcrowded in the poor world, women in nearly every society and minorities in too many countries. The world cannot afford to let so much human potential be under-utilised. It is irresponsible, it is unfair and it ignores the benefit everyone would gain if those marginalised were full and effective performing members of society.

Just as we do not use people well, neither do we take care of our habitat. Every year, as the world's wealth grows, we put more pressure on it, by far the most of the strain coming from the twenty percent of mankind who are its most prosperous. Fish stocks, tropical forests and watersheds are currently being used at an unsustainable rate. The few international controls that do limit the damage caused by our ever-increasing appetites and habits of consumption are not strong enough to be truly effective.

We have no choice but to change our governing economic institutions, to make them both more expert and sensitive, more democratic but less centralised, more global in scope yet more concerned than they are at present with the "small picture" as well as the "big picture". If we are to harness this remarkable surge of human economic energy so that it develops in a way that most fulfils the potential of humankind then we need effective global institutions. A river cannot run without banks and a train without tracks.

The ones we have in place – the World Bank, the International Monetary Fund, (IMF) the World Trade Organisation and the Group of Eight all are weighted in the interests of the old industrialized countries. Powerful though they are, the distribution of economic muscle is changing fast. China, India, Brazil and Russia must already be counted among the top ten economic powers. Yet they have little influence on international economic decision-making. Neither do Mexico, Indonesia, Taiwan and South Korea which are only a few steps behind.

The major powers, in fact, live with an economic paradox. It was, in significant measure, the practice of democratic participation in their own societies that enabled them to develop their economies so successfully. Yet they deny replicating this experience on the world stage.

Democracy, not so long ago limited to a handful of nations, is now spreading fast to all parts of the world. Even countries that do not practice it give it lip service. It is, perhaps, the most potent of all the forces of change in the new century. Autocrats have been pushed aside, personal power has been relegated to the dustbin of history and people everywhere are winning the power of choice in political matters.

Elections, of course, are the public marker of the new order. But in reality they are but the first step in the pursuit of democratic life. The tradition of democratic behaviour takes decades to inoculate deep enough into the body politic so that it becomes second nature. It also has its dangers – as it allows free expression to those who would seek to constrain and deny the freedom of others. Democracy, as with the Weimar Republic, can be its own undoing, if electorate and leadership take its precepts too lightly and bargain away its essential principles in the process of political manoeuvre.

In international institutions, too, we have to make progress towards democratic participation. In the UN and in other international organs larger and more powerful nations often wield more than a single equally weighted vote, yet the principle of equality of status is as important in the community of states as it is in any national or local community.

Corruption can quickly undo the trust of the peoples however well delivered democracy is. Power confers enormous advantages upon incumbents, power that can and is, increasingly, being turned to personal advantage. Drugs, arms sales and real estate, enterprises where fortunes are quickly made, are all danger zones for the political official. The business community of the industrial world has not set a good example in ensuring that its members follow ethical business practices.

The strength of civil society can be reinforced at both the national and the international level by clearly defined commitments to human rights, democracy, anti-corruption, sovereignty and self-determination.

Most of these are incorporated in the UN Charter. Some have been given added weight by the Universal Declaration of Human Rights, by the conventions on civil and political rights and on economic, social and cultural rights, by regional human rights charters, and by the Declaration on the Rights and Duties of States.

Yet our new sense of civil society raises the question – is it enough to have rights that are almost entirely defined in terms of the relationship between people and governments?

We must think, more and more, of individuals and private groups accepting the obligations to help and protect the rights of others. And into this flows naturally the tributary of the river of rights which is responsibility. We have to give as well as receive, to put in as well as take out, to see the other person's perspective as well as our own.

If one day nations could make use of law in their international dealings, economic and political, as much as they do at home then it would be possible to start conceiving of a world without war, where disputes between countries are adjudicated rather than fought over and where those countries that do wrong are penalised and compelled to ameliorate their practice without military or economic confrontation. This would be civilization of the highest order – ensuring, by the observance of law, that tyranny is kept in check, that liberty and justice prevail and that the strong do not trample on the weak and vulnerable.

The development of international law offers the world its best choice of avoiding war. Indeed if law were observed, military might, or even the enforcement procedures of the Security Council, would become increasingly redundant. Yet if there is no law all the enforcement in the world will not achieve its objective.

It is a question of degree. We have progressed a long way already and many of the norms of international law – particularly on human rights – are already respected by domestic courts. Many regional institutions already exist that practice international law, albeit on a more localised basis, such as the European Court of Justice and the European Court of Human Rights. The World Bank has its own legal tribunal for arbitrating investment disputes. More recently we have the International Criminal Court to try those accused of war crimes and crimes against humanity.

It is a question of attitude – how far we are prepared to go to sublimate our national loyalties before a law that transcends individual cultures and societies but nevertheless wins our respect because it is just and because it avoids conflict.

We live in the most extraordinary times, an age of an enormous potential yet with the capacity to self-destruct still intact. In that we are no different from our forefathers. Yet what is different, as we stand at the onset of a new century, is that never before has there lived a generation that shares so many common aspirations and accepts that humanity is bonded together in a way that their parents and grandparents could have, even with the best imagination, only dimly perceived.

When problems erupt they become everyone's problem. Wherever we are we know about Bosnia or Rwanda or the Sudan or bird flu. We are neighbours, but are we good neighbours? Can we help? How can we help? How can we help better than last time?

If we give in this way we also receive. A world where the raw edges of political and social disputes are softened, even in far away places, is a better place for us. Disruption and mayhem in an age of such fast telecommunications, the aeroplane and the intercontinental missile have the ability, if not contained, to transport themselves to our own backyard. It is the same with our environment. As Barbara Ward said thirty years ago, "we only have one earth" and there is little or nothing that modern society does in one part of the world with its productive energies that does not affect another. The world we inhabit now is too small for that to be avoided.

Blueprints are important. We cannot build anew without careful forethought. But nothing will work out well in practice, even with the best design, unless a quality of leadership is tapped that can give tangible and perceptive direction to those many strands of change now in process.

We need a leadership that knows how to transcend mankind's divisions, to diminish our most primitive instincts and to enhance our nobler ones. It must have the power of personality that inspires the best of us and takes us onward and beyond what we do now so often unsatisfactorily and insufficiently to what we could do if human energies were liberated from the confines of too simple and too narrow a perspective. We need to move beyond country, race, religion, culture, language and life-style to being part of what Martin Luther King called the beloved community. "We seek only", he said "to make possible a world where men can live as brothers."

Leadership, we know, is an intangible quality that can only be described as it is observed. But we can list some of the ingredients it will need if it is to have any chance of working in today's world. It must understand the need to pre-empt crises as well as have the ability to persist with their resolution once they occur. It must believe that the application of force is the signature of defeat and that true peace comes from careful compromise where no-one is asked to abase themselves before their opponent. It must be inspirational and take us into the reaches of our best performance, even enabling us to move far beyond what we have ever achieved before. It must be practical and down to earth, sifting the essentials and concentrating on what really are the priorities of living. It must be moral, selfless and yet convinced of its own audacity. In the end it will be immensely courageous for the problems it faces can appear at times quite daunting and near to overwhelming.

We inhabit a precious but vulnerable planet. We can make the best of it or the worst. We can live by law, respect and a sense of community or we can pull apart from both each other and the habitat of which we partake and live in division and disunity, all the time diminishing the quality and expectation of daily life.

# 1 Can We Avoid A Clash of Civilizations?

If we are going to discuss Islamic fundamentalism a good place to start is Christian fundamentalism. It is actually more demanding to be a Christian fundamentalist than an Islamic one. You are only allowed one wife, you should probably live in poverty ("It is easier for a rich man to go through the eye of a needle than to enter heaven") and you should be non-violent ("Turn the other cheek"). Moreover you should regard all human life as intrinsically sacred, which means whilst opposing abortion, one is also against capital punishment and, as the early Christians thought, warfare.

What present day American Christian fundamentalists concentrate on seems only a half-lit portion of the true picture. They are tough on sex and alcohol (though there is not much in the Gospels about either of them, apart from the account of Jesus' presence at the wedding feast of some family friends in Canaan which seems to record a good boozy celebration). But they are totally unchristian-like about gun ownership, capital punishment, war making, atonement and forgiveness.

Compared with Christian fundamentalism, contemporary Islamic fundamentalism is almost licentious – many wives and any number of divorces are permitted (although Mohammed thought divorces probably upset God). Young unmarried couples in fundamentalist Iran can even get a license from a Shi'ite imam for a night or two of passion, even for longer, a trial marriage, not to mention, according to some local religious authorities, promises of multiple wives in the life beyond it they sacrifice their lives in the cause of the jihad. (But what is the increasing number of female suicide bombers promised?)

At the other end of the spectrum of human existence, the spiritual, Christendom had no reason to be surprised at the outcry that followed the publication of the Danish newspaper cartoon drawing of Mohammed with his turban pierced with a bomb. Iconoclasm – the destruction of the figurative depiction of God and his prophets – was one of the important factors that in the ninth century strengthened the split between Roman Catholicism and Byzantine Orthodoxy. In fact the iconoclastic movement of the Eastern Church was in part a sympathetic reaction to the puritanical values of Islam. Later the Reformation led to similar moves against Catholic practices with fundamentalist

Protestants stripping out of their churches images of Mary and the saints, and the crucifix became bodiless.

Islamic fundamentalists, unsurprisingly, can be found across the religious spectrum in every country where Muslims congregate, although many Western observers attribute its centre of gravity to Wahhabism, the rigid Islamic brand of Sunni Islam prevalent in Saudi Arabia. Christian fundamentalism also spreads its wings. It may have deep roots in southern Baptist Churches in America, but President George W. Bush is a fundamentalist Methodist and Pope Benedict, who remains unmoving and unshakeable on birth control, abortion, capital punishment and is against most wars – at least he is relatively consistent – is head of the Roman Catholic Church and regards himself as a Thomist scholar not a fundamentalist.

It ought to be easier to decide who and what is right in Islamic fundamentalism than Christian. Islam after all is the faith of a single text, but Christianity has many, including four rather different versions of the life of Jesus, a record of the letters and missionary work of St Paul and a final work of apocalyptic prophecy announcing the imminent end of the world and the Second Coming of the Messiah. (It is another of many ironies that Jewish fundamentalists extend a warm embrace to the American fundamentalists who support ultra Zionism, despite the fact that their belief in the Second Coming, if it came about, would involve the end of Judaism.)

Given the plethora of texts and the fact that Christianity is a religion riven with many denominations and sects, not to mention its complicated formulations of God not being just one but three, one might assume that one might expect more harmony in Islam. Indeed Islam is a more austere monotheism. But it is not particularly harmonic – the religion of the single text and single God is riven too. It is also, along with Judaism, the more violent of the original traditions.

We have no alternative but to go back to the beginning if we are to have a hope of understanding the despair and anger that burst on the world with the demolition of the twin towers of New York's World Trade Centre by the suicide pilots of the "fundamentalist" Al Qaeda movement on September 11, 2001. This will not give us all the answers to all our questions. Nevertheless, this is the only way to start. Otherwise we fall into the trap set by ignoring history as George W. Bush and Tony Blair have done: of entering a drama that is already in its fifth or sixth act but assuming they were somehow at the beginning. Undoubtedly at the moment there is something of a "clash of civilizations" but to conclude that this has a long unbroken pedigree is a serious misreading of the history of the two religions. And to project it into the future as a development already determined by the past is to base an argument on the emotions of the moment, not reason. There is nothing inevitable about it at all.

Muslims believe that God first sent his revelation to Jews and then to the Christians, but that both religions distorted God's true message. God then finally sent down his pristine revelation one last time through Mohammed, the last of a long line of prophets. This is why Muslims believe the Koran, the revelation of God as spoken to Mohammed by the angel Gabriel, supersedes Jewish and Christian scriptures.

Although we do not know too much about Mohammed, we do know more about his life than we know about Moses, Abraham, Jesus or even Buddha and Confucius. He was born in modern day Saudi Arabia in 570 AD. He was orphaned as a child and at twenty-five married a wealthy widow, Khadija.

Arabia at that time was mainly polytheistic – tribal religions full of cults and pagan practices, although there were a number of Jewish communities and even a few Christian ones. Besides stressing belief in only one God, the message of the new revelation as transcribed in the Koran was a condemnation of the exploitation of the poor, the orphaned and the widowed. It forbade corruption, fraud, cheating, false contracts, the flouting of wealth and arrogance. It prescribed strict punishments for slander, stealing, murder, adultery and the use of intoxicants and gambling.

After ten years of preaching, Mohammed had had little success. His wife had died and also the uncle who raised him. His small band of followers was persecuted by the commercial aristocracy of the thriving trading town of Mecca. Then in 622 he was invited by the city fathers to the neighbouring oasis city of Medina to establish the first Muslim community. It was at that point that his movement began to grow. Mohammed was both its religious and political leader, and also its judge, chief tax collector and social reformer. Later he was to be its military chief and in 630 led his Muslim troops to conquer Mecca. By the time of his death, two years later, most of the Arabs of the western part of Arabia had joined the Umma, the community of believers. Yet although Islam from its early beginnings was undoubtedly a warrior religion, Mohammed did also bring a message of peace: Muslim must not fight against Muslim.

Within 20 years after Mohammed's death the Muslims had conquered large parts of the Roman Empire and absorbed the Persian. Within 100 years his followers had established an empire greater than Rome at its zenith. By 718 the Muslim armies had conquered Iberia. By the thirteenth and fourteenth centuries Islam ruled as far east as India, Indonesia and parts of China. In total contrast, Christians submitted themselves to the lions rather than fight and not until the Emperor Constantine converted to Christianity some 300 years after Jesus' death did Christianity take on the role of running a state with all its well-embedded military traditions.

If Mohammed was most unChrist-like in his attitude to war and to killing he differed just as profoundly in his attitude to women. Although Jesus obviously enjoyed the company of women he apparently remained both single and celibate. Islam, in marked contrast, allowed a man to take up to four wives (but not commit adultery) and Mohammed admitted that his own great weakness was his sexual appetite and, confessing human temptation, bent his own rules to take on multiple lovers. But of course Mohammed never claimed to be anything more than a man!

There is much in the Koran that brings it close to Christianity. One of the chapters of the Koran is devoted to venerating the Virgin Mary, and respectful references to Jesus and his teaching are found repeatedly in its pages. One has to remember, however, how important it was for the Arabs to have "a monotheism of their own, with scriptures in their own language, holy places in their own heartland and their own ways of setting about worship and decent living."

By the seventh century the Christian faith was very much bound up with East Roman order, which the Muslims sought to overthrow even as they absorbed its system of governance, of taxation, bureaucracy and written records. In everything but religion the early Islamic caliphate based at Damascus from 661 to 750 was the successor state to the Roman Empire.

In 750 the Islamic world took another equally remarkable political step forward. Abu-l-'Abbas staged a coup in Damascus, installing himself a caliph after murdering the ruling dynasty. Twelve years late his successor, al-Mansur, moved the capital of the Islamic Empire to Baghdad. It was known as the Abbasid dynasty after the prophet's uncle al-'Abbas from whom they claimed descent. They ruled until the Mongol invasion in 1258.

Under the Abbasids enormous energy was spent on absorbing the intellectual heritage of the Greeks, Persian and Roman civilizations. Much of the important writings of Aristotle on philosophy, Ptolemy on astronomy, Hippocrates and Galen on medicine were translated into Arabic. The Abbasids also reached out to the east, learning from the Chinese the techniques of papermaking in the eighth century. This knowledge did not spread to Europe until the twelfth century. (It arrived first in Christian Spain.) The Muslims also imported from India the concept of zero which revolutionized mathematics.

But the Islamists didn't just copy and preserve, they initiated new departures. Ibn Sina, working from the medical treatise of Galen, took the ideas forward into the then modern era. His medical textbook became a standard work for centuries.

A contemporary was al-Biruni who described five times as many medicinal plants as had Dioscorides, the greatest pharmacologist of antiquity. His calculations of the radius and circumference of the earth were respectively only 15 and 200 kilometres from today's reckonings.

Major urban centres of learning with vast libraries developed. In Cordova and Palermo in the west, in Cairo and Baghdad in the Arabian world and Nishapur in India. Europe remained in the Dark Ages, turning its back on the learning of antiquity. Indeed, without the cultural renaissance of the Abbasids most of the knowledge of antiquity would have been lost.

Schools of law sprang up in these centres of learning – four remain to this day. They drafted a vast body of laws regulating marriage, polygamy or polygyny, divorce, inheritance, theft, adultery, drinking and issues of war and peace. This law came to be regarded as the essence of the Shari'a – the way of life ordained by God for mankind.

Whilst the caliphs ruled, the learned men – the ulama – developed over a number of centuries the science of Muslim law. None of the schools could claim a monopoly of correct interpretation but they tend to agree on the essentials, although since there is no Pope nor anyone like him they can and do produce conflicting judgements in particular cases. Shari'a law can be said to be still evolving. However, the ulama are only interpreting law. The law had been made by God. When they agree it is taken as binding. Although Mohammed made no provisions for a successor or a priesthood the ulama are in essence a clergy, albeit unlike Christian priests who administer sacraments and pardon sins and were inaugurated, according to Catholic tradition, by St Peter.

After the fall of the Abbasids in the tenth century political authority in the Muslim world became secular, although rulers needed the ulamas' support to rule. Indeed, in many instances, the clergy have become so powerful, as in the Iran of Ayatollahs Khomeini and Khamene, that they pre-empt political decision-making. To become an important and influential imam – leader of prayer and learning – is not a question of appointment but of personality and following.

Islam has been torn asunder by a great divide that occurred within a generation after Mohammed's death. The first people to break away from the mainstream community of the Sunni were the Kharijites who killed the third caliph, Omar, and replaced him by Mohammed's cousin Ali. Whilst the Kharijites were later to fade into marginal communities in Oman and in East and North Africa the Shi'a, the other early breakaway group, as they became known, spread far and wide the notion that the rightful leadership belonged to Mohammed's family. It was an uphill battle. They were repudiated by the Abbasids, but nevertheless over the centuries grew into the force they are today forming a majority in Iran, Iraq and substantial minorities in Saudi Arabia, Lebanon, Turkey, India and Pakistan. Still they are a mere 10% of the worldwide community of Muslim. The Shi'ites emphasise more than the Sunnis the spiritual authority of the clergy who through a kind of apostolic succession are descendants of Ali. Shi'ism, unlike Sunnisim, also in practice makes a distinction between church and state.

The rule of the Abbasids was undoubtedly a golden age. But Islam continued to be a dynamic force long after. The Sufi (mystic) orders spread Islam to black Africa and South-east Asia. In the sixteenth century new and powerful Muslim states evolved with the Moguls in India, the Safarids in Persia, and the Ottomans in West Asia and Eastern Europe became the world's leading military power until the seventeenth century. Until the sixteenth century Muslim thinkers continued to lead the world in astronomy, medicine and other sciences.

Still, the fall of the Abbasids was a watershed. Islam lost much of its coherence. The split between Sunni and Shi'ite had widened with the Shi'ite founding of rival caliphate in Cairo in 969. In Baghdad factionism and military coups took their toll, weakening Abbasid rule.

Meanwhile, the Byzantine Christian empire based in Constantinople had led Europe's climb out of three centuries of economic stagnation, cultural strife and military defeat. New leaders came on the scene and were insistent on re-conquering old Christian lands. They had their first success in 969 in the capture of Antioch. This was balanced at first by the rise of the Seljuk Turks who defeated a Byzantine army in eastern Turkey encouraging a Turkish take-over of Asia Minor. The Turks then pressed north and west. They conquered first Bulgaria, Serbia, Albania, Northern Greece, Kosovo and Hungary and reached the gates of Vienna in 1529. In the east the Mogul empire was growing fast.

Christendom in turn responded by launching the Crusades, which meeting mostly defeat especially at Necropolis in 1396, led to Byzantine overstretch and the fall of Constantinople to the Ottomans in 1453. Only in the west did Christendom overpower Islam. Gradually during the twelfth and thirteen centuries the Christian monarchies pushed the Muslims back from northern Spain to the south and by 1250 only the emirate of Granada was still in Muslim hands.

The marriage of Isabella of Castile and Ferdinand of Aragon in 1474 signalled the end for Granada. They re-united Spain under Christian rule in January 1492 with their own personal crusade. But within a short four year period Islam, although losing power in the west of Europe, gained even more in the east of Europe.

Yet if Muslim political power continued to wax from the fifteenth century on, West European scientific and technological innovation gradually but steadily superseded that of Islam. The historians seem unable to explain this paradox.

The West was changing fast, escaping the rut that Charlemagne's anti-intellectual rule of Europe had pushed it into in the eighth century. Scholars realised they had to learn from Islam and during the twelfth and thirteen centuries the Arabic corpus that incorporated Greek, Persian (and Roman) learning was translated into Latin. Adelard of Bath's translation of the Arabic version of Euclid's *Elements* made Western scientific scholars aware of the most influential handbook of geometry ever written. The rise of the West took the Islamic world by surprise. They coped with it by largely ignoring and disdaining it – a terrible mistake.

Ironically, thanks to Muslim scholarship, Western philosophers were able to acquaint themselves with Aristotle and his arguments that the world was intelligible without revelation. It was left to Thomas Aquinas in the thirteenth century to integrate reason and revelation. Without his intellectual intervention the Renaissance and the Enlightenment might have occurred even earlier. Still, by the standards of the times it was a big step forward. By 1500 the scales between the Islamic world and Christendom had tipped in the latter's favour, even though in the sixteenth century the Ottoman Empire still remained the most powerful state in the world and remained so until the late seventeenth century.

No-one can doubt that there was a clash of civilizations. Too much blood was spilt by the Crusades on the one hand and the rapid expansion of the Ottoman Empire on the other. But for the intellectuals the contest was by no means as bitter as the chronicle of battles suggests. Fifteenh-century pronouncements on the justness of going to war were much more reserved and nuanced than those before. Many theologians and philosophers believed that they should study Islam and then pursue a dialogue that was essentially courteous rather than antagonistic.

The Spaniard, John of Segovia, who died in 1458 and the German, Nicholas of Cusa, who died in 1464, were particularly influential. John translated the Koran and sought to foster academic conferences in which scholars from the two religions could meet and debate. But the primate of Spain ignored him and continued with his policy of forced baptisms.

Nicolas was a cardinal yet wrote a work that argued that the Koran is compatible with the New Testament. There was more that bound the two religions together, he argued, than separated them. Since human intellect could never plumb ultimate truth it had to rely on mystical intuition and seekers in both religions could find it in their own way.

This thinking caught the imagination of many intellectuals, yet it wasn't enough to overcome conservative and militaristic impulses on both sides.

The unexplainable paradox of the co-existence of Islamic military and political expansion and growing intellectual and scientific weakness continued to deepen. Islam seemed intent on shooting itself in the foot. Whereas Gutenberg was printing his first Bible in 1455 (on paper that Islamic knowledge had provided) the Sultan of Constantinople in 1515 made it a capital offence for Muslims to use printing presses. It was Christendom in the course of the sixteenth century which developed presses for the printing in Arabic script. Islam, despite its continuing military prowess, for reasons that remain unclear until this day, had lost its intellectual and creative edge.

In all these 600 years of the spread and development of Islam one of the most intriguing aspects is Islam's tolerance for Judaism and Christianity, an attitude not always reciprocated. The Koran requires that Muslims should respect the Ahl al-Kitab, "The People of the Book". In practice, however, the early Muslim conquerors demanded that non-Muslims wear a distinctive sash and were not allowed to build new synagogues or churches. Sexual relations with Muslims were forbidden, as was proselytising among Muslims. (Under the Mogul king, Akbar (1542-1605), Muslims in India were also compelled to be tolerant to Hindus. The Taj Mahal with its fusion of Islamic and Hindu styles is a testament to his benign attitude.)

Mohammed himself was intimately aware of Jewish belief and practices. There were Jewish communities all over central Arabia and Mohammed clearly revered the heroes of Jewish history, even though, as an uneducated illiterate, he couldn't read the Old Testament for himself. Likewise he treated Christians and their beliefs with something approaching affection. Mary, Christ's mother, is mentioned more in the Koran than in the Gospels. Mohammed accepted that Jesus was born of a virgin and, as with his own prophecy, the archangel Gabriel had been a guiding force. But he did not accept that Jesus was the Son of God. Nor that he died on the cross. ("They killed him not, nor crucified him. But it was made to appear so.")

When his early troupe of followers was persecuted by traditional Arab rulers he chose Christian Abyssinia as a place of refuge for them. The prophet's daughter, Rugayyah, and fourteen others travelled by boat down the Red Sea to Abyssinia.

Although there are many examples through the ages of Christian and Jewish communities, which thrived under Islamic rule, according to Shari'a law there is no formal or legal acceptance of their right to worship or own property. The Turkish millet system later changed this but this was not because of changes in the Shari'a. It was the Sultan's secular law.

Islamists, often seeking to emphasise the tolerance of their religion, recall Saladin's conquest of Jerusalem in 1187. For the next 700 years Jerusalem remained under Muslim rule. The churches were open. The Jews were given funds to rebuild their synagogues. This was in marked contrast to the way the Crusaders had ruled Jerusalem before when Muslims and Jews were mainly forbidden from living within the city walls.

Likewise, from the fifteenth century on, when the majority of Arabs lived under Ottoman rule, for its five hundred years of life Christians and Jews were recognised and protected. Many of the Jews who were expelled from Iberia were granted refuge in the Ottoman Empire. Likewise German, French and Czech Protestants fleeing Catholic persecution were given protection.

Andrew Wheatcroft's *Infidels*, a study of the conflict between Islam and Christendom, is probably the best historical treatise on the subject. Wheatcroft chronicles in detail the Islamic colonisation of Spain. After the Muslim conquest of Al-Andalus in 720 although there was no systematic campaign of forcible conversions within a couple of centuries most Christians had converted to Islam. The term *"La Guerra Fria"*, the Cold War, was first coined by Christians to describe their relationship with Muslims. While Christians and Jews were tolerated, Muslims "must not massage a Jew or Christian nor throw away his refuse, nor clean his latrines." Catholic priests were often seen as "evil-doers, fornicators and sodomites". In fact both sides held mythical views about each other's unbridled sexuality. But there were also signs of a reaching out. A gold dinar struck in 713 AD carries the Muslim profession of faith in Latin, not Arabic. (There is no other known case when Arab rulers forsook Arabic when quoting scripture.)

In marked contrast when Christian Spain finally conquered the last Islamic redoubt, Granada, the victorious Christians decreed a radical policy of mass conversion, which ended with the ethnic cleansing of all the descendants of the "Moors". And the Jews became the main target of the so-called "purist legislation" and later the Holy Inquisition. Relations between Christians and Jews were a "ritualised antagonism" often flaring into violence. In the 1391 pogroms in Christian Spain an estimated 100,000 Jews were killed. In a decree of 1492, the year they sent Columbus away on his voyage, Ferdinand and Isabella legislated the expulsion of the Jews. Some 50,000 to 80,000 left, some to North Africa and many travelling by ship to Italy or Constantinople. A great many perished of hunger on the way.

The Balkans was the third area where Islam met Christendom. Even though the Balkans were Europe's "wild frontier", for the Christian powers the Ottoman occupation of the Balkans "seemed a cancerous intrusion within the natural bounds of Christendom." Many local Christians in Albania and Bosnia converted to Islam and are Muslim to this day. The struggle here was more the virulent than its predecessors in Spain and the Levant and became "the mis en scène for the final act of Europe's encounter with Islam, the last crusade"– at least until September 11th 2001 unleashed a new wave of emotions and antagonisms. Robert Kaplan has observed, "In modern times, it all began here."

Around Easter 1821, the Greek peasants of the Pelononnese began to kill all the Muslims in the land. Then later in 1876 came the mass killings of Christians in Bulgaria, prompting a great outpouring of moral outrage in the West. Nothing said or written had a greater impact than Gladstone's pamphlet "Bulgarian Horrors and the Question of the East". The anti-Ottoman cause became a juggernaut. "Wherever they went", wrote Gladstone of the Ottomans, "a broad line of blood marked the track behind them, and as far as their dominion reached civilization vanished from view." It seemed Shakespeare's witches brew of "nose of Turk and Tartar's lips", Dante's portrayal of Mohammed in hell, Voltaire's *Fanaticism or Mohammed the Prophet* and Delacroix's painting, "Massacre of Chaos," with Christian women pursued by Turkish lancers, had finally come to life as it was meant to be in the eyes of the Christian beholder. The killings of the Muslims in the Peloponnese were neither depicted nor remembered. (Lest this seems too one-sided I hasten to remind my audience that there were countercurrents: in Mozart's day Vienna – despite the Ottoman siege of 1683 – was in love with all things Turkish. Hence his *Abduction from the Seraglio* a happy, light opera about a Turkish palace and its harem.)

1798, the year of Napoleon Bonaparte's invasion of Egypt, was the moment when the political tide of Islam began to ebb. Although this brief occupation of three years was defeated by the British it highlighted the weakness of Islamic rule and marked the onset of the European powers' competitive urge to conquer Muslim lands.

Then in the next century the British, their sea and administrative power enabled by the fruits of the Industrial Revolution, which in turn had been built on the capital provided by the slave trade, conquered the Islamic-influenced lands of India, Burma and Malaysia. At around the same time the Dutch conquered

Indonesia and the Russians the Caucasus and Turkistan. From India the British expanded their dominance to Aden, the Persian Gulf and Afghanistan.

In 1830 the French invaded Algeria and from there conquered much of Muslim black Africa, with the exception of the emirates of Nigeria ruled by the British. The British then conquered Egypt in 1882 and sailing up the Nile took Sudan. Spain reached out to the Western Sahara and part of Morocco. France took the northern part.

This was the beginning of the end for the Ottoman Empire. The mainly Christian territories of the empire were also re-claimed from it: Montenegro, Serbia, Greece, Romania, Bosnia, Bulgaria and Macedonia.

Trying to save their fading reach the Ottomans allied themselves with Germany in 1914. It was a terrible mistake. The Ottomans were defeated and its empire dismembered. The Arabs, believing British promises of an independent Arab state, rose in revolt against the rule of Istanbul. Betrayed, they are still reeling from decisions made then by Britain and France, who divided the Arab Middle East into spheres of influence – Britain took Iraq, Palestine and Transjordan; France took Lebanon and Syria. "A French General, arriving in Damascus," writes Edward Mortimer in his classic study of Islam, "rode to the tomb of Saladin, the Muslim leader who had defeated the Crusaders 700 years before and, knocking on the gates, proclaimed, "Saladin, we have returned."

The Muslim world was finally dominated and controlled by the Christian West. The house of Islam, once the repository of one of the world's most advanced civilizations – only China could have challenged it at its zenith – was reduced to its religious shell. No wonder Muslims began to think that they had failed by not being true to their faith. The seeds of a religious resurgence were planted even if it took another generation for them to sprout.

Roger Scruton is not alone in concluding, "It is difficult to see the destruction of the Ottoman Empire as anything other than a disaster – a disaster whose consequences threaten to match those of the Russian Revolution and the rise of Hitler." The artificial regimes created by the British and the French quickly withered to be replaced by oil-rich feudal despotism, hereditary monarchy and in Syria and Iraq by the quasi Leninist/gangster rule of the Ba'ath party. Later in Iran, in the 1980s, there was the overthrow of the dictatorial and decadent Shah by the fundamentalist Shi'ite revolution of Ayatollah Khomeini. "War is a blessing for the world and for every nation." Khomeini said in a speech in 1984. This was the first major public political event in the modern day "Clash of Civilizations", even though the roots of al-Qaedaism are more traceable to Sunni Egypt and to a lesser extent Sunni Saudi Arabia.

Ironically most of the energy of new Islamic-orientated Iran went into a long war of attrition with Iraq. Its ability to take on the West was limited to a spontaneous taking of hostages at the US embassy in Tehran by young militants.

The real action of consequence was elsewhere – in Egypt.

During the nineteenth and most of the twentieth centuries terrorism in the Muslim and Arab world was not significant. Towards the end of the last century there was a profound change. With the Palestinians it was aimed at Western support of Israel. On the Indian sub-continent it is centered on Kashmir and the Muslim urge to claim this state from Hindu-dominated India. In Saudi Arabia it was the revival of Wahhabism, the teaching of an eighteenth century puritanical sect. But the epicentre was in Egypt, even though the fundamentalists were always marginalised politically in local politics.

Islam, as we have seen, has long been a tolerant religion. But the resurgence of fundamentalism brought in its wake fanaticism and that in turn has bred a particular kind of cruel terrorism that spares neither women nor children, nor even believers. The worldwide decline in terrorism that marked the 1980s and early 1990s came to a shuddering halt and then a quite terrifying reversal.

But before elaborating what evolved in Egypt we need to examine the full spread of Islamic revivalism, for most of this movement, long in the making, was anything but violent.

The Islam resurgence became a potent force in Muslim politics in the 1970s and 1980s. It affected nearly all of Islam – in Indonesia, in Malaysia, in the Sudan and Nigeria, not just in the Middle East. It infected resistance movements in Afghanistan and Kashmir and led to the development of Islamic opposition parties in Egypt, Tunisia, Algiers, Morocco, Palestine and Indonesia. Their ideological range is enormous. In Saudi Arabia they support the status quo, even if that means being pro-American. In Egypt, in total contrast, they have been radical revolutionaries.

Although often taking political form this revivalism was based on a growing sense of the importance of pious belief at the personal level, leading to increased attendance at the mosque, a greater emphasis on Islamic dress, the revitalization of Sufism (mysticism) and less tolerance for breaking traditional values.

Some of this had to do with the growth of Israeli power and the reaction that this caused. Nasser had fought the 1967 Anti-Israeli war in the name of nationalism and socialism. His successor, Anwar Sadat, although more pro-American, fought a similar war in 1973 as a "holy war".

It also owed much to the rise of the oil powers and the initiation of the Arab oil boycott in 1974, which suggested to the Islamic masses, albeit misleadingly, that at last they had a counter weapon to weald against those colonialists and imperialists who had brought them low.

A third, if passing, influence was the Iranian revolution of 1978, which deposed the secular pro-Western Shah and fired the imagination of the Muslim world. Religious activists and militants now had a role model. Even though this was a revolution led by Shi'ite clergy, Sunni radicals in Egypt, Pakistan and Malaysia were emboldened by it.

By the 1990s revivalism had moved from the fringe to the mainstream with a new class of educated Islamically-orientated elites. Its influence is now everywhere, in schools and universities and in the social services. Much of it, even most of it, is moderate and content to work within the system non-violently. Many revivalists have pushed for political liberalization and democratic policies. But beginning in Egypt in 1928 with the founding of the Muslim brotherhood, a more militant form of Islamic revivalism has spread its tentacles throughout the Islamic world.

Although initially the purpose of the Brotherhood was the dissemination of religious propaganda and social responsibility, by the 1930s it had become much more radical. It developed a military wing that was in the forefront of the struggle against British rule. Later they overreached themselves when they attempted to kill Nasser and the government responded with a draconian suppression. Even though in 1964 Nasser amnestied the organisation they continued with their attempts to overthrow the government.

It was around this time that one of the militants imprisoned by Nasser, Sayed Qutb, a theologian, began to write and preach, the substance of which is clearly traceable to the teachings of the leadership of Al Qaeda today. Qutb taught that not only was Islam the only true religion but that all other religions and civilisations were barbarian. Even in prison he wrote prolifically, some twenty books. When with other militants he was released in the 1964 amnesty he continued to plan to take Nasser's life. He was re-arrested. This time he was hanged.

Since his death millions of his books have been printed and he inspired many underground organisations. El-Jihad and Gama'a Islamiya became big threats to the government, inspired by a living guru and follower of Qutb, Sheik Umar Abdel Rahman, who fled to the US in 1990 and for reasons still little understood was given refuge there. In 1993 he was arrested after the first bombing of the World Trade Centre.

These Egyptian militants for their part chalked up a long line of assassinations from President Anwar Sadat in 1981 to fifty Western tourists in 1997 in Luxor.

By the mid 1990s the leading members of el-Jihad had moved to Afghanistan, tired of the repression at home and out of sorts with the Muslim Brotherhood which they rightly claimed had become tame and reformist. In Afghanistan one of their leaders Ayman Al Zawahiri struck up a friendship with Osama bin Laden. He became his deputy.

At home in Egypt Gama'a still continued with its terrorism, providing a home for restless university trained young people who, a generation or two before, would have joined the Communist party. But by 1999, just as Al Qaeda came to the boil, it was over at home, at least for now. Their leaders in jail called for the terrorists to halt hostilities. 2002 saw the publication of a four-volume series of books written by Gama'a's mostly jailed leaders, confessing their past mistakes. Although they did not renounce jihad altogether, they admitted that they had been wrong to attack both fellow Muslims and civilian tourists and said that their members had been forbidden to join Al Qaeda

"It is human to hate," writes Harvard professor, Samuel Huntingdon, in his influential book *The Clash of Civilizations and the Remaking of World Order*. "In this new [post Cold War] world, local politics is the politics of ethnicity; global politics is the politics of civilization. The rivalry of the superpowers is replaced by the clash of civilizations."

Huntington first published his ideas in an essay of *Foreign Affairs* in the summer of 1993. The Cold War was barely over. The strategists of the think tanks and universities, the planning staffs of the Pentagon and State Department were then suddenly without a task in life. Editors were no longer interested in their op-ed articles, research grants began to dry up and most important, their own self-worth and motivation was seriously undermined. A few wise ones, like Colin Powell, then chairman of the Joint Chiefs of Staff confessed, "I'm running out of demons."

When Huntington published this essay it was as if a benign wind had rekindled dying embers. Here was a new enemy and a new cause. The applause was deafening. With the advantage of a great deal of financial support and a large team of graduate students within three years Huntington published his book. It reads as if he passed out section headings to each of his researchers and told them to find the worst-case examples and readings of history to back up what is an extraordinarily one-sided argument. It is doubtful if a single, high-powered academic, if he or she had to sift through the historical record unaided, could have come up with such an unshaded opinion at book length.

On cue came the rise of Al-Qaeda. What should have been seen as a small band of violent dissidents on a par with the Palestinian plane highjackers, the ruthless Baader-Meinhof terrorists of Germany or the IRA of the 1980s, came to be interpreted as the spearhead of new Islam, revengeful, millennialist and intent on laying Western/Christian civilizations low for all time. Generally overlooked in the ideological hubbub was the great irony that most of the terrorist shock-troops of Al Qaeda would never have come into organised being if they had not been trained at the CIA's behest (and finances) by Pakistani and Saudi Arabian intelligence in the then united Islamic/Western effort to defeat the Soviet occupation of Afghanistan by force of arms.

Then came September 11th. In one vivid masterstroke, but using no ultramodern technology, Al Qaeda provoked the wrath of superpower. Led by a self-declared Texan "good old boy" the US president, George W. Bush initiated a series of ill-considered, heavy-handed policy initiatives that made Osama bin Laden (and later Saddam Hussein) the pin-up star of much of the Islamic and Arab world. Around the world Muslims felt that the anger of America and its partner in arms, Britain, was directed not so much at the terrorism of one small troupe but at their culture, their religion and their self-dignity. US and British policy succeeded in converting Osama bin Laden's band of earnest followers into an Islamic-wide mood. Al Qaeda has become a state of mind.

Despite the obvious failure of the attempt to bomb and knock out Al Qaeda in its Afghani redoubt and the attempt, by military might, to turn Iraq into an oasis of Arab democracy, and despite their consequence – the (US organised) opinion polls that showed that almost 90% of Muslims are today pro bin Laden and anti the US – too many in the US still seem enthralled by Huntington's prognosis. "So long as Islam remains Islam and the West remains the West, this fundamental conflict between two great civilizations and way of life will continue to define their relations in the future even as it has defined them for the past fourteen centuries," he wrote in his book which by now has become a sort of gospel for American policy-makers.

Huntington spent much of his book's effort in attempting to persuade his audience that "the underlying problem for the West is not Islam fundamentalism. IT IS ISLAM, a different civilization whose people are convinced of the superiority of their culture and are obsessed with the inferiority of their power."

It is not surprising that so myopic a conviction led him to see a future where the West would end up in an all out nuclear war with Islam and its apparent ally, another perennial antagonist of the West, so he says, Synic civilization. "The twentieth-century conflict between liberal democracy and Marxist-Leninism is only a fleeting superficial historical phenomenon compared to the continuing and deeply conflictual relationship between Islam and Christianity."

There is little historical evidence for Huntington's extreme view, as the previous pages have made clear. Although, as Huntington does, you can argue persuasively that Islam almost from the beginning was a religion of the sword, Christianity, once the Emperor Constantine converted, was absorbed into the militaristic culture of the Roman Empire. In succeeding centuries there was indeed often and regularly a clash of civilizations. But there was one spectacular difference between the two religions. Islam was, by and large, a tolerant religion, that respected the "Peoples of the Book" giving them always when it ruled over them a great deal of autonomy. (The Ottoman Empire was even more tolerant than the unusually benign Hapsburg Empire.)

The Christians for their part were rarely tolerant, always angling to recapture Jerusalem which they considered part of their heritage and unable to come to terms with Islamic and Jewish minorities in their midst. Indeed, the long persecution of the Jews which culminated in Hitler's gas chambers was always pursued by Christians not Muslims. Today we are seized by the clash between Jew and Arab over the ancient land of Palestine. It has produced a poisonous, deadly relationship between Islam and Judaism. But this is a comparatively new phenomenon unlike what went on for most of their centuries of co-existence. If it hadn't been for the Christian sentimentality of the British government of Lloyd George that led to the Balfour Declaration and the creation of a Jewish homeland on British-occupied Palestinian territory, and if it hadn't been for the Nazi Holocaust which drove so many of Europe's Jews away from their almost equally ancient homelands, there would not be today's Islamic/Jewish clash of civilizations on Palestinian soil.

Because the West, the Christian world, has taken a pro-Israel stand for most of the time since the British left Palestine in 1947, the wrath of the Islam/Jewish clash has spilt over into a distrust of the Christians. In recent years the Europeans have attempted to distance themselves from their American brethren as the tempo of events has quickened between Israel and the Palestinians and as a new European generation, one or two steps removed from the guilt of the Holocaust, could look at the situation in a more balanced way.

Enmity between Islam and the Christian world has certainly grown frighteningly fast, but as yet it is only the militant fundamentalists who drive it into sheer murderous hatred. As Professor Michael Howard, the Oxford and Harvard historian of war, wrote in *Foreign Affairs*, "bin Laden is about as representative of Islam as Ian Paisley is of Christianity."

What exactly is this fundamentalism, that is not, according to Huntington, but is according to a majority of sober, informed, observers, the driving force of a bitter, no-holds barred conflict on the Islamic side?

A common view of a majority of Western scholars is to blame fundamentalism on Wahabism, the influential rigorous Islamic sect that governs the religious life of Saudi Arabia, the country of bin Laden's birth and youth. This is a relatively recent development. They used to blame it on Ayatollah Khomeini, who in 1974 led a successful revolution against the rule of the Shah and established the first modern Islamic fundamentalist state. Women were forced to dress in burqas. Money and arms were poured into the guerrilla group, Hezbollah, that is fighting the Israeli occupation of the Lebanon. The media was tightly controlled. Young militants, acting with the blessing of the clerical establishment, seized the diplomats at the US embassy provoking a crisis with the US that was a major factor in the unseating of President Jimmy Carter, a moderate leader, and his replacement with the rightist government of Ronald Reagan.

At the time much was made of Iran's capacity to electrify much of the Islamic world with its fundamentalist message. "It is Allah himself who commands men to wage war, and to allow the infidels to stay alive means to let them do more corrupting," said Khomeini. In reality nothing of the sort occurred. The majority Sunnis (90%) of Islam were not particularly enamoured of this Shi'ite, clergy-dominated revolution. Its neighbour, ruled by the then very secular Saddam Hussein, wore it down with a war of attrition that lasted the best part of a decade. At home a younger generation grew up unmotivated by the zeal of the Khomeini generation and gravitated towards democracy, economic development at home, isolationism abroad and tolerance in personal behaviour. The clergy still maintain a grip on domestic policy, and indeed reasserted their influence in the election of 2005, but the straightjacket has been loosened to such an extent that few worry today about Iran as a source of violent fundamentalism that can pose a threat to the outside world, even if it does go ahead and develop nuclear weapons.

The new *bête noir* of a majority of today's scholars is Saudi Arabia's Wahhabism. The Wahhabite movement has its roots in the sect founded by Mohammed Ibu Abdul-Wahab who was born in 1703. He was a founder of one of the four classical schools of Sunni jurisprudence. He was a Martin Luther figure in Islam – opposed to an absolute and unquestionable authority. Abdul-Wahab rebelled against the society he grew up in with its tolerance of adultery, poverty and superstition and the worship of saints' tombs.

Like Luther he also sought support from a local prince, Mohammed Ibin Sa'ud. And like Mohammed he believed that his ideas could be spread by warfare. Indeed, in a very non-Koranic way, he believed that jihad could be conducted against other Muslims, if it could be shown they were compromising their beliefs. He also appeared, unusually for a Sunni, to accept an implicit separation of powers – between temporal and spiritual authority.

In the early twentieth century a group of Wahhabis collected around a descendent of the original Iban Sa'ud to form a brotherhood, again to revitalize the faith. They called themselves Ikhwan. This movement led by Ibn Sa'ud "gradually drove the Turkish clients from their paper thrones in the Arabian peninsular." By the time the Ottoman Empire collapsed in the wake of World War I, Ibn Sa'ud was able to declare the Kingdom of Saudi Arabia that covered most of the peninsular.

The Ikhwan have maintained their cause as a minority movement within Saudi Arabia, who have regularly seen themselves at odds with the compromises of the ruling family. In 1979 a group of Ikhwan tried to forcibly take over the Sacred Mosque at Mecca. In an attempt to distance themselves from the Ikhwan, many of the puritan "ulema" (religious authorities) no longer call themselves Wahhabis but Salafis – believers who are true to the forgotten piety of the Salaf (or companions of the Prophet).

It is a matter of some passion among scholars whether bin Laden and the Taliban are Wahhabis. Haneef James Oliver, a Kenyan scholar, says the Taliban are not Wahhabis. "They belong to what is known as the Sufi Deobandi movement, founded in the Indian Himalayas in the 1860s". Bin Laden himself, he argues, although he now says he is not concerned with differentiating between matters of creed, was probably originally a Sufi, which is better known as Sufism, a mystical sect that is the antithesis of Wahhabism. This he puts down to his family's Yemini origins (and the origin of most of the September 11th highjackers) which has been a long time base of Sufism.

Oliver goes further and states that bin Laden's present day affiliation is with the Egyptian Qutbists. On this point many Western observers agree with him. "If one man deserves the title of intellectual grandfather to Osama bin Laden, it is probably the Egyptian writer and activist Sayyid Qutb," wrote the *New York Times'* Robert Worth. Roger Sctruton observes, commenting on Ayman al-Zawahari, bin Laden's deputy, and Mohammed Atta who led the attack against the World Trade Centre, "Although bin Laden is a Saudi by birth, his most active followers are Egyptians shaped by Western technology (al Zawahiri is a surgeon and Atta an engineer) and Qutbist Islamism." Malise Ruthven makes the interesting additional point that "part of the problem is caused by the way fundamentalist ideologues trained in technical subjects such as engineering treat religious texts as operational manuals. And Walter Laquer in his latest study of terrorism observes, "The heartland of Islamic fundamentalism was Egypt ... Al

Zawahari and those of his comrades who had gone to Afghanistan eventually to become part of Al-Qaeda lost contact with the militants inside Egypt. They strongly disapproved of the leaders in prison who had opted for a truce ... The pillars of the new organisation (Al Qaeda) were the Egyptians and bin Laden."

One of the big questions is how Islamic is this extreme militancy? John Grey, writing in *The Independent*, has argued that Qutbism is not rooted in Islamic tradition, but rather is very much a Western-based ideology. Qutb, he says, "incorporated many elements derived from European ideology into his thinking" and as such Qutbism should be seen as an "exotic hybrid, bred from the encounter of sections of the Islamic intelligencia with radical Western ideologies". He adds, "The inspiration for Qutb's thought is not so much the Koran but the current of Western philosophy embroiled in thinkers such as Nietzsche, Kierkegaard and Heidegger. Qutb's thought – the blueprint for all subsequent radical Islamist political theology – is as much a response to twentieth century Europe's experience of "the death of God" as to anything in the Islamic tradition. Qutbism is in no way traditional. Like all fundamentalist ideology it is unmistakably modern." Perhaps Gray should have substituted the word "extremist" for "fundamentalist", but otherwise his analysis is hard to fault.

For totally different reasons the rise of extreme fundamentalism in Islam has been matched by a surge of fundamentalist belief in the West, particularly in the south of the United States and particularly among those who vote Republican and see George W. Bush as sympathetic to their views.

Not only do many of them appear to have an instinctive abhorrence of Islam, brought to the surface by September 11th, they have allied themselves with Israel, at what could not be a worse time when Israeli/Muslim relations have deteriorated sharply. Many American fundamentalists (Evangelicals) believe that the founding of Israel in 1948 is a part of a divine scenario. This, they argue, "was prefigured in the Book of Revelation and will lead to the return of Christ and the conversion of the Jews to Christianity." It should strike the Jews, if nobody else, that political support from such a source is not exactly in their long run favour, especially when these Evangelicals maintain that a thousand-year earthly reign of Christ is imminent. Yet such is the polarised state of opinion between Islam and Judaism, Israel has welcomed the supporters of this credo in droves as they parade around Jerusalem and campaign on behalf of Israel in Washington. "Islamic extremism depends for its following on the paranoid assumption that the West is virulently anti-Islamic," argues Malise Ruthven. Yet the West, driven by the policies of George Bush and Tony Blair, has done little or nothing to reverse this perception. Quite the opposite. By its bombing of Afghanistan which took more innocent lives than perished in the World Trade Centre, by its unfailing support for the right of the Israeli political spectrum and by its war with Iraq it has done more for the cause of Islamic "paranoia" than bin Laden on his own could ever have done.

Bin Laden is in the enviable position of watching his ideas self-combust among young Islam militants – in Indonesia, where bombs in the tourist resort of Bali claimed over 200 lives, in Saudi Arabia where the authorities appear on the defensive as the rate of bombings increases aimed at removing the skilled expatriates on which the economy depends and in Palestine where already charged militants feel they have a magnificent, successful, patron saint on their side. But these cells are also proliferating in Western Europe and the US.

The bombing at a main railway station in Madrid – on the eve of a general election, claiming over 200 lives – appeared to be the work of autonomous, disaffected Moroccan immigrants. In France, Britain and Germany bombs are made, sometimes go off, Islamic preachers stir up emotions, and bin Laden's appeal radiates much as did Ché Guevara to a young Western generation in the 1960s and 70s.

The unanswered question is can bin Laden's appeal be dealt with as effectively as was Ché Guevara's – although it should not be forgotten that was not as easy as it seems in hindsight.

One can say it was the steady progress on social reform made by the capitalist economies, the greater respect for human rights, the advance of democracy especially in Latin America and a growing intolerance for violence of any kind from the young politically engaged.

Charles de Gaulle, the great leader of France, made the mistake during the 1968 uprising of students (partly inspired by the civil rights, black power and anti-war movements in America and partly by revolutionary Marxism à la Guevara) of thinking his days as president were numbered, he later confessed. Middle of the road opinion seemed, passively at least, on the side of the students. But a brutal in-the-streets crack down by the police and the open support of the army for de Gaulle quickly reversed the tables. And before long de Gaulle was in power for another term. In the US a combination of big city riots and shoot-outs by the Marxist gun-toting Black Panthers led to a backlash among white voters and the election of Richard Nixon, who in turn engaged in what his Administration accurately termed "repression." Black Panther groups – as in Chicago – were raided by sharp-shooting police, a number killed and most intimidated.

In Germany, the Baader-Meinhof gang, a ruthless anti-capitalist group who sought out key figures in the establishment to murder, were eventually broken and subdued by police tactics that were much more humane than those used in Paris and Chicago.

Likewise, it was the steady police work of Interpol that led to the capture of the most famous and elusive of all international terrorists of the 1970s and 1980s – the Venezuelan, Ilich Ramirez Sanchez, better known as "Carlos". He had become a hired gun for the intelligence services of Iraq, Syria and Libya and also the Popular Front for the Liberation of Palestine. He was convicted in a Paris court in 1997 of numerous offences of hijacking, bank robberies and murder.

Repression can work. In Latin America it is quite clear that the brutal repressive tactics of the army against young dissidents sympathetic to Guevara worked in countries as varied as Chile, Peru, Uruguay, Argentina, Brazil, Guatemala and El Salvador. It also worked very well in Egypt. The police and the army used tactics and methods (in particular torture) that would never be condoned in the Western democracies, not even in the Chicago of Major Richard Daley.

But in other situations – Sri Lanka, Kashmir, Chechnya, East Timor, Palestine and Iraq – repression has exaggerated the problem, driving more people into the terrorist camps and recruiting more young members for suicide missions. On balance it is better to find a way, as the Germans did with the Baader-Meinhof gang and the British eventually did with the IRA, of defeating terrorism without indulging in the severe tactics of too cruel a repression.

During the 1980s and early 1990s there was a worldwide decline in terrorism. The left-wing terrorists for the most part disappeared. The right-wing ones lost influence and the nationalist-separatist ones – the IRA and the Basques – began the slow path of negotiations. Sponsors of terrorism like the Libyans, Syrians, the Sudanese and the Iranians pulled in their horns. Even the Palestinians, during the 1990s, took big steps away from violence. Diplomacy, mediation and the use of economic incentives have often been more effective than they are given credit for.

Even today, most of the world is quieter and less violent than it has ever been. Not only is there peace among the big powers for the first time since 1870-1914, the Stockholm International Peace Research Institute, which closely monitors conflicts, reports that since 1991 the number of conflicts worldwide has steadily fallen each year of the last fourteen years. At the same time democracy has been spreading rapidly, as has the appreciation of the norms of human rights.

But, it is true, as Huntington argues, that most violence today is generated by Muslims – not just Al Qaeda and the Palestinians, but by Kashmiris and Chechnyans.

However, it does not help to roll these together into one package as Huntington does. It is a fortuitous combination. Each has its own history quite separate from the others. Only with Al Qaeda and the Palestinians can one argue that there is today a mutual charging of each other's batteries. Yet the Palestinian cause is an old one – reaching back to British policy in the 1920s. Al Qaeda is a modern movement, concerned primarily with the American stranglehold on the politics and policies of Saudi Arabia, which has driven it into an obsessive hatred of America. (From 1991 to 2003 the US had a large military base in Saudi Arabia. For many Muslims, not just the militants, this was sacrilegious in the country that contained Islam's most revered holy places.) The fact that Al Qaeda has ignited support among disaffected Muslins as far apart as Indonesia, the Philippines and Western Europe was not part of Al Qaeda's original game plan – it fell into their lap because of the alienation that those groups were feeling as minorities in a hostile culture.

Perspective is important. Otherwise we can talk ourselves very fast into a situation where, by extrapolation and cross-cutting, we can make a worrying picture a quite terrifying one. We end up with a scenario of terrorists everywhere getting their hands on nuclear weapons and holding Western civilization hostage.

It is always important when confronting a problem to disaggregate it. The trouble with the policies of Bush/Blair is that they have done the opposite and by their recklessness they have aggravated every problem and created a unity in the Arab and much of the Islamic world that did not exist in this virulent form before. But of course Al Qaeda would never have had its ready supply of shock troops if the tunnel-vision of the Carter and Reagan era had not armed, with no questions asked, the Islamic militants who fought the Soviet army in Afghanistan. It was this that created the first cadres of professionalized Islamic terrorists with an anti-American agenda.

Today, with the Islamic Jihadists, Al Qaeda and the Palestinian groups, we face more complicated dangers. The counter-terrorist operations of Bush and Blair on the one hand and the Israelis on the other, rather than quelling the militants, have fed the flames of bitterness and resentment, widening enormously the constituency of the militants and leading us a step closer to a war of civilizations. Moreover, we live in an age when Western society is so technologically complex that it is much more vulnerable than it ever was to small bands of men determined to undermine it. Moreover, the chance in future years of the terrorists being able to manufacture a crude, so-called dirty "nuclear bomb" and smuggle it by small boat or plane into one of the West's largest cities is a real one. We live in an age when the nuclear-have powers have been recklessly irresponsible about both the export of nuclear technology and the guarding of stores of plutonium, enriched uranium and even the weapons themselves.

Moreover, the fifth column, disaffected Islamists, resident as immigrant workers or the offspring of immigrant workers, inside all the Western countries, has shown alarming signs of sympathy for the work of the militants. Despite many positive signs of integration among educated immigrants, there are increasing numbers of what Marx would call a "lumpen proletariat" who feel unwanted, spurned and rejected and who are fertile recruiting ground for militants.

The fact that Islamism as a political governing movement has manifestly failed where it has been recently tried – in Iran first and foremost but also in Afghanistan, Sudan and Algeria – is not to be counted on in every situation. The militants work with a well-honed message, exploiting simple and basic frustrations and are not engaging their recruits to ponder the complexities of political life. And even when militant Islamist government fails as it did in Iran, it can do a lot of damage while it exists.

Nevertheless, despite the opinion polls in the Muslim world that show an alarmingly high proportion of people becoming anti-American and anti-Western, there is evidence that in two of the most important countries in the Islamic World the tide is not running in just one direction. It is important not to forget that the Arab countries make up only 20% of the world's Islamic population. Despite the bombing in a tourist resort in the Indonesian island of Bali that claimed over 200 lives and guerrilla activity of an Islamic nature in two parts of the country, militant Islamism gets little traction in Islam's most populous country. Following the recent peaceful and well-supported general election in which Islamists of the more radical hue played little part, the indications are that for the future Indonesians will not be part of the catchment zone of Al Qaeda. Indeed, it is likely to become what Turkey is fast becoming in the West – a solid outpost of Islamic moderation, tolerance and democratic practice.

It is also likely that Turkey will end up as a member of the European Union (It has long been a member of NATO.) This would be the culmination of Turkey's long courtship of Europe that reaches back to Attaturk, the revolutionary general of the 1920s who founded modern Turkey on secular principles, clearly separating state and religion, and driving through, often ruthlessly, a series of political and social changes whose consequence is today that a majority of its people now feel more at ease in being part of Europe, at least politically, than being part of the East.

Turkey and Indonesia may be the most important countries that exhibit deeply rooted traditions of religious tolerance, but this trait can also be found among the vast majority of India's Muslim population of 150 million, Nigeria's 50 million Muslims, Bangladesh's 120 million, not to mention smaller but influential nations like Malaysia and Tunisia. In all of them Muslims behave as they have through the centuries, earnest about their religion, but tolerant of other religions especially those of "The Book"

In his book *Faith and Power,* Edward Mortimer, when writing about Rishid Rida, the great Islamic intellectual of the first half of the twentieth century, asked himself if Rida was "fundamentalist", since he was an admirer and defender of the militant Wahhabi puritans. "I do not think so" concluded Mortimer "although I must admit that the precise meaning of this word when used in the context of Islam eludes me."

It is astonishingly difficult to define fundamentalism either in Islam or Christianity. If it means "an effort to define the fundamentals of one's religion and a refusal to budge from them once defined then surely anybody with serious religious beliefs of any sort must be a fundamentalist in this sense."

In Christianity there are many strains of fundamentalism. The Catholic Church, which abhors Enlightenment liberalism, is clearly fundamentalist when it comes to issues like birth control and abortion, a position which allies the Vatican in international population conferences with many Muslim states and wins plaudits from many evangelical Church groups in the US. But this kind of fundamentalism is anathema to the powerful black Baptist Churches of America who consider themselves also part of the fundamentalist tradition of being "born again" believers. And where does the fundamentalism of Northern Ireland's Protestant firebrand, Ian Paisley, fit in? His refusal to countenance any compromise with the Catholic population and his tolerance of the ugly Protestant militias make him unacceptable to the opinion of fundamentalists in the southern United States that consider religious toleration as an important part of their American credo.

Likewise in Islam the so-called fundamentalists have many strands, even as they overlap each other and sometimes intertwine. Wahhibism is not Salafism despite the mutual respect they have for each other. And bin Laden's fundamentalism is neither, despite his appeal to many who call themselves Wahhabis. It is profoundly ironic that the "fundamentalist" bin Laden, with his Egyptian-influenced credo, has adopted a philosophy whose true pedigree reaches back to the tolerant, enlightened reformism of Jamal al-Din al-Afghani and his disciples Mohammed Abdul and Rishid Rida. Labels cannot only be seriously misleading, they have led Western policy, particularly American and British, in a dangerous and totally counterproductive direction. There has been no clash of civilizations since September 11th, merely a clash between one strain of so-called fundamentalism in the US and one strain in parts of the Middle East and Afghanistan.

What can the West do to diminish this Islamic hostility that has now reached unprecedented levels in some parts – but by no means all parts of the Islamic World?

It means a rapid winding down of the American and British military presence in Iraq and Afghanistan. It means, whatever the state of Iran's putative nuclear armoury turns out to be, forswearing "pre-emptive" military act as a way of dealing with it. It means deciding that a new way of dealing with Israeli intransigence and Palestinian political chaos is put in place. This would mean a carrot and stick approach – an offer of membership of the European Union for Israel if it is accommodating and accepts Crown Prince Abdullah's peace plan, coupled with the sticks of the US agreeing to respect the World Court's ruling on Israel's wall of separation and the EU leading the way with strong sanctions on the Israeli economy. On the Palestinian side it means the EU withdrawing its substantial aid programme unless Hamas agrees to accept Israel's right to exist. In Saudi Arabia it means unwinding the highly personal network that exists between parts of the Saudi establishment and the Republican hierarchy in the US. With Egypt it means making clear that future large amounts of US aid will be contingent on progress towards democracy. In Kuwait and the Gulf states it means withdrawing US and British troops as they have been withdrawn (one outstanding decision by Bush) from Saudi Arabia. With Turkey it means accelerating the negotiations for membership of the European Union whilst recognising that the country be allowed to maintain its essential cultural and religious values.

None of these on their own are concessions to Al Qaeda. They should have been done long before bin Laden came on the scene. They are simply overdue changes to policies that should never have been put into place.

The political level, however, is only one way the West should work. The churches and universities need to be more active in initiating dialogue with their counterparts in the Islam world. This is not missionary work. Quite the reverse. It is work to be done with humility, to learn from this great religious and intellectual tradition. The knowledge gained needs to be programmed to filter down our educational systems so that young people grow up without the ignorance and insensitivity of their parents.

Besides this we need a more frank debate on certain aspects of our own Western culture. At the moment Islamic societies, if they know anything about Western culture, know the populist version transmitted by satellite. It is football and "Sex in the City" and advertising under-the-armpit deodorants. A relatively insignificant effort goes into raising awareness of the cultural inheritance of the West, its rich tradition in music, art, architecture and literature. Very few of the great writings of Western literature, either past or present, are translated into Arabic or Urdu. Likewise the occasions when organisations like the British Council have the financial wherewithal to mount an exhibition of great Western art in Saudi Arabia or Indonesia are few and far between.

And what about our evolving idea of tolerance? When we debate same-sex marriages or the reach and extent of pornography in the hotel industry or even how young women dress, are we sensitive to the fact that we don't just live in our own communities? We are part of the global village and we can upset and hurt other peoples by displaying our own extreme personal ideas of liberty. This is not to suggest that Western girls should dress in the headscarf or burqa, but a look at young Turkish women in Istanbul would be instructive: the feminine figure, the elegance of high-heeled shoes, the artful use of make-up are all there. But at the same time the allure is sublimated just a few degrees, so that what is suggested is not gratuitously flaunted. A woman's best friend is what she can hint at, not what she can wave like the football fan's flag. As Jean-Christophe Rufin, the winner of the Prix Goncourt, wrote in his novel, *Brazil Red*, "The genius of civilization lay precisely in making sexuality blossom while keeping it hidden away, in revealing through dissimulation, in moving the very soul through modesty and artifice."

Some modest effort on the cultural side of the presentation of Western life might reduce the instinctive Islamic hostility, born often of ignorance, by quite a few degrees.

Many "born again Muslims" have become militants. But there are other trends in Islamic society. Islamist intellectuals like Rashid Ghanoushi, the Tunisian leader and Abdal-Wahhab el-Affendi, the Sudanese writer, are now arguing that restoring the Shar'ia "from above" by political action is "a recipe for tyranny and violence". But one should go back even further.

Jamal al-Din-al-Afghani, who lived from 1838 to 1897, was born in Iran and then lived in India. He preached a message of reform that has been dubbed the "protestant Islam". He argued that just as Islam had been open to absorbing Greek philosophy in the Middle Ages so it should be open to European ideas of liberalism today. His protégé, Mohammed Abduh, started the Salafiya movement, identifying with the salafi (elders) of the early Muslim community. He preached the compatibility of revelation and reason, and condemned the blind following of tradition. He had a great influence in Cairo as mufti (chief religious leader) of al-Azhar University (whose mufti today is still one of Islam's most outspoken liberals and influential preachers). He criticised polygamy, argued for the improved status of women and his associate, Qasim Amin, went further, denouncing veiling and social seclusion and the male's unfettered right to divorce.

It was the First World War and the defeat and break-up of the Ottoman Empire, the bulwark of Islamic identity, the expansion of European imperial influence in the Middle East and the creation of Israel that undermined the appeal of these new ways of thinking. European culture appeared destructive, no longer appealing, just as the American destruction of Iraq and support of Israel is weakening the cause of the Islamic liberals today. The Salafiyas, then led by the Syrian intellectual, Rishid Rida, based in Egypt, were split between radicals and liberals. The radicals, anti-Western and increasingly conservative, reacting to the Western-influenced secularisation of life, grew in strength and gave birth to the Muslim Brotherhood. The liberals, a much smaller group, moved left, only maintaining influence among intellectuals, high school teachers and journalists.

These days the liberals are beleaguered by the radicals. In 1994, long before we had heard of bin Laden, the Nobel Prize winning Egyptian novelist, Najib Mahfuz, a strong liberal, was stabbed and seriously wounded by a radical militant. Today the liberals, despite their intellectual and relevant doctrines, exist only on the fringe, concentrated in the universities and non-governmental organisations. Only in Turkey and in Indonesia do these thinkers have significant following. Many choose to live in the West, like Ishtiaq Ahmed, an associate professor of political science at Stockholm University who, writing on Shari'a law, has made the point that "since the time of Afghani the Shari'a has been interpreted rather flexibly. The limits set by Shari'a are not easily fixed ... Some 150 years ago fatwas were issued against travel by train, photos were considered unIslamic and the telephone and radio subversive gadgets". Ahmed recalls how Afghani observed that Islamic civilization was a religion of progress and reason whereas Christianity was full of superstitions.

Even in Pakistan liberals are speaking up. The scholar, Altaf Hussain, the founder and leader of the MQM, wrote in the Karachi newspaper, *Dawn*, last year that "It is the crying need of the times that Muslims take control of their lives by reinterpreting their religious values and mores in the light of their own age. Islam is a dynamic force that can't, and shouldn't, be held hostage to any one time frame or period."

The liberals do continue to exist and the growing Islamic revulsion of the terrorism of Al Qaeda, which has now killed more Muslims than Westerners, is encouraging them to become more outspoken. As Graham Fuller, a former vice chairman of the National Intelligence Council of the CIA has observed in *Foreign Affairs*, "Contemporary Islam is a dynamic phenomenon. It includes not only bin Laden and the Taliban but also liberals who are clearly embarking on their own reformation with potentially powerful consequences. Deeply entrenched traditionalists find these latter stirrings a threat, but many more Muslims, including many Islamists, see such efforts to understand eternal values in contemporary terms as essential to a living faith."

Fuller also highlights that these days nearly all Islamists are pushing hard for democracy. They have been convinced this is the only way to escape the stranglehold and repression of quasi-fascist modernist Arab regimes. In Algeria a decade ago Islamist parties actually won a general election only to see it overruled by the incumbent militant with the support of France and the US anxious about the consequences. A similar sequence of events happened in neighbouring Tunisia.

The battle is well underway. President Mohammed Khatami tried to uphold civil liberties in Iran in the face of determined resistance from a hard line clerical faction, only to see his liberal policies pushed aside by a mixture of American intransigence and a conservative shift in the electorate at home (the latter very much a reaction to the former). In Turkey where Islamists were voted into power three years ago the government seems to have found a way for the secular establishment, in particular the military, to accept a moderate Islamic government. Although previous governments have long been democratically elected and could not be described by any means as quasi-fascist like their Arab neighbours, they gave short shrift to human rights, the rights of minorities including the Kurds or to Islamist religious expression.

The fact that today these three things are changing for the better in harness goes to show what a powerful weapon for political change is the clarion call for human rights. It provides an umbrella for diverse interests who are united only in the need for free expression and their abhorrence of repression. If that leads them to democracy this can only be for the good. In the short-run it may lead to a rigid Islamist-dominated regime, but even if it does, if democracy can be maintained, it is inevitable that in time the government will be forced to become more open and tolerant.

Human rights are a wedge that can open this door and keep it open. The Islamists have faced enough persecution, prosecution, imprisonment, torture and repression to form an instinctive empathy for the calls and cause of the international human rights lobby. As the Nobel Peace prize winner, the Iranian, Shiri Ebadi, has argued, if the West, in particular Washington, had insisted on human rights standards in Iran whilst at the same time dropping its instinctive hostility and engaging in friendly diplomacy, the urges of the hardliners to develop Iran's nuclear weapons would have been sidelined by a more liberal and democratic climate at home.

It is important too that the Western world, the original home of contemporary human rights values, not cast aside its own adherence to them for the short-term needs of the moment. As one CIA intelligence veteran put it succinctly in a recent anonymously authored book, *Imperial Hubris*, "the US remains bin Laden's only indispensable ally."

By isolating Iran over twenty years, choosing an unnecessary war first in Afghanistan and even more so in Iraq and the Lebanon, the US and Britain have provoked an Islamic backlash that has made militant Islam a force its adherents could only have dreamed of. At the same time those two Western democracies have tarnished their lustre by suspending at home habeas corpus, one of the most elementary and important of all rights, and substituting administrative fiat and dictat for lawful practice.

If the accent of activity in the West, post September 11, had been on human rights it would have found more than an echo in the Islamic world. The liberal Islamic activists would have been emboldened to fight their corner. Now in most countries they are on the defensive before popular opinion that is roused in a visceral hatred against America and Britain (and to a lesser extent the rest of the West) and exhibits a frightening amount of sympathy for the persona of Al Qaeda, even if initially most Muslims were repulsed by the sheer horror of September 11th.

Historically, there has never been a sustained, continuous, clash between these great civilizations, Islam and Christianity. Undoubtedly there have been particular clashes and until the fall of the Ottoman Empire as a consequence of the First World War the Muslim world won most of them. Yet in victory Muslims invariably showed greater magnanimity and tolerance than did the Christian powers when they triumphed. Moreover, since 1914 the West, now in the ascendancy, has inflicted one grievous blow after another on the Muslim world, particularly on the Middle Eastern peoples. It should have come as no surprise that there was an almighty reaction, even if no-one could have imagined quite the ferocity that Al Qaeda brought to bear. Yet without the equally almighty reaction of Bush and Blair it is quite possible that with more temperate policies Al Qaeda would have fairly quickly withered away, as have already its Egyptian roots.

All might have been different if the Western world had remained true to the precepts of its own Greek and Christian founding and the wise notions of the philosophers of the Enlightenment with their emphasis on the importance of reason and their enthusiasm for democracy and human rights.

# 2 Can We Allow the Free Movement of People?

It was Walter Lippmann, the great American columnist of the *New York Herald Tribune*, who reminded us that news and truth are not the same thing: "The function of news is to signalise an event, the function of truth is to bring to light the hidden facts, to set them into relation with each other and make a picture of reality on which men can act."

We are – and have been for forty years or more – almost blinded by news about immigration. There is, by the month, an outpouring of reports and studies, often contradictory or even downright confusing. Hardly a day goes by when we are not told some interesting and provoking item, about black Africans in a small boat taking in water in a wild Atlantic, desperately using their mobile to call, via the network of the nearby island of Fuerteventura, a cousin in Spain to alert the coastguard who duly rescues them, or an altercation between once ever-so-friendly political leaders in Sweden and Denmark over the merits of Denmark's newly fashioned conservative immigration policies, to the point where the leader of Denmark's Peoples' Party threatened to "pull up the drawbridge" – the new (unpullable up) bridge that now links Sweden to the European mainland.

I have contributed my own quota of stories – reporting from the Mauritanian desert on the migrants who brave all to cross the Sahara and the Mediterranean to find their way to the decrepit dormitories in abandoned factories circling Paris, from where they venture to work washing the street gutters of Paris every morning, making it the most pristine of all Europe's capitals. Or spending days interviewing in the shantytowns, awful contraptions of discarded corrugated iron and cardboard that used to disfigure outer Paris in the 1970s when Algerians and Africans first poured into high growth, labour-short, Europe. Or journeying to the fields of Wisconsin to yet more shacks to report on the Mexican migrant workers, picking peas and canning vegetables, without access to a doctor or even a nurse, unless some local Church worker found them a contact. Or standing, my burning thirst almost forgotten, in a northern Senegalese village, bordering the Sahara, astonished at the glittering white cement of the newly renovated mosque and the women, erect, dressed in exquisite damask, gaudy parasols aloft, walking handsomely along the river bank, the cares of a bygone harsh era banished by the monthly remittances from their menfolk in France.

We have it all at our fingertips now, but are we any nearer at getting at the truth, at understanding either what is really going on or what our policies at the receiving end should be?

Was Enoch Powell, the cerebral, racist Conservative politician of the 1960s, perhaps right after all when he foresaw that one day British streets would be like "the River Tiber, foaming with much blood"? Overcoming our distaste for the way he put things, pronouncing Negro almost like nigger in one not-to-be-forgotten Third Programme discussion, should we have listened to the substance of his warnings more carefully? As William Deedes, a former cabinet colleague, wrote recently, his speeches "forced everyone in authority to make light of all the problems Commonwealth immigration was creating."

Are we now in danger of arriving in incremental, almost unnoticed, steps over the last 40 years at David Ricardo's "iron law of wages," so perfectly elastic has become the supply of immigrant labour over the years, thanks to the increasing inter-connectedness of nations and peoples and the often superb organisation of the long-distance people smugglers? Has one unfortunate consequence of globalisation, of which emigration plays a major part, been to begin the creation of a pool of cheap labour in the industrialised West that is almost unlimited, forcing wages to stabilize at just above subsistence level? Until recent years, in Europe, if not America, Ricardo's theory could not work as once feared, because of geographical, political, craft and trade union barriers, not to mention pro farm policies, all of which have worked to limit the available supply of labour. But now? (According to a study made by Harvard professor George Borjas, the rapid rise in immigration from Mexico into the US has pushed the wage levels of immigrants relative to natives sharply down.)

Have we already allowed in such vast numbers that we have crossed the Rubicon of political and religious tolerance by the host societies? Was the cultured and sophisticated Italian writer, Oriani Fallaci, speaking for large numbers of ordinary working class people, who usually are the ones who play host to the immigrants, when she wrote in a leading liberal paper of Italy, *Corriere della Serra* (which in the aftermath of September 11th was more than happy to print altogether 12,000 words of her anti-Islamic invective), of her experience of trying to get rid of Somali immigrants living in a tent, performing all their bodily functions next to Florence's Cathedral: " I don't go singing Ave Marias or Paternosters before the tomb of Mohammed. I don't piss or shit at the feet of their minarets. When I find myself in their countries I never forget that I am a guest and a foreigner. I am careful not to offend them with clothing or behaviour that are normal for us but inadmissable to them... Why should we respect people who don't respect us? Why should we defend their culture or presumed culture when they don't respect ours? I want to defend our culture and I say that I prefer Dante Alighieri to Omar Khayyam. And the sky opens. They crucify me 'Racist, racist!'" Of course she sounds like one, the way she puts it, but when eighteen years ago Muslim leaders in Bradford publicly burnt *The Satanic Verses* or when, more recently, Muslim youths in Marseilles burnt down synagogues and school buses it was difficult even for hardened liberals not to let such similar thoughts cross their minds.

Can immigration go on? Why should it go on? And, anyway, what real, long-term, benefits does it bring? During the 1970s and 1980s the question became relatively muted. The European economies under-performed and many European governments had put into place restrictive immigration policies that weakened a flow that was diminished anyway by the slackening of demand.

But then came the Yugoslav, African and Afghani wars and a hectic rush of refugees into Western Europe. An economic turn for the better made political generosity rather easy. For a while it looked as if the whole 1960's belief system was being dusted off: that immigration oils the cogs and wheels of the economy, especially the bit below decks where the heaving lifting is done. Many industrialists, eager for cheap labour, claimed that immigration relieved labour bottlenecks and countered inflationary pressures.

But then as quickly as the new tide of welcoming came in it ebbed. The big and difficult questions of the 1960s and 70s are back with a vengeance. Although the refugee numbers are far down from their early 1990's peak, the debate has never been so fast and furious, and understandably so. All over Europe asylum numbers are creeping up again. In Britain immigration is at its highest levels since records began. Even to those pro the free market and pro the intermingling of people there is a sense, albeit expressed reluctantly, that enough is now enough. There is a growing feeling that the earlier massive migrations, first of the 1960's and them of the early 1990s, whatever good it did to a few sections of the economy, to many of the first generation of the immigrants themselves and to our ignorance of the music, cuisine and culture of faraway peoples, created a series of hard-to-deal-with problems for which society is now paying the bills.

Immigration, we now see, has enabled society to put on hold older problems it should have been forced to confront earlier. In particular, it postponed the re-organisation of economic life in the most humdrum parts of the economy, putting off the day when menial jobs would have been reshaped to attract unemployed locals. It also postponed the day when a lot of businesses – textiles and agriculture are the worst examples, but in fact a wide range of industry from steel manufacture to shipyards to automobile plants, all of which at various times begged successfully for government aid – should have packed up thirty years ago, not ten years ago as most of them were eventually forced to do, and relocate in lower cost, often Third World, emigrant-producing countries.

For society at large, each new wave of immigration, particularly in those periods of high economic activity, greased the wheels and kept the inflationary demons at bay. But it was never quite clear and even today it is the subject of much ingrown debate, did the costs outweigh the benefits? Once the immigrants are settled, their families reunited or reproduced, did their own "demands" – housing, schools, social services together with the burden of juvenile delinquency and rising crime – cost society more than what they were putting in?

Even in America, which for now accepts, if not always as uniformly as it once used to, that it will continue to be a country whose vitality partly comes from immigration, and where the process of social adopting and adapting is more smooth, economists find it hard to prove that latter day immigration has been a significant economic plus over the long run. One fairly recent study by the US National Academy of Sciences estimates that migrants make an annual net contribution to the economy of $10 billion, truly peanuts. The debate continues, and each side has its points, but it is certainly no longer as clear-cut as the Americans always presumed it was. (See the illuminating review of some recent literature by Harvard professor, Christopher Jenks, in the November 2002 issue of the *New York Review of Books*.)

Readers, I hope, will forgive me if I only briefly refer to the economic debate. It truly has become an extraordinary theoretical one for the specialists. It's not that it is incomprehensible, it is simply inconclusive and often contradictory. In as much as I would attempt to summarise it, I would say that immigration is a good thing for certain industries, a useful anti-inflationary tool in the short run, usually good for the majority of first generation immigrants themselves, but not for low paid natives (in California American-born workers have left the state as fast as immigrants have moved in, so extreme has been the impact of immigrants on keeping wages down), and of questionable and uncertain value to the sending countries which, while they gain often handsomely from remittances, lose their best and brightest, often those most entrepreneurial, driven to distant lands. But even this inevitably partisan summary can be challenged.

If only one could say, as a card-carrying free marketer that I am, that the free movement of labour would be as beneficial to all parties as is the free movement of capital and free trade. But if there are enormous costs in implementing the latter two in a too simplistic way, they pale into insignificance when one examines the complexities of the free flow of human beings themselves.

The economic debate, even if it were to be settled one way or another, cannot be the only one. Besides it, there has to be and equal debate on social stability and another on social responsibility (what some might call social morality). The plumbing of the complexities of these two is more a layman's task – doubtless why Enoch Powell, bright as he was, concentrated on these and ignored the economics.

In the 1960s the social question rarely extended beyond the issues of open doors and equal opportunity. Was citizenship easily granted? (In Britain and Holland it was automatic for ex colonials, in France and Sweden not so difficult to obtain, in Germany almost impossible.) Were the new immigrants getting a fair share? What were the chances of upward mobility? Should the inward flow be regulated? Germany had no inhibitions about this. Its *Gastarbeiter* (guest worker) programme was built round the notion of returning home after a couple of years. But most countries tied themselves in knots with all sorts of "braking" legislation, seemingly unaware, as was shown back in an early study made in the mid 1960s for the outstanding British report, *Colour and Citizenship*, that inflows correlated with unfilled vacancies – migrants in effect "braked" themselves. They simply did not come if the grapevine reported there were no jobs at the other end.

Later came debates about prejudice and colour bars, and gradually the countries of Europe, while often loudly protesting it wasn't a problem, legislated against discrimination. Later still, as the migrants put down family roots – even in Germany too – came the issue of children's opportunities. With often a disturbed childhood, shunted between parents in Europe and grandparents at home, with the inevitable language difficulties for lack of native playmates, with more than their fair share of taunts from native children, with teachers who often resented the extra complications of a mixed classroom and, not least, confined to often already bad schools in slum or poor neighbourhoods where sometimes their numbers just swamped native children, it was exceedingly difficult to grow up with the same flow of adrenalin that had driven their parents to cut through every barrier on their road to a better life.

What made a difficult situation worse was the tendency of host societies to assume immigrants were more prone to crime, an attitude that police forces everywhere magnified quite counterproductively. In reality, the crime levels of the first generation were significantly below that of the host population. But bad policing worked to make the prejudice self-fulfilling. Moreover, it helped lay the conditions for the second generation to embrace crime. Persecuted and hounded for what they hadn't done, it led to political militancy on the one hand and a devil-will-take-me attitude to the binding constraints of society on the other. Coupled with poor achievement at school and closed doors in the job market place for those who, unlike their parents, would not settle for dirt, docility and low pay, the ingredients for a tormented and unfruitful life were well mixed.

As the second generation matured so did the questions that immigration and its consequences threw up change complexion. Like a dye thrown in the river to highlight the course of its currents, the settlement of large numbers of immigrant families in the worst parts of Europe's major urban areas – inner cities in Britain and Germany, outer rim housing estates in France and Holland – threw into perspective the poor social and scholastic amenities and crime that in more monochrome days had received little publicity.

Although most European countries had social housing programmes of varying effectiveness, few were geared up to deal with what appeared to be a mushrooming of social problems in the new immigrant communities, which were compounded by a growing friction between old and new communities, between those who were essentially, for all their leftward voting patterns, traditional, conservative and nationalistic communities, and newcomers whose tastes and practices of life were often simply alien. While the educated and much travelled often revelled in the surface manifestations of new music, cuisines, religious practices and lifestyles, it was the poorer members of the native working class who had to live and work alongside the immigrants, without anyone ever asking them was this the way they would choose for their country to change.

Looking back over the last couple of decades what is astonishing is perhaps not so much the rise of extremist anti-immigrant political parties and the growth of anti-immigrant violence and intolerant police behaviour, but that a majority of immigrants, even the second and now sometimes the third generation, have found a reasonable niche in the host society and that the native working class has come to terms with much of immigrant life, accepting them in their workplace and unions, tolerating them in their pubs and sporting events, indeed in football, once the most rigid bastion of working class aspirations, accepting them as equals. The plusses may be more than the minuses, yet they are not sufficient. Resentment in host societies is building up- in some countries at a horrific pace. In France, Holland, Denmark, Switzerland and Austria it has found a demagogic, but influential voice, and other countries may suffer the same experience before very long. It is only a question of time before the 17% of the vote threshold (Le Pen's high watermark) moves up to a threatening 25%.

There are now too many combustible situations provoked by immigration. Too many, that is, if one of the important aims of government is the building of a sober society in which one can enjoy an un-threatened lifestyle. To be more precise – in which there is an on-going state of social and political harmony that does not countenance the turning over of cars in Frankfurt, firebombings in Rotterdam, publicly setting fire to high-class English literature in Bradford, burning down synagogues in Marseilles, voicing loudly their support of the activities of bin Laden, and fighting the police with cobblestones, slates and petrol bombs in Paris and Oldham, not to mention the sharp rise in everyday criminal activity all over Europe.

There is no doubt, however, that the violence against immigrants came first – the turds through the letter box, the gang attacks, the knifings, the shootings, the fire-bombing of immigrants shops and homes. First there was action and then re-action. Indeed, if anything the reaction was slow to materialise. The first generation of immigrants was essentially passive, but the second, particularly if they were jobless, were ripe, not for revolution – that did not much interest them – but for spite and mayhem, perhaps even revenge.

There is not much reason to believe that improvement and amelioration can come quickly. In northern England, the Midlands and in parts of London, around numerous French, German, Italian and Spanish cities, in the suburbs of Amsterdam, large numbers of immigrants partly out of comfort, partly out of misplaced housing policies, have been thrown together in concentrated heaps. Whilst in some cases it satisfies an urge to live close to one's countrymen, more often it has led to a social segregation from the host society that allows the immigrants to cut themselves off from the rather rapid evolution of contemporary European societies. At one extreme this can lead, as it did in the Swedish university town of Uppsala, to a father (a Turkish Kurd) murdering his daughter for dating a Swedish boy. At the other it leads to a false politicisation, whereby a small but not insignificant number of immigrants become the expatriate supporters of extremely violence political causes back home, re-establishing abroad the repressive, violent prone or feuding societies they were at one time only too happy to leave behind.

Oriani Fallaci overstates it in an unpleasant way. But she bites on the bitter kernel of an essential truth of human experience – not to adjust to the norms of a host society is either an extreme narrow mindedness or an arrogance of the highest order. I think of my Swedish doctor friend who recently decided to go and work to build up his pension (Swedish doctors are the most poorly paid in Europe) in the King Fahd hospital in Riyadh, whose wife laughingly accepts without question that she should wear a headscarf in public, give up driving and be ultra-discreet about their drinking. It wouldn't cross their minds as reasonably sensible people to have any other attitude. Immigrants who come to us have to realize that they come not just to a job, but also to an organic society with its own long history and its own strong traditions. They can ask for freedom of belief for themselves and uphold the personal moral standards they believe in, but they cannot try to impose their views on the society around them, whether it is religious values or political persuasions, especially if it means breaking the laws and the more important conventions of the host society. Besides, for their own peace of mind, they seriously need to weigh the consequences of their children growing up in an alien culture and accept that, if they have made a decision to leave their roots, changing mores are inevitable. It must be made clear that to them that part of emigrating is not just because they aspire to a particular job, but also because they aspire to be part of the culture and political life of the receiving country.

If they cannot see this for themselves, then they must be educated and informed as part of the process of formal admittance. If they cannot swallow it, which is a quite understandable position to take, then there is no good reason to allow entry. The American immigrants, once they decide to seek citizenship, must take an "oath of allegiance". That is rather a good idea. This argument is water under the bridge for the 20 million or so immigrants already inside the European Union, but it is quite relevant for the refugees who queue at our gates, the illegal immigrants who periodically win an amnesty and become legalised and the skilled immigrants that most of the governments of Europe are intent on recruiting. Europe simply cannot allow its major cities in the course of the next decade or two to become replicas of Northern Ireland.

Europe has prided itself on its economic and political liberalism, but there has been simply too much *laissez-faire*, both in anticipating the social problems of the marginalisation of fast-growing numbers of immigrant settlers and in accepting the politicisation of closed cells of hard men within certain immigrant communities. In an era when misguided post-September 11th American and British policy is ratcheting up increasing degrees of anti-Western hostility across what was an already charged Islamic world, we have no choice but to watch our backs.

The issues of social responsibility here intrude. We should be open to sharing our wealth and our opportunities. Why should we be taking down barriers for fellow Europeans but putting up barriers for the darker poorer peoples of Africa, Asia and Latin America? The answer is we shouldn't have to, but we have made such a mess of the way we have done it so far that a moratorium while we work hard at ameliorating the pile-up of problems is essential – perhaps extending for a generation. Besides, there is another side to this coin which liberal society doesn't care to look at very often: what damage are we doing to the sending societies by encouraging emigration?

There is something almost repulsive about the way the health services of European countries have milked both consciously and unconsciously the Third World for their doctors and nurses, leaving countries that are desperate for medical care bereft of those their hard won tax money has often educated and trained. The British government encouraged one of its most eminent immigrants, the ex-Egyptian heart surgeon Magdi Yacoub, to poach fellow specialists from the hospitals of the world. Inevitably the greatest response to his recruiting campaign, given the use of his name and the modest salaries offered, came from Third World and Eastern European countries. The same pattern is being repeated more quietly in the filching of other skills – computer specialists, engineers, chemists, teachers, businessmen and university professors. Many European governments today, putting their charged immigration debates momentarily on one side, are relaxing immigration restrictions for such groups.

If we truly had the welfare of emigrant societies in our sights we would make it the more difficult to enter the more skilled or educated the immigrants were. Not only would this make Africa, India and countries such as the Philippines and Mexico healthier and better educated, it would do more than any amount of foreign aid to encourage the kind of development that would provide jobs and opportunities for those mass of unskilled who too often see their only chance of escaping poverty as migrating overseas.

Emigration, observed Simon Jenkins in a column in *The Times*, "is the Third World's contribution to globalisation." If it is, it is coming at a great cost to the Third World and a great initial benefit to the First World. Back in 1970, Madeleine Trebous made a telling study of Algerian emigration to France and observed that France receives young migrant workers whose "economic value" is at a maximum and whose "rearing" has cost France not a franc. Nothing has changed in thirty years. Remittances may be a windfall for macro-economic policy in the emigrant countries, but at the micro level they tend to have minimal productive effect, concentrated as they are on spending on consumer goods, the upkeep and education of children left behind, modern housing (where showcasing merely increases the urge to further emigration) and the financing of relatives who also want to emigrate. Only when the barriers to further emigration have been tightened do the remittances of earlier generations have a benign effect on a local economy.

Yet the pressures on us to close our eyes to the dilemmas of immigration appear to be mounting. Rates of population growth are falling all over Europe, in some countries such as Italy, Spain and Germany, frighteningly fast. One forecast, made by the UN's chief population statistician at the request of Pat Buchanan for his apocalyptic book, *The Death of the West*, predicts that if the present German low birth rate continues and immigration is zero Germany's population will fall by over half by the end of the century. Increasingly, the question being raised is who is going to pay for the pensions of the present aging workforce? As the *Financial Times* bluntly answered the question in a recent editorial, "Europe must now prepare to open its doors."

But what does that mean? Should Europe bring in 170 million immigrants by mid century if it wishes to keep its population aged 15 to 64 at today's level (which it would have to if the German kind of arithmetic were applied across Europe)?

A trend we all know is not a final statement. Sweden, the mother of not only the sexual revolution but of the working mother and the government-funded crèche, after years of a dramatically falling birth rate now exhibits signs of a reverse (likewise, Finland and Denmark). Italy, Germany and Spain are now introducing incentives that will encourage couples to have more children. In the UK and France the decline in population is happening rather slowly and probably could easily be reversed with the same kind of encouraging policies that the Scandinavian governments have fashioned. Among the wealthier members of the middle-class across Europe larger families are already more popular than they were a generation ago, suggesting that while increased general prosperity may at first encourage a low birth rate as young couples become consumer conscious, sustainable wealth may work the other way. Moreover, there is evidence that as the divorce rate continues to climb, still fertile women who take another partner sometimes start a second family. Assuming income levels keep rising at the rate they have the last fifty years, the falling population scare may turn out to be one of those Club of Rome-type overstatements.

If ever a social argument has been overdone it is the current one about the ageing of our population and the likely future pensions' crisis. The widespread notion, touted for example by a recent special government-appointed commission in Germany, that to counter the country's ageing population "policy should be to attract highly qualified foreigners" is so much nonsense. A few tens of thousands of professionals can do nothing for a society that is ageing from top to bottom under present social conditions. Such an argument would have to admit that the unskilled were needed as much as the skilled – and in vast numbers. Otherwise, who would do the work and who would pay enough taxes and social insurance premiums?

Every study has shown that the simple expedient of the rising of the retiring age by a few years, together with a concomitant rise in labour force participation, will knock the bottom out of this problem. Undoubtedly, there will be resistance to this, but compared with the social instability that a loosening of the immigration spigot would bring about, it pales into relative insignificance. In an age when people are living longer and healthier lives (a French child born today has a 50% chance of reaching 100), it is quite ridiculous both for themselves and for the social welfare of the societies to which they belong that people should renounce working for their bread and butter so early in life. In Holland, with its low jobless rate, recruiting the elderly into new jobs, as government has felt compelled to find an alternative to new immigration, has become a growth industry. In Rotterdam "55+", an employment agency, has seen demand soar for health-care workers, teachers and librarians. Who these days at 70 or even 75 cannot drive a bus or sell tickets in a railway station? As for the professions, is it not true that, in an economy that is increasingly brain-led, the knowledge and experience that only comes with longevity is more useful than the adrenalin of youth? To change our cultural attitudes, which perversely have gone in the reverse direction in recent years, governments need to give society some fiscal shock treatment, like sharply cutting taxes for the working elderly or doubling the normal state pension if one waits to retire until the age of 75.

Europeans often become tangled up when thinking about the American experience of a historically liberal immigration policy (although relatively tight on refugee admissions) and the resulting more youthful population. This is something of a red herring. It actually doesn't matter if in the US the population is growing faster and is younger. The critical issue for Europe is how it uses its work force – can it use its older people effectively and productively? Can it avoid the cultural attitude, prevalent first in America, but now common throughout Europe, of throwing people on the scrap heap, often at 55 (as with French railway drivers) but at 50, as is common in some professions, not least journalism and banking, in marked contrast to say judges or, once upon a time, politicians, who in Britain at least go on until they are 75 (which merely goes to underline how culturally induced these artificial retirement ages are)?

Indeed, it could be said that the US is shooting itself in the foot by putting such a premium on absorbing a youthful, immigrant-fed population. Research that I have quoted above shows us that the net benefit of mass immigration might be as little as $10 billion a year, peanuts for an economy the size of America's. This is too little gain for a society that has to balance the gain with the loss – first and foremost, that of cultural and social identity; second, its openness to a fifth column of al-Qaeda-type dissidents; and, third, to a general suppression of wages and living conditions for its poorest 20%. (Although one should add the caveat that the importing of brain power – a relatively small percentage of the total inflow of migrants – is another matter. For the US this can only be a net gain, but one very much at the expense of the progress of the developing countries.)

My bias by now is perhaps obvious – I appear to be arguing in favour of immediate tight controls on future immigration. But that is to misread me. I know full well that the tighter the restrictions the more the flows of manpower will go underground. This was the lesson of American immigration thirty years ago and in my book of that time, which compared immigration in the US with that of Europe, I predicted that Europe would repeat America's experience of massive illegal labour, which it has.

It would be rather incongruous, to say the least, for one who has long argued that drugs should be liberalised in order to undercut the black market and the mafias who thrive on it, destabilising so many Latin American and Caribbean countries, to turn round and shrug off the problems of a black labour market. Trafficking in individuals is now the fastest growing business of organised crime. There is no simple solution, although tighter controls, as Denmark has shown, will help somewhat. Stiff penalties on employers who are found employing illegals would help even more, even though in Britain's case it would mean the introduction of some form of national identity card.

Part of the answer to this, paradoxically, is to liberalise the immigration market – to take down all the artificial barriers of government controls. The Cato Institute, a libertarian US think tank, argues that then immigration will become a circular process, instead of having immigrants, once in, clinging like limpets to the rocks of the host country for fear of ejection. This would be good for the immigrants, good for the host society and good for the further pursuit of the human rights of both sides.

The United States has conducted what is in fact a pilot project on liberalization with Puerto Rican immigration, which has always been unrestricted because of its special political status within the USA. Even in the 1980s, nearly half of the immigrants coming from this then underdeveloped, poor, Caribbean island, stayed on the mainland for only two years. In the 1990s the traffic ceased of its own accord, as Puerto Rico rapidly developed. The truth is that migrant workers, if given a choice, usually prefer to get home once they have achieved their goals. One sees the same phenomenon with Polish workers today who have recently gained the freedom to work unimpeded in half the states of the European Union. Cheap airfares make it even easier for them to keep their roots at home intact. The excellent Polish carpenter I recently employed in my Swedish flat spends three weeks of every month in Sweden and one week a month back home with his family. He has no intention of settling in Sweden although he is free to do so. He has cost me half of what I would pay a Swedish carpenter.

Immigrants who cause the kind of problems that now rattle receiving societies often act as they do in a desperate attempt to cling onto what they think is the way of doing things back home or simply because they feel trapped. Moreover, liberalization would destroy the evils of the black market.

Step by step, we have to move the immigration phenomenon back to where it was in the 1960s, unrecognised though it generally was at that time, when emigrants only decided to uproot themselves because they knew there would be jobs at the other end. No unfilled vacancies, no migrant flows or, at least, much smaller ones. This doesn't only mean using the older member of our society better, it means often re-fashioning many low-paid jobs so that they have more appeal for native workers (who now include the large numbers of second and third generation offspring of migrants).

Once we get hold of these issues, the contemporary problem of masses of asylum seekers (who often, perhaps in a majority of cases today, are disguised immigrant workers) might begin to fall into place.

Meanwhile, to help the process along, there is much we can do at the sending end to reduce the push factors. First and foremost, it means a more determined approach to the lowering of tariff barriers on typical Third World labour-intensive exports, textiles, shoes and agricultural products in particular. Second, it means, by the deft use of aid policies, encouraging land reform and small farmer productivity in the Third World's rural backwaters. Third, it means being pro-active politically in situations where we can see conflict brewing and which are likely, if they spin out of control, to produce hundreds of thousands of new refugees. In Yugoslavia, the main source of European refugees in the 1990s, Europe involved itself very late in the day, when Milosević and his destructive apparatchiks already had their tails up. Defence budgets have to be re-directed towards peace-making in failed states, rather than building up armouries of expensive modern weaponry, only suitable for counterproductive wars with the likes of Iraq. Earlier intervention – political and economic – could perhaps have avoided the later military deployments and bombing in ex-Yugoslavia.

The great immigration debate has to become the great re-thinking and re-structuring debate. Charlie Brown is right, of course when he says, "No problem is so big and complicated that it can't be run away from". But then "backward" situations, as Sartre once said, can be also a point of vantage when people are questioning the results of forward movement.

# 3  Can We Diminish War?

"It is hard to deny that war is inherent in the very nature of the state. States historically identify themselves by their relationship to one another, asserting their existence and defining their boundaries by the use of force or the imminent threat of force; and for so long as the international community consists of sovereign states, war between them remains a possibility, of which all governments have to take reasonable account ... Who fights with Dragons, said Nietzsche, shall himself become a Dragon. [But] the other horn of the dilemma is: he who does not fight with Dragons may be devoured by them."

This observation by the eminent historian of war, Michael Howard (*The Causes of War and Other Essays*, Harvard University Press, 1983) contains a large element of truth, but it is not the whole truth. War and even more so the preparation for war, the building and trading of armaments, is commonplace. Yet it is diminishing. The body count, to use that repugnant yet unforgettable term of the Vietnam War, may have increased with the world's rapidly improving technological prowess, but the occasion of war has unquestionably diminished.

Indeed what we see today is the culmination of a long process. The decline in the amount of warfare in Europe, the epicentre of most wars on earth the last six hundred years, if not longer, has been in process for some 150 years.

Undoubtedly, the European Union's great achievement has been to realize what in fact was its founders' purpose – to cement the often warring nations of Western Europe into a peaceful whole. So easy to summarize the achievement. So easy too to underestimate the historical magnitude of this quite astonishing and unprecedented success story.

Moreover, for the first time in history, there are a not insignificant number of states that have been free from war for the best part of two centuries. In Europe there are Switzerland and Sweden, both despite a long tradition of warfare. In the latter's case the pedigree of war stretches back to the Vikings and whose modern day emergence as a nation state owes much to the aggressive militaristic leadership of Vasa in the eighteenth century, who not content with putting the whole of Scandinavia under the Swedish yoke tried, with some success at first, to extend Swedish power eastward over Russia and southward over Germany.

Latin America, Venezuela, Costa Rica and Brazil have now lived out a century, much longer in the latter's case, without war.

Indeed, entire regions of our planet have long escaped internal war – North America most importantly. Neither Canada, nor Mexico, nor the United States maintains troops on each other's borders. Likewise the South Pacific has long been peaceful, apart from a brief invasion by the Japanese in the Second World War and relatively small-scale conflicts in West Iranian and East Timor.

Today the largest economic power in Asia, Japan, formally abjures warfare, an undertaking written into its constitution, the consequence of the nuclear bombardment by the US of Hiroshima and Nagasaki, and its subsequent defeat in the Second World War, which left great intellectual scars as well as the more obvious emotional ones.

In due course I will argue that there is enough evidence at hand to suggest this poorly reported balance of peaceful existence between neighbouring states not only belies Michael Howard's summation, but could in fact be extended in our lifetime in a quite significant way.

But first there must be an accounting of Professor Howard's view, not least because he speaks a lot of sense and there are a lot of rather high-powered thinkers who not only agree with him, but also believe the world must continue that way if it is to survive and prosper.

Arguably the greatest practitioner of the so-called "realist" thinking about war these days is Professor Mersheimer of the University of Chicago, who walks heavily in the footsteps of his intellectual mentor, former Secretary of State, Henry Kissinger. Following the collapse of the Soviet Union and of the long and bitter Cold War in 1992, he wrote, in *Rethinking America's Security: Beyond Cold War to New World Order,* in a perfect echo of Michael Howard, "With the Cold War now relegated to the dustbin of history ... optimists believe those changes can serve as the basis for a more peaceful world in the 21st century. In fact, however, there have been no fundamental changes in the nature of international politics since World War II. The state system is still alive and well and, although regrettable, military competition between sovereign states will remain the distinguishing feature of international politics for the foreseeable future."

I don't know if Professor Mearsheimer has ever read Nancy Mitford's delightful biographical work, *Voltaire in Love*. Voltaire, the *eminence grise* of the Enlightenment, was a passionate pacifist (although not entirely a consistent one), a man so convinced of the argument against the deployment of state violence in any cause that his friendship with the young prince Frederick of Prussia developed into a litmus test of his ability to translate his beliefs into the actions of statecraft. In what over the years became a major intellectual effort to woo the man who was surely by inheritance eventually going to become the fulcrum that would lever war and peace in Europe, he appeared to have much success. Frederick became his disciple, writing a tract, *Anti-Machiavelli,* in which "he was going to refute the cynical maxims of that Italian enemy of the human race, mouthpiece of Satan, and prove that it was to the interests of a ruler to be good, honest and above board." The central theme of *Anti-Machiavelli* was the wickedness of those rulers who seek self-aggrandizement at the expense of other men's lives, the uselessness of territorial conquest, the importance of learning and, above all, of pleasure.

There was much sincerity in this man, despite his madcap playboy image of a prince known to cavort in homosexual orgies whilst Voltaire was visiting, although he found time enough for earnest discourse with the great philosopher. Yet when his father died and he became King of Prussia, later to be known as Peter the Great, all changed. He now believed that with power in his hands he should extend the wealth and realms of his kingdom. Elements of his early idealism remained: he abolished censorship, capital punishment, child labour and torture, which was not used again in Prussia for nearly 200 years. But he stepped into the role that, if Howard and Mearsheimer are correct, is pre-ordained and quite unavoidable – the never-ending power struggle of the state and its perpetual need to assert its interests, peacefully if possible, but failing that by recourse to arms. When all states have the capability for doing each other harm, Mearsheimer argues, each is driven to amass as much power as it can to be secure against attack. "A state's ultimate goal", he says "is to be the hegemony in the system."

In today's world, global hegemony can only be achieved, Mearsheimer argues, by "crystal clear cut nuclear superiority", which he defines as "a capability to devastate its rivals without fear of retaliation".

The United States is the only regional hegemon in modern history because of its ability to dominate the affairs of the western hemisphere. Other states such as Japan and Nazi Germany have tried to achieve this status, but failed in the attempt.

Rather than criticise the morality of this, Mearsheimer matter-of-factly observes that "states are disposed to think offensively toward other states even though their ultimate motive is simply to survive. In short, "great powers have aggressive intentions" and he quotes John Herz's original statement of the so called "security dilemma" with approval: "Striving to attain security from attack [states] are driven to acquire more and more power to escape the impact of the power of others".

Is this realism? Or is it pessimism? In truth it is not even realism when projected backwards into history and as for the future its pessimism is arguably outrageous.

As Professor Glenn Snyder has argued in the Harvard quarterly, *International Security*, neither the United States in 1900, when it was already a hegemon in the western hemisphere, expanded into Europe and Asia, nor did Great Britain during the peak of its power in the nineteenth century expand into Europe. Mearsheimer calls these anomalies, explicable by "the stopping power of waters" – the Atlantic in the American case and the English Channel in the British one. Yet his supporting argument is thin and it is not surprising that

Snyder concludes that "one wonders whether the 'stopping power' resides in the water, or the strength of opponents – or simply a lack of interest in expansion?"

So when Mearsheimer now posits great instability, perhaps war in Europe and Northeast Asia over the next 20 years, one finds it easy to treat his pessimistic foreboding as little more than the wishful thinking of one who believes his theories are true for all time. For Europe he sees, after the US withdraws its troops, Germany acquiring nuclear weapons, and a security competition for central Europe developing between Germany and Russia. In Northeast Asia he sees two possible scenarios. The first, after a US withdrawal, would see Japan developing a nuclear deterrent which both Russia and China would be tempted to pre-empt. The second scenario sees China economically overtaking Japan. The US retains its military presence to balance China, to stop it becoming the regional hegemon. So earnest is he about this possibility that he counsels the US to do all it can to head off such a contingency by doing whatever can be done to slow down China's rapid growth rate.

But are great powers really as ambitious, self-centered and single-minded as Mearsheimer's hypothesis argues? I think the evolution of history in all its complexity tells us something else. Even though human beings have made war as far back as we know this doesn't predetermine our future, and it doesn't necessarily prove that there will be more of the same. The truth is the post World War II and even more the post Cold War world is a different animal from what existed before. I want to take these two points in turn. But to do so we have to wind the historical clock back to the fifteenth century. It is then we can take advantage of Evan Luard's fascinating study of war in European society. He has divided up the history of warfare into five periods: The Age of Dynasties (1400-1559), the Age of Religions (1559-1648), the Age of Sovereignty (1648-1789), the Age of Nationalism (1789-1917) and the Age of Ideology, from 1917 onwards.

By dividing up history in this way we can see rather vividly that whilst wars continued to break out somewhere every one or two years, even more often in some past periods, the determining cases and motives changed if not quite with the fashion but with the age, its political sophistication and its overriding ruling arrangements. On occasion a particular personality at the helm could make a big difference to the frequency of war – Vasa in Sweden was a compulsive warrior king, Elizabeth I of England, contrary to her modern day reputation, kept her powder dry, as did James I, keeping England out of wars on the continent for over a century. But, by and large, if we take the long view, personalities seem to have only marginal effect on the general dynamic, even if a conciliatory figure like Maximillian II could by sheer force of personality keep an empire out of war.

In the Age of Dynasties when kings, queens and dukes ruled uncertain fiefdoms, war was often "private" – the cause of some noble or knight, even an independent rabble of disbanded troops, not unlike in Africa today. In England the House of Lancaster seized the throne, and soon faced a rebellion in

Wales. Most wars were short, and only a few, like the Hundred Years war, when England claimed the French crown, rather long. Casualties were not high and usually limited to the professional soldiers.

The Age of Religions brought more intense wars and more costly too. This was the age of the birth of Protestantism and dissent from Rome. Religion became the most important reason for waging war and this was especially so of civil wars which erupted on all and every occasion, as religious minorities battled against intolerance from on high. Indeed, for much of this era states had little conviction or energy for fighting abroad. Hence English governments under Elizabeth I and James I were primarily concerned with home-inspired threats and kept to a minimum their involvement in upheavals on the continent. Only once it was decided which faith would dominate in which sovereignty did the major powers of Europe resume their quest for dominance.

In this period war became more lethal. The musket and artillery made their appearance and civilians if they were regarded as beholden to the wrong faith were assumed to be fair game.

The third period, the Age of Sovereignty, was the era of state building. War tended to come about as king and princes sought to extend or consolidate their national territory. In this period war over faith practically disappeared. In its place was the prestige and honour of the state. Yet it was a frustrating business. Very few wars ended in outright victory. Usually it was war fought to a draw. As with the 1991 war with Iraq, the power with the upper hand often drew back from pursuing total victory for fear it would upset the local balance of power. Indeed, the horrors of the religious war with their massive toll on civilians receded.

Wars decreased in number and decreased further in the next era, the Age of Nationalism. Despite the Napoleonic war and the first three years of the First World War, France was involved in international wars in Europe in only 32 years out of 128. Prussia, although more at war than any other power in the hundred-year period 1815 to 1914, was at war in only five of those years.

There were long periods (1815-1854) and (1871-1914) when the major powers of Europe did not fight each other at all. Yet civil war was more common. And outside Europe it was a different story. War-making, it appeared, was translated to the urge for territorial control and the search for colonies and trading routes far from home. They were fought almost entirely against under-armed native forces. The major powers did not fight each other overseas despite their competitive instincts for slices of Asian or African real estate. (However, France, Britain and Spain did go to war with the United States, Russia with Japan and Japan later with China.)

For adherents of the balance of power school this era throws up interesting questions. What had changed in the balance of power in Europe to explain the difference between the war years of 1854-71 and the peaceful decades before and after? Nothing. Right throughout this era there was a rough balance of power between the five or six major powers. Much of the time it succeeded in keeping the peace, but it wasn't foolproof. All that one can say by way of explanation is that war broke out, as in 1914, because the issues were more complicated – the degree of influence Russia was allowed to enjoy in the Ottoman Empire, whether or not Austrian power could prevail in Italy, the balance of power between Prussia and Austria in Germany and that between Prussia and France across Europe. In that situation the balance of power, so beloved by theorists like Mearsheimer and Kissinger, simply broke down. Interestingly, US Secretary of State Condoleezza Rice, in a speech to the International Institute for Strategic Studies, condemned "balance of power" politics as outmoded and dangerous. She said: "We tried this before; it led to the Great War."

For most of this period wars were much shorter than earlier eras. Some of the important wars were over in a few weeks, thanks to overwhelming firepower and the clever use of railways to transport large armies, and military strategies that were based on high mobility and the concentration of large forces. All this was to be turned on its head by the carnage and endless duration of the last war of this era, World War I. The generals on both sides, by now masters of the craft of industrial warfare, drove each other to a bloody standstill. 12 million people died, probably sixty times as many as the Franco-Prussian war that preceded it.

The final era was the Age of Ideology, as the countries of Europe, along with Japan and the US fought each other, the liberal democracies first against the fascists and then against the communists. Although the superpowers never came to direct blows – indeed not a shot was fired in anger during the whole span of the Cold War – at the time of the Cuban missile crisis they came dangerously close to a nuclear exchange and they continuously fought each through proxies. (Now it appears to some that we are entering a new era of ideological war, against Islamic fundamentalism, and one combined with a new age of nationalism as the US seeks to best any country that might challenge it with weapons of mass destruction.)

Warfare in this era of ideology, while less than the first four earlier eras, has probably not been less than the immediate preceding period. Europe, the centre of most of the world's wars in recorded history, has enjoyed a period of peace for longer than it has ever known before.

But war, repressed by empire, flared up all over much of the Third World, apart from Latin America, long a continent of few wars and short wars, apart from the civil war, "La Violencia" in Colombia and the guerrilla-type, proxy US/Cuban wars in Guatemala, Nicaragua and El Salvador. Many of the wars were anti-colonialist wars. Some were proxy wars or supposed proxy wars between the superpowers, notably Korea and Vietnam. Some were frontier disputes arising from independence. Indeed, the two most dangerous of all those conflicts, overwhelmingly so, between India and Pakistan and between Israel and the Palestinians are old-time, unresolved, colonial-era boundary disputes.

Wars since 1945 have been almost entirely civil wars, fought between the adherents of different political philosophers, either pro-West or pro-Communist or so it has been made to appear, although Europeans may recognise them as more akin to dynastic rivalries or the age of religious wars.

The arrival of nuclear armaments surprisingly has not had the impact at one time was thought likely. While they are said to have frozen the superpower conflict between Russia and the West and also between China and Russia and China and the West (I will look at this question of nuclear deterrence in my next chapter) they didn't seem to affect the incidence of war between nuclear and non-nuclear powers. In fact in Vietnam and Afghanistan the non-nuclear power was victorious. Nevertheless, modern conventional weapons have become extraordinarily sophisticated and possessors of the finest equipment – Israel with the Arabs, the British with Argentina, the US with Iraq – often prevail, but not always, as the Afghanis and Vietnamese both showed. As the Hussites showed 350 years ago, morale is everything.

Arguably, the most appalling development of the era has been the sharp rise in civilian deaths, partly because of aerial bombardment, partly because of the use of nuclear weapons against Japan and partly because, as ethnic wars have spread in the wake of de-colonisation, the level of violence appears to have been ratcheted up compared with previous eras. This is certainly because of the easy availability of high-powered armaments, but also it is because of the longevity of many guerrilla wars, and the spread of anarchy, particularly in large parts of Africa, where post-colonial governments quickly lost their bequeathed authority.

Looking back over this vast historical panorama, one can see that although the stage directions for war were given by different leaders in different ages the frequency of war changed only modestly. Over time wars have become, according to Luard's meticulous arithmetic, less frequent and the number of years in which an average country has been involved in war has declined steadily over the centuries. But there is a contrary trend – the scale of war and the cost of conflict.

Going back through the ages we see from our perspective (one can do this exercise in every era apart from the first) that the reasons wars were fought were not issues that would now engage us. Would we fight to keep our prince in power? Would we fight for our tribe – and Europe is still full of tribes, Bavarians, Lancastrians, Piedmontese and Skåningars? We certainly wouldn't fight for our religion and it is extremely doubtful if we would fight to expand the territory of our country either into that of our near neighbours or overseas. The urge for national independence is now well satisfied, although it is only in recent times that this could be said of much of the Third World. Interestingly, there is little evidence that countries have ever fought over economic issues. Despite the arguments over the price paid for raw materials, monopolies established to protect trade in particular products, the level of tariffs, interest rates or the rescheduling of debt, it is rare, if ever, that the rows have escalated to armed conflicts. More likely there would be war over a trivial item of face and prestige – did Dutch ships dip their flags to the English fleet? Was the Chinese responsible for the death of an English sailor punished? Was the German Kaiser discourteous to the French Ambassador? And so on.

Apart from the trivial, which has intruded more often than we perhaps like to think, the issues that usually provoke war are conflicts of expectations and ambiguous sovereignty. Yet even allowing for this, the truth is that questions that seemed of paramount importance in one era, a reason for bloody war, the killing of the innocent and the mayhem that goes with it, are matters of indifference in a subsequent age. What was in one age solved by the brutal application of force is either ignored or solved by quiet diplomacy in another.

Governments of whatever hue, in whichever age, may not desire war for its own sake, but they have been all too easily motivated to war, even though alternatives have usually been within reach. Now we are under the thumb of a relatively new war-causing ideology: the desire to see governments of a particular political persuasion in power. This was very rarely the cause of war in previous centuries. Today, as with Iraq, it is in danger of being taken to extremes. Only one thing is certain: humanity one day will come to see it as yet one more convention of the times, for which it would never shed blood in the age in which it now resides.

The change over 600 years boils down to this question of the legitimacy of war – what is illegitimate by the reasoning of one age is quite foolhardy, unnecessary and even illegitimate by the lights of another. "Just Wars" may in one age mean preserving the balance of power, in another preventative war, in another the overthrowing of a tyrannical government. How we arrive at the morality of war is an interesting and important debate in its own right, if only to find out what is so special about our own age. Because "special" we believe it is, as has the inhabitant of every passed age.

War, the systematic and organised use of violence with all it bestial destructiveness, is peculiar to the most advanced of animals, man. Writing in the early sixteenth century the Dutch philosopher and theologian Erasmus, one of the earliest critics, considered wars "unnatural". "Animals do not make war on one another. Whoever heard of 100, 000 animals rushing together, to butcher each other, as men do everywhere."

Yet many, as devoted to their Christian beliefs as Erasmus, have found reason for war. Moreover, the horrors of war could not be averted by simply complaining about the perfidy of humankind. Thus in the seventeenth and eighteenth centuries the great international lawyers Grotius, Pufendorf and Emeric Vattel attempted to codify its rationale and civilise its means. In 1623 the French monk, Emeric Cruce, published his pioneering proposal for a United Nations-type of an Assembly in which international differences would be settled by compulsory arbitration. Cruce also profoundly touched on what is a powerful theme in academic writing today – peaceful political intercourse could be encouraged by free trade, a theme I shall return to later.

By the beginning of the eighteenth century such thinkers as Frances Bacon and John Locke had ceased to look at war as a moral issue. War occurred, as Locke wrote, merely because "Want of a common judge with authority puts all men in a state of nature". War was a necessary evil in a world of states which had to check the evil desires and ambitions of other states.

In France, with the Enlightenment bursting forth, Voltaire and Rousseau had convinced many liberal thinkers that wars happened not so much for lack of international peacekeeping structures but because they were a way of life among a militarised, aristocratic ruling class. Indeed, it is probably true that if a young nobleman wanted to make his mark in life it was expected that he pursue his fortunes in war. As Michael Howard has put it in his book *The Growth of the Liberal Conscience,* for this class warfare was "little more than an agreeable and far from uncomfortable extension of their ordinary life style. The officer's armies, when not fighting, treated each other in the most courteous fashion. They believed in order and the balance of power. They did not see themselves, as the philosophers accused them, as partakers in a gruesome and unnecessary game."

The movement of intellectual dissent grew. The wars of the eighteenth century took such an economic toll that Francois Quesnay and Jaques Turgot on the French side and Adam Smith in England began to argue that a true concentration on the production of wealth would lead men to realise that war was quite counterproductive. In Prussia, Immanuel Kant, arguably the one of the three or four most influential philosophers of the Enlightenment, published in 1795 his *Perpetual Peace*. He slammed the typical sovereign who "abates nothing of his feast, sports, pleasure, palaces or court festivities during a war, and can therefore declare war as a sort of pleasure on the slightest provocation." What is needed to avoid war, Kant argued, was that "The Civil Constitution shall in every State be republican.... [since] if the sanction of citizens is necessary to decide whether there shall be war or not, nothing is more natural than that they would think long before beginning such a terrible game."

Kant was not a pacifist. He saw much of life as a Hobbesian struggle against evil, and even that war is sometimes unavoidable. But he also strongly believed it was unjustifiable. In a foreshadowing of today's human rights movement he wrote that he believed, "The general and continuous establishment of peace constitutes not only a part, but the entire end and purpose of a theory of rights within the limits of pure reason."

For the philosophers and free market economists of Europe it was the creation of a republic in the US, whose constitution was the first clear political statement of the values of the Enlightenment, that offered the historic opportunity to put reason into practice. The philosophers conveniently turned a blind eye to the fact that there would have been no republic had it not been for a drawn out war with Britain.

It was the pro-revolutionary Thomas Paine in his pamphlet *The Rights of Man* who, more eloquently than any of his contemporaries, drove the argument home. The answer to war, he said echoing Adam Smith, lay in free trade, and of course republican government. Barely were the words out of his mouth than France, home to the Revolution, and liberty, equality and fraternity, was plunged into the carnage of Robespierre, the tumbrel and the guillotine and, shortly after, the Napoleonic wars, the worst in Europe for 200 years. Still, every one of Napoleon's foot soldiers carried a copy of the *Declaration of the*

*Rights of Man* in their knapsack and the seed was sown for the end in Europe of brutal monarchic government and the game of war and, on the other side of the street, the advance of human rights.

Thomas Paine's synthesis of the views of the Enlightenment, weathered by a hundred subsequent revolutions and wars, has lived on, deeply implanted in both the liberal and the socialist half of the culture of Europe and the United States, and has through colonialism spread itself into the Indian sub-continent, parts of Southeast Asia, Africa and South America, and through the American post-World War II engagement, into the far reaches of east Asia, into Japan, South Korea, Taiwan, and the Philippines in particular. On the way down through history the thought process diversified and adapted into thousands of fragments, sometimes dispersed, sometimes knitted back together in new forms, but all the while preserving one common theme, an abhorrence of war and a belief that the single greatest impediment to war was the "Establishment", which blocked popular participation in government and promoted artificial barriers to international intercourse.

Jeremy Bentham, who published his *Plan for a Universal and Perpetual Peace* in 1789, was probably the most influential of those in Britain who tried to apply these ideas to real life situations. There could be no universal peace, he argued, unless Britain and France ceased to fight each other over their colonies. Such was his ability to distil the wisdom of the philosophers to his own warlike country that he is credited with devising a programme that was central to British foreign policy up to the onset of World War I. Peace would come, Bentham said, by abandoning the colonial cause, reducing armaments, avoiding alliances on the continent and, echoing Adam Smith, by free trade. He also, prophetically, saw the need for a World Court to adjudicate disputes between nations.

The Napoleonic wars, although deeply upsetting and unsettling for those who had thought the French Revolution would usher in a great new era, spurred the peace cause on. By its end there was in being in Britain, France and the US a powerful "Peace Movement", an organisation of middle class liberals, many of them businessmen, working to secure the abolition of war. John Stuart Mill was one of them, writing that, "It is commerce which is rapidly rendering war obsolete." While much of the initiative in the Peace Movement on both sides of the Atlantic was engineered by the Christian pacifist followers of George Fox, the Quakers, it was the businessmen and the free traders who gave it its political muscle.

The great flaw in this, by now quite long, tradition, in seeing war as unnatural, bad for trade, and an activity foisted on society, by first kings and princes and later by closed establishments, was that public opinion was too rarely on the side of the peacemakers. The influential free trader Richard Cobden tried to explain away the crowd's reaction to the appearance of the great warrior and defeater of Napoleon, the Duke of Wellington, at the Great Exhibition of 1851, by suggesting that the entire English people had been infected with aristocratic vices. "The aristocracy had converted the combativeness of the English race to its own sinister ends."

But what he observed was nothing more than the same martial spirit that inspired French volunteers to swarm into Napoleon's armies convinced that the army was the nation and the nation had a purpose, to upset the old repressive kingly order, or later, inflamed the British schoolboys who could not wait to serve in the trenches of Flanders against Bolshies, deeply imbued with deep shades of patriotism. War was terrible, yes, but it was also necessary and sometimes splendid. It rings out in the poetry of Rupert Brooke and can be found in prose form most stirringly in Pat Barker's bitter evocation of World War 1, *Regeneration* and in Norman Mailer's *The Naked and The Dead*.

Every mood has a philosopher to match and in Europe Guseppe Mazzini was the righteous, thoughtful, war-monger. "The Map of Europe is to redraw!" he exclaimed in 1845. Nationalism was an honourable creed and national liberation was the cause. War was inevitable – "desperate and determined war that knew no true end save in victory or the grave". Of course he had a point. Europe was still, years after Napoleon, replete with tyrants and foreign rulers and very short of democracy. The middle decades of the nineteenth century witnessed, as I have earlier pointed out, large scale, nationalistic driven warfare after forty years of peace, and in the US there was the Civil War, in which the northern side found much support from members of the Peace Movement. Nevertheless, it rather looked that with the US under the control of the industrial classes and the peoples of Italy and Germany now united in their respective nation states that an era of peace had indeed arrived. And from 1870 to 1914 that is how it was. Trade and commerce took over. It was an era of globalization, at least among the developed nations. In a historic development, international arbitration by special courts was introduced for commercial disputes. The Peace Movement grew with renewed vitality (and the greatest number was in Scandinavia). Maybe war, after all, was going to be abolished. Yet there was plenty for the anti-pacifists to get their teeth into – the need to roll back the bloody repression of both the Russian and Ottoman empires. The British people, said Prime Minister Gladstone, must not "shrink from the responsibility of undertaking them." The warrior ethic flourished side by side with the peace movement and in England public schools were founded to instil the spirit of discipline, service and patriotism. In France the Dreyfus affair revealed how deep rooted was narrow-minded militarism. Michael Howard writes that at the dawn of the twentieth century Europe was "a very bellicose, very militaristic society" and no longer "could the inflated spirit of patriotism and xenophobia that had impressed thinkers from Erasmus onwards be laid at the door of the old aristocracy". It was now virulent even among the industrial classes.

Even Howard with all his knowledge of the history of warfare is stumped to find an answer to why the martial spirit had become so rabid. It certainly went in the opposite direction of profit making unless one was in the armaments business, which although brutally well organised as a pressure group was then, as it is even more so today, a minority economic interest.

Perhaps it was a question of status, he surmises, the desire for the new middle classes to make themselves acceptable in societies where a warrior ethic was still dominant. "Historians and political scientists," writes Howard "who try to explain the First World War simply in terms of the accumulation of capitalist rivalries and capitalist search for markets are like the drunk in the story who, when asked why he was searching for his lost watch under a street lamp rather than further up the road where he had dropped it, explained that it was because there was most light there." Still the Marxists and the Socialists held firm to their conviction, only divided about whether violence was justified to defeat the Capitalist interests. The socialist intelligentsia all over Europe tried their damnedest to dampen the martial spirit of the proletariat. But as the Socialist playwright, George Bernard Shaw, wrote, perhaps somewhat exaggeratedly, "All classes in proportion to their lack of travel and familiarity with foreign literature are bellicose, prejudiced against foreigners, fond of fighting as a cruel sport – in short, dog-like in their notions of foreign policy." And as Victor Adler, the Austrian socialist said, observing the enthusiasm with which the Viennese crowds welcomed the prospect of war with Serbia, "It is better to be wrong with the working classes than right against them."

But if World War I proved all the philosophers and liberals wrong it proved the practitioners of real politik were, to use a working class expression, "up a gum tree". The balance of power meant to avoid war precipitated it.

Arguably, the only good thing that came out of the First World War was the idealism of the American president, Woodrow Wilson. Inspired by Thomas Paine he tried unsuccessfully at Versailles at the end of the war to argue against revenge and reparations upon a defeated Germany and to create a powerful League of Nations, with America as its spinal cord, that would seek to arbitrate future conflicts and to head off war. On both counts he failed. World War II was built on the ashes of World War I. The pacifist cause flared once again, to be sidelined one more time. The architects of the balance of power built new edifices only once again to see them crumble and Hitler swept all in front of him. In the end even the liberals and the socialists saw the second global conflict of the century as a "good war".

It is not my purpose here to pursue the history of the Cold War, the cold peace of Europe and its various hot wars on the periphery, in Korea, Vietnam, Angola and Central America. Suffice to say that we have all learnt the hard way that, as Howard says, "Peoples if left to themselves are naturally peaceful, like its converse that they are naturally belligerent, begs for more questions than it answers." We are still hard at work, as Kant would add, "establishing" a state of peace. The fact that we have many of the building blocks in place – the UN, the World Court, the International Criminal Court and countless international conventions outlawing everything from torture to the abuse of children to genocide, should be a cause for comfort. The way to go is a long road. But the astonishing thing is that we are going down it at a faster clip than I suspect Erasmus, Kant, Adam Smith, Voltaire and Thomas Paine could ever have imagined.

As we begin the new century, certain trends are clearly apparent that suggest that mankind in the round is putting war on one side. It can be said with some certainty that, in many of the more economically developed parts of the world that war is only seen by a modest minority as a source of glory and renown. Indeed, for two generations now it can be fairly said it is now no longer, after Vietnam, seen as a sacred duty in our one remaining military super power – how else to explain the rise of Bill Clinton to the presidency, a self-confessed draft dodger, who defeated two able World War II heroes? How else to explain the seeming paradox of his successor, George W. Bush and his most militant right-hand man, Vice-president Dick Cheney, are also draft dodgers? It has certainly been a factor – though by its nature an immeasurable one – in explaining why George Bush had more problems in raising an international posse to confront Saddam Hussein in 2003 than his father did in 1991.

Another sea-change of importance is that no longer can governments anywhere get away with publicly declaring a desire to acquire the territory belonging to another country. Indeed the only time this has happened since the Second World War was when Iraq claimed its neighbour Kuwait, at which point Saddam Hussein became an international outcast.

Yet it is only two centuries ago that Frederick the Great was doing it all the time and only seventy years ago that Mussolini would proudly pontificate on his territorial ambitions.

On the other hand we must not become too sanguine – there are contrary trends. Frederick was a man who had his principles – his armies were made to treat non-combatants with respect, and so too their crops. Today war seems to brook no divide between soldier and civilian – the saturation bombing of Dresden, the burning alive of civilians in Vietnam, the use of helicopter gun ships to destroy whole villages in Afghanistan and Chechnya, the abandonment of the traditional immunity to attack merchant shipping, (and the old convention of rescuing sailors from the sunken ships), the indiscriminate bombing of guerrillas, and the particular virulence of modern day ethnic warfare in places as diverse as ex Yugoslavia and Rwanda where civilians rather than solders became the main target. This is not to mention the nuclear bombing of Hiroshima and Nagasaki when even its perpetrator, President Harry Truman, argued as his justification for destroying a city of mainly civilians that it was to avoid the heavy casualties of American soldiers if they had to fight their way on the ground to subdue Japan.

Still, the use of nuclear weapons, it must be said, stopped humanity in its tracks. It has become the ultimate taboo. Whilst both sides in the Cold War built their whole defence around the threat to extinguish the other, whilst India and Pakistan do it today, while George Bush (and his father before him) threatened Saddam Hussein with them should he have given the order to use his chemical and biological weapons on advancing American troops, the very cold dose of modern day realism that runs right through the higher reaches of American military ranks suggests that the human impediment to their actual use in a real situation would stymie any president who gave the order.

I think it is not far reached to suggest that there is a process underway that signifies quite clearly that there is no inherent reason why the world we inhabit should not be able to resolve its conflicts without recourse to war. Some states have lived for centuries without war. Some regions, now including Europe, Japan, China and many countries in Latin America and two of the countries in North America, have lived for many decades without it.

We can see quite clearly now that whatever our current disputes in the perspective of history a vast majority of wars in the past no longer make a great degree of sense. In one age, tens of thousands of lives will be sacrificed to win succession to a throne, while in another, only 200 or 300 years later, no government anywhere will fight for such a purpose. In one age the great majority of wars will be fought over religion while a mere century later such a cause was considered almost irrelevant.

Indeed the difference that exists between individuals, say between Donald Rumsfeld and me, in one period of time, pales into insignificance compared with difference in attitudes between one age and another. We are simply prisoners to the ideology of the times in which we are born.

Perhaps this is because of the changing class structure in different ages, particularly the character of the elites who wield power. When power is held by dynasts this influences the thinking of everyone, even those who are not dynasts. When the clergy and their close adherents become influential, their ideology will govern society and influence the direction of war-making. When those who care deeply about national rights and national independence rise to positions of power their preoccupations hold sway. More recently it was ideological questions, still apparent in the wary way Washington looks at China. Already it is hard to explain to the present generation how difficult it was to avoid all out nuclear war that may have destroyed a quarter of the planet over Russia's decision to place nuclear missiles in Cuba when the US already had them very close to the Soviet Union in Turkey.

Today, we might be, although it is too early to be sure, living in an age without major war. Of course there are many small wars going on all the time all over the place. A decade ago, at the time of the wars in ex-Yugoslavia and the pogroms in Burundi and Rwanda, politicians panicked that the world seemed to be catching alight with wars – Secretary of State Warren Christopher, viewing the apparent multiplication of ethnic wars as the lid of the Cold War came off the boiling cauldron beneath, exclaimed, "Where will it end? Will it end with 5,000 countries?"

The evidence, however, suggests that for well over a decade now the number of wars have been falling. This is the conclusion made by close yearly monitoring of conflict zones by the Stockholm International Peace Research Institute and also by the Minority at Risk Project of the University of Maryland. The latter makes the point that when one considers the number of serious ethnic disputes of recent years that have been resolved without killing, the glass looks rather more than half full than empty, as the journalistic and political wailing of our era suggests.

Many will still argue that we in the West emerged unscathed from the Cold War because the nuclear deterrent worked. Superficially perhaps it did. Certainly it became an easy intellectual prop whenever a crisis did arise and the more level-headed politicians and generals had to give a reasonable explanation, one acceptable to their more warlike peers, why war was not an option. But the truth maybe lies elsewhere. Nuclear weapons, everyone accepts, did not stop countries waging war against nuclear armed opponents, which was a great surprise to the early first generation of nuclear theorists – the North Koreans (with Chinese support) against the Americans and their allies in 1959, the Vietnamese against the same forces in the 1960s, the Afghanis against the Soviets in the 1980s and the Argentineans against the British a few years later. But perhaps they didn't avoid war in Europe or between the superpowers either. Perhaps the age in which we have all lived made too much of the issue of ideology, more than the facts really bear. Perhaps the truth is there was no great reason for war and the majority of people on both sides after World War II felt something akin to revulsion to the very idea of another great war. Even more to the point, there was no good reason for war. War in Europe, in the last two centuries, had come to pass because there were dissatisfied powers eager to right a grievance and what grievances there were during the Cold War – the division of Germany or the subservience of the East European states by Moscow – were not judged by their war-weary peoples as worthy of even guerrilla action, much less a full-blown war. After the wars of the nineteenth century and the world wars of the twentieth, the Balkans apart, the map of Europe had been re-drawn sufficiently as to take care of most of the major ethnic and national ambitions, urges and grievances. European frontiers, even the Order-Neise line dividing Germany and Poland, were more firmly established and more widely accepted than at any time in history.

Even that is not quite sufficient explanation for the absence of war. Another surely is the quite unprecedented rise in the standard of living experienced over the last hundred years, and its concomitant, a rapidly expanding technology that gave birth among many of its other rather useful progeny one less so, the ability to manufacture increasingly, by a geometric measure, destructive armaments.

These two forces emerging in tandem, uneasily so at first, appear as the twentieth century progressed to work against each other with what may be grudgingly called "personal satisfaction" gradually winning out – the higher the standard of living, the less attractive is the prospect of war. Unlike earlier ages, voters know it won't bring prosperity or territory or even secure for very long the supply of critical raw materials like oil. Many of the voters have lived long enough to know that today's war is soon forgotten and within a decade, two at the most, no-one quite knows why their sons gave their lives. Once the revisionist journalists, novelists, film makers, historians, church leaders and penitent former political and military leaders have done their work, arguing that in retrospect that Vietnam was not a "good war", who still living has the stomach for another one? Very few it appears in Europe and a bare majority in America that only becomes a workable majority if the political leaders are clever enough to persuade them it will be a quick one – hence American public opinion turning so quickly against the war in Iraq. Not for nothing is the Vietnam memorial in Washington so different from its more flamboyant, patriotic forbears. Instead of eagles and rifles there are only stark slabs of black marble with names of all the American dead on them. As Michael Mandlebaum has written "it represented the soldier not as a hero but as an innocent and literally faceless victim."

The stability of the post war Western World reinforces this trend. National consciousness is generally at peace with the situation we have now inherited. No-one frets in the US about the North/South divide, real though it still is in important ways. There is not in Europe an Austrian or Turkish Empire about to disintegrate. Germany's borders are secure and unquestioned. Since a substantial number of twentieth and nineteenth century foreign wars originated in internal conflicts this relative new era of stability is a change of circumstance of understated proportions.

One can see the same forces at work in many parts of the more advanced Third World – in South Korea, most strikingly of all. But also in Malaysia and Singapore, in Taiwan and Thailand and in much of South America and the Caribbean.

Today the occasions of war are usually ignited by the same forces that triggered wars in old Europe – civil conflicts where other ways of security change appear closed, either because of dictatorship, maladministration and often a combination of both. Democracies are these days usually exempt from civil war, but most important, although they are still quite capable of making war, as with Iraq, they do not appear to go to war with each other. The empirical debate over the research on this, perhaps rather amazing statement, has long progressed in the confines of academic journals, in particular Harvard University's quarterly *International Security*. It now appears to be firmly settled. Democracies, of which there are more every year that passes, settle their disputes with each other by diplomacy, arbitration, conciliation, but not force of arms. Indeed it almost looks as if Erasmus' question about how man could behave worse than the beasts has found an answer: he will not if he has the vote that can change his government and if the foreign countries he interacts with have the same system. Erasmus who doubtless turned in his grave right through the last century may, this century, get the rest he clearly deserves – but that, of course, depends on the expansion of democracy.

Already we can say, after the steady, even rapid expansion of democracy, following the end of World War II and accelerating since the taking down of the Iron Curtain, the "pool" of democracy is now large enough for it to generate its own culture – one that is contagious and infectious to the millions who know they need democracy in China, in Africa, in parts of Latin America, or if they have it know they need a better version of it with an independent judiciary, a freer press, the abolition of torture, capital punishment and the abuse of women, and an extension of the practice of human rights at every level of society.

Michael Mandlebaum has best captured the spirit and dynamic of this relative new turn of events in his book, *The Ideas that Conquered the World*. What he shows is that not only was Erasmus on target, if rather ahead of his time, but so were Adam Smith and John Cobden with their conviction that free trade was the route to developing not just a higher standard of living among trading nations, but the means of bringing nations into a more amicable relationship. "In the last decade of the twentieth century social scientists found a strong relationship between democratic politics at home and peaceful conduct abroad. For the politicians and citizens of the democratic Western core this finding had a double attraction. It was flattering, for it meant that the more the world reproduced their own political arrangements the more tranquil it would be; and it posited that their form of government, which they valued and promoted for its own sake, had an additional, unexpected benefit – as if cherry-topped cheesecake had turned out to be not only tasty but nutritious."

Liberal economies beget liberal politics which beget liberal security policies. It is hard to disagree. In my own book *Like Water on Stone* (Penguin 2001) I drew attention to the close relationship between the free market and free political institutions. Particularly noteworthy, I pointed out, was a study carried out by a pro-democracy think tank, Freedom House, that published a report in 2001 observing that "there is a high and significant correlation between the level of political freedom measured by Freedom House and economic freedom as measured by the Wall Street Journal/Heritage Foundation survey." This study effectively answered the old conundrum of whether the large number of prosperous countries are free as a consequence of their prosperity and development or whether prosperity is a consequence of basic political and civic freedoms. Economic growth is certainly possible in an un-free political culture, but political freedom accelerates it. Repressive, militaristic, countries with high and sustained growth rates, such as China, are an exception rather than the rule.

We can see now that the mature democracies are living with a social fact of consequence, what Mandlebaum calls "debellicisation." What has happened to the status and legitimacy of war in western society is comparable to the fate of religious faith and the acceptance of political and social inequality. At the beginning of the last century they were still robust. At the beginning of this they are all but eroded.

In the twentieth century, as William Pfaff has argued, mankind tried all the variants of political thought that industrial society and the concomitant growing power of the political centre had made possible – fascism, Marxism and liberal capitalism. Only the latter survived and prospered, both nurturing and feeding off the gradual development of democracy, as the franchise was steadily widened. Human ingenuity might well in the future come up with another ideology that is more attractive than economic liberalism, but so far there is no sign of it, neither in China, still nominally a Marxist state, nor in much of the Arab world, still shunning democracy in its political forms, and desperately searching for justification of the present feudal arrangements in ancient Islamic texts, but increasingly accepting the liberal ideas of the market place.

One suspects, if its stagnant political arrangements were not buffered by the astonishing revenues of the oil economy, a change from feudal and often despotic rule would be much further advanced than it is today.

Much will depend for the future on the development of democracy and therefore peace among nations on how Russia and China develop and, to a lesser degree, how quickly the Israelis and the Palestinians come to a modus vivendi. It will also, it should be added, depend on how quickly the Western nations, who allowed their nationals to earn a living by trafficking in the ingredients of weapons of mass destruction, learn a more artful way of containing the newly armed so-called "rogue" powers; and also how by revising their instinctively repressive attitude to turbulence in the fast-evolving Islamic world we learn how to counter the rising tide of fundamentalism and the power of a few on the fringes of that movement to wreak immense havoc on the scale of September 11th.

In both Russia and China there is little direct experience of political liberalism to draw on, although the former has a rich cultural affinity with the western world. The land of Tolstoy, Dostoevsky, Tchaikowsky, Rimsky-Korsakov, not to mention Solzenitzen and Sakarov is not bereft of the deepest yearnings of civilized humanity – for order, equilibrium, caring and compassion – all of which are part, if only part, of the liberal experience. Despite all the early confusion of the re-establishment of Russian democracy, following the collapse of the Soviet Union, it can now be seen that under President Vladimir Putin that progress is being made. It may still on occasion seem uncertain and often contradictory but there are clear signs of forward momentum.

China, whilst economically free in a way that Mao-tse Tung, the founder of this Communist state, would have abhorred, still appears in its political arrangements to possess a type of governance that he would recognise. The Communist party remains supreme and the system of political appointment in Beijing owes everything to patronage. Nevertheless, partly contested elections are being encouraged at the local level and the parliament, the People's National Compress, although not freely elected, occasionally exhibits a mind of its own. Moreover, some parts of the press exhibit an unusual measure of freedom and the academic world is increasingly allowed to pursue, unmolested, the rigour of independent thinking. Not least, on its flank Beijing is paced by the freedoms (although actual democracy is severely controlled) practised by recently absorbed Hong Kong and by the thriving and fast maturing democracy of Taiwan which Beijing claims as part of China. For now, and perhaps the long term, China's foreign policy seems to be one of keeping a low international profile, maintaining a stable relationship with the US and capitalising on globalisation to achieve super economic growth.

Mandlebaum in an earlier essay summed it up rather well, "The great chess game of international politics is finished, or at least suspended. A pawn is now just a pawn, not a sentry standing guard against an attack on a king." If major war between the great historical powers remains highly unlikely, although not impossible, we still live in fear of local wars of war with Iraq or North Korea or Iran where local strongmen have sought by building weapons of mass destruction to make themselves immune to overbearing influence by outside powers, in particular, the US, and the US in particular feels correspondingly threatened by these developments. It is not so much it cares about nuclear proliferation – that care has always been somewhat ambiguous, if not, half-hearted – but it is immensely bothered about nuclear weapons being in the hands of those it regards as potentially hostile. All this has been driven in part by self-sustaining momentum of the military / academic / industrial complex that, "unemployed" after the end of the Cold War, almost desperately cast around for new enemies. Not for them was the biting conclusion of the then Chairman of the Joint Chiefs of Staff, General Colin Powell, who perhaps too innocently said, "I am running out of demons" and advocated serious nuclear disarmament. Historians will one day determine the extent to which in-built American hostility made the forces of Al Qaeda (which doubtless would have existed anyway such is the bitter legacy of the Cold War in Afghanistan and the continuing provocation of an unsettled Israeli / Palestinian conflict) much mightier than they would otherwise have been.

Whether we have ahead of us a century of relative peace will depend not so much on the "enemy" but on the principal power of our modern world, the United States. Will the Kissingers and Mersheimers have the upper hand (although the latter actually opposed America going to war with Iraq on the grounds that deterrence was already working satisfactorily enough)? Or will we listen more to Robert McNamara, the former Secretary of Defence under presidents Kennedy and Johnson, who was responsible for many of America's bad decisions during the Vietnam War and who was party to all the most difficult decisions made during the Cuban missile crisis, but who is now convinced that "realism" in foreign policy is actually "unreal". "Realism creates enemies where there need not be enemies. It leads to missed opportunities for sustainable peace that may never come again."

Increasingly in his writings McNamara not only argues that the possession of nuclear weapons is profoundly immoral but that in a deep crisis "things often spin out of control and, no matter who started the crisis, it is the very existence of nuclear weapons themselves – the possibility they will be used and that the conflict will escalate – that becomes the biggest threat." He is also convinced that what pushed him and the presidents he served to continue the wrong-headed attitudes that perpetrated the Vietnam War quite unnecessarily was "lack of empathy".

The tragedy of Vietnam, he writes, "was, in many ways, a tragedy of American unilateralism." "It became obvious (during the course of the war) how monumentally wrong were so many of the US assumptions, perceptions, judgements and calculations that led to the Americanization of the war."

McNamara today advocates a moral imperative to avoid war whenever possible, combined with multilateral imperative which will put constraints on the particular interests or influences in the American body politic that tend to be too ready to go to war.

The protestant theologian Reinhold Neibuhr, McNamara writes, used to ask, "How much evil must we do in order to do good?" And McNamara answers the question, "Posing the question in this way will be painful at times, because not to intervene will seem to many like an endorsement of the killing that is in progress. It need not be. It may rather be an honest acknowledgement of the limitations of the international community to intervene successfully in these sorts of conflicts. As difficult as it is to accept, we may have to admit that at times some of these conflicts have no solution, at least no solution achievable by the application of external military force."

If policy makers in the great powers could be persuaded to think like this much war could be avoided in the coming centuries. And, if at the same time democracy and with it the recognition of the importance of living by international law, expands its frontiers, even to include China, the Middle East and Africa, then we will undoubtedly find that the urge to resolve differences by military might will become muted. Not least, if we learn to build and use a more robust United Nations in the way I have outlined in Chapter 7 then we have a chance of reaching Kant's "state of peace."

Freedom from war is not an illusion. The life of civilization and of humankind is not predetermined by unshakable physical causations or tough-minded political theorists. We can intervene and shape its direction. We need reason, faith, generosity and imaginative experiment. Then we might find, as some parts of the world have already found, what Erasmus said was indeed prescient: "God hath shaped this creative man not to war, but to friendship, not to destruction, but to health, not to wrong but to kindness and benevolence."

# 4 Can We Get Rid of Nuclear Weapons?

The art of war has now advanced to the point where it can threaten extinction, if not of the whole planet certainly of whole societies. The arsenal of nuclear weapons, at one time, only a few years ago, was powerful enough to destroy whole continents. The blasts on the eve of the end of the Second World War, at Hiroshima and Nagasaki, can now be repeated one million times. The remains would not be merely the broken arches of the Caesars, the abandoned viaducts and moss-covered temples of the Incas, the desolation of one of the pulsating hearts of European civilization, Dresden or the human emptiness of Hiroshima, but millions of square kilometres of uninhabitable desolation, and a suffering which would incorporate more agony than the sum of past history. It would be a time when "the living would envy the dead" and it would be a world which might well have destroyed the legacy of law, order and love that successive generations have handed over the centuries to one another, often enough each one determined to improve on what went before.

The use of nuclear weapons would be the worst human rights abuse that man could inflict on mankind. In 1996, in testimony before the International Court of Justice, the mayor of Nagasaki recalled his memory of the American nuclear attack. "Nagasaki became a city of death where not even the insects could be heard. After a while, countless men, women and children began to gather for a drink of water at the banks of the nearby Urakami river. Their hair and clothing scorched and their burnt skin hanging in sheets like rags. Begging for help they died one after another in the water or in heaps on the banks. The radiation began to take its toll, killing people like the scourge of death expanding in concentric circles from the hypocenter. Four months after the atomic bombing, 74,000 people were dead and 75,000 had suffered injuries, that is, two-thirds of the city population had fallen victim to this calamity that came upon Nagasaki like a preview of the Apocalypse."

At the height of the Cold War the superpowers, together with France, Britain and Israel, possessed 100,000 nuclear warheads, equivalent to two million of this weapon dropped on Nagasaki.

The great president of France, Charles de Gaulle, observed, "After a nuclear war, the two sides would have neither powers, nor laws, nor cities, nor cultures, nor cradles, nor tombs." Nikita Kruschev who presided over the Soviet Union in the days of the Cuban missile crisis later wrote, "When I learned all the facts about nuclear power I couldn't sleep for several days. Then I became convinced that we would never possibly use these weapons, and I was able to sleep again." The scientific chief of the Manhattan project that developed the first American nuclear test, Robert Oppenheimer, wrote, "At that moment ... there flashed through my mind a passage from the Bhagavad-Gita, the sacred book of the Hindus: "I am become Death, the shatterer of Worlds." And Arundhati Roy, the prize-winning Indian novelist, wrote after the first Indian nuclear weapons test in 1998, "If there is a nuclear war, our foes will not be Pakistan, China or America or even each other. Our foe will be the earth itself. Our cities and forests, our fields and villages will burn for days. Rivers will turn to poison. The air will become fire. The wind will spread the flames. When everything there is to burn has burned and the fires die, smoke will rise and shut out the sun. The earth will be enveloped in darkness, there will be no day – only interminable night."

There are two main issues in any discussion on nuclear weapons, moral and political. For some nuclear armaments are so wicked, so evil, in their capacity to execute life as we know it that there can be no talk of modifying or controlling them; they must be banned, if necessary unilaterally renounced. Deterrence, even if it could be proved to have kept the peace, is profoundly immoral in concept and in tone, for the threat to destroy is as wrong as the act itself.

This latter observation is true. But equally it can lead to the conclusion that we have to deal with the problem by multilateral means – by agreement between the antagonistic nuclear parties – rather than by unilateral cuts. The means of getting rid of them is as important a moral issue as the means of deterrence. If the reduction of a part of the stockpile were done in such a way as to increase instability and the likelihood of war, this would as reprehensible an act as one which provoked war by initiating a new round in the arms race, or which caused untold suffering and grief by being the first to use nuclear weapons.

Thomas Nagel, in his essay "War and Massacres" (in *Just and Unjust Wars* by Michael Walz, Allen Lane, 1978) has suggested we are working between two poles of moral intuition. We know that there are some outcomes that must be avoided at all costs and we know that there are some costs that never can be morally justified. We must face the possibility, Nagel argues, "that these two forms of moral intuition are not capable of being brought together into a single coherent moral system, and that the world can present us with a situation in which there is no honourable or moral course for a man to take, no course free of guilt or responsibility for evil."

But we have to be careful not to be carried away with the tortuous logic of such an argument. I suspect that John Mearsheimer, America's pre-eminent balance of power theorist, might even find comfort in this rather fine moral balancing. He has called nuclear weapons "a powerful force for peace", that worked as they were meant to as the perfect deterrent during the Cold War.

Today, he advocates "well-managed" proliferation. He would like to see Germany armed with nuclear weapons and even would "let proliferation occur in Eastern Europe".

One thing that is quite remarkable about the proponents of nuclear weapons is not so much their moral certainty that they are saving the world from more and more wars than already occur, it is the elegance with which over more than half a century they have refined their arguments. One mark of entry into the rather exclusive circle of high level strategic thinking is the intellectual ability to be able to turn a bald argument into a graceful phrase – what Barbara Ward once called "the fatal felicity" – that distinguishes their books and articles from what might otherwise be termed Machiavellian gobblygook. Their chat, when stripped of its well cut cloth, is as banal as a man disrobed. As General George Lee Butler summed up his life as head of the US Strategic Command (the man responsible for putting into action a president's order to begin a nuclear attack), "I spent hours at the blackboard, walking my students through those convoluted corridors: flexible response, assured destruction, essential equivalence and the dynamic between strategic offence and defence ... As I puzzled through all this, I became, to some extent, enthralled by it. Here was an intellectual riddle of the most intricate kind – a puzzle to which there appeared to be no solutions. The wonderful title of Herman Khan's book, *Thinking the Unthinkable*, captured the dilemma perfectly: that it is unthinkable to imagine the wholesale slaughter of societies, yet at the same time it appears necessary to do so, in the hope that you hit upon some formulation that will preclude the act; but then in the process you may wind up amassing forces that engender the very outcome you hope to avoid."

At the time of the relatively long history of nuclear deterrence during the Cold War there was always something going on that gave the more sophisticated insiders a reason for doubt. During the election campaign of John Kennedy much was made by him that the US was vulnerable to a pre-emptive attack by the new Soviet heavy missiles. Partly under the impetus of this so-called "missile gap" the US then developed its own heavy missiles armed with multiple warheads. Only later did the great theoretician of nuclear balance, Henry Kissinger, admit that this development had made the process of negotiating missile limits with the Soviet Union much more complex.

Similarly, much later on in the 1980s, under the threat of the newly deployed short range heavy Soviet missile, the SS20, in Europe, Chancellor Helmut Schmidt led a mighty campaign that tore at the heart of European political life to introduce into Western Europe a new American rocket, the Pershing, to counterbalance the SS20 and to tie more closely America's destiny in with Europe's. Yet it was never clear, as again Henry Kissinger disarmingly confessed, if America would launch a nuclear assault, once Europe had been attacked, since this would mean making US cities vulnerable to a similar bombardment. Speaking in Brussels in 1978, Kissinger made it clear that he believed the US would never initiate a nuclear strike against the Soviet Union, no matter what the provocation. "Our European allies should not keep asking us to multiply strategic assurances that we cannot possibly mean or, if we do mean, we should not execute because if we execute them we risk the destruction of civilization." Moreover, as McGeorge Bundy, the former National Security Advisor to President Kennedy, wrote, the Pershing deployment row was all quite unnecessary, because if an imbalance had developed in Europe all that had to be done was to move an American nuclear-armed submarine into the Baltic and Moscow would be under the hammer of a missile with a flight time of less than a minute. (Leningrad even less.)

Even at the apogee of America's nuclear arsenals there was always the worry that with its submarines close offshore to Washington the Soviet Union could decapitate the American command structure almost before it had time to blink. (Desmond Ball of the International Institute for Strategic Studies and John Steinbrunner of the Brookings Institution were the single most influential contributors to this argument.)

In the early 1970s Bruce Blair served as an air force launch control officer for Minuteman nuclear missiles in Montana. Now he is a senior fellow at the Brookings Institution and has become, as the *Washington Post* described him, "the leading expert" on nuclear command and control. More than anyone else, apart from General Butler, he has shown up the startling inconsistencies of US launch policies. In public the position has been consistent over many administrations – in order to deter the Soviet Union the US must possess an invulnerable force capable of surviving a first strike and then retaliating afterwards. The purpose of this posture was to give the President a second choice on receiving a warning that a Soviet nuclear attack was on its way. On the supposition that the warning could be wrong (and there had been many such due to computer malfunction and other deficiencies in the system); or that the attack was an unauthorized one (launched by a "rogue" or mentally deranged Soviet officer – and the US itself had two or three near disasters with its own officers); or that the Soviet leadership had decided only on a limited attack ( the US had spent years persuading them that if nuclear war should ever come to be it should start gradually to give diplomacy a final chance before Armageddon), the belief was the President needed time to judge what was actually occurring and the flexibility to go with it.

Blair demonstrated, however, that he was almost never called on to carry out a drill in which he fired off his missiles after the US had sustained a full-scale Soviet attack. Instead they were drilled to fire in a situation where no Soviet attack had occurred. The US was preparing either to launch on warning of an incoming attack or even pre-emptively.

The short answer to those who say "deterrence" worked during the Cold War is that, technically speaking, it never quite existed. George Butler has made this point in his uniquely devastating way: "[Deterrence] is fatally flawed as a logic in two respects. First and foremost deterrence required that you make yourself effectively invulnerable to an enemy's attack. In the nuclear age, the requirements are especially high, because the consequences of even one nuclear weapon slipping through your defences are going to be catastrophic.

Yet your perfect invulnerability would spell perfect vulnerability for your opponent, which of course he cannot accept. Consequently, any balance struck is extremely unstable and each side is led to build larger and larger arsenals, to discover more and more elegant technologies. Yet these never strike the desired balance either – the second logical flaw – because in the history of warfare from which nuclear war is not immune, neither the offence nor the defence has ever remained dominant for any significant period."

What Butler has convincingly demonstrated was that although deterrence was the aim, the competitive nuclear arms race effectively turned the doctrine of deterrence on its head. It became a circle that could never be squared. By conveying to the enemy the ability to retaliate massively even if attacked, your forces are in a state of alert that from the enemy's point of view looks as if you are preparing for a pre-emptive first strike. Whatever the theorists have said at the operational level the requirements of deterrence have proved to be impracticable. "The consequence was a move in practice to a system structured to drive the president inevitably toward a decision – one that he would have at the most one or two minutes to think about – to launch under attack or on warning of one. Indeed it would be difficult for any president (assuming he were still alive) to override a decision to fire. Since there were provisions to delegate this authority down the line if the president were incapacitated, who is to say what might happen under the stress of a supposed attack? Senior officers might assume, if communications were interrupted, that the president was incapacitated and take the decision into their own hands. Besides, submarine commanders at sea have long possessed autonomy when submerged and unable to make radio contact with headquarters. There has always been a contradiction between the necessity to be submerged to ride out a supposed attack and the need to surface to receive an up-to-date order.

It is true of course that this nuclear stand-off did work to produce great caution among the protagonists. But it worked best when needed least. When there was a crisis as over the decision by Kruschev to introduce short range nuclear-tipped missiles into Cuba "deterrence appeared to become almost irrelevant."

"Talk to Robert McNamara (Kennedy and Lyndon Johnson's Secretary of Defence) and others", says Butler, "They will tell you there was no real talk of deterrence in those critical thirteen days. What you had was two small groups of men in two small rooms, groping frantically in an intellectual fog, in the dark, to deal with a crisis that had spun out of control."

It was this experience together with the failure of his Vietnam policy that led McNamara to question the whole basis of nuclear deterrence. In fact the doubts began early during the first year of his time in office. He told both Presidents Kennedy and Johnson that he "recommended without qualification, that they never initiate, under any circumstances, the use of nuclear weapons. I believe they accepted my recommendations."

He confessed this in an article in *Foreign Affairs* magazine in 1983 and he was immediately accused of single handedly destroying the West's nuclear deterrent. "In reality", he later wrote, "I was destroying the *illusion* of nuclear deterrence." He knew from the inside, so he believed, that no American president "under any conceivable circumstances" was going to authorize the use of NATO nuclear forces in response to an attack on Western Europe using only conventional Soviet-controlled Warsaw Pact forces. "In truth, for nearly 40 years, with respect to our stated nuclear policy, it could be said the emperor had no clothes."

Outsiders may wonder how this policy to use nuclear weapons in the case of a Soviet conventional attack survived unmarked for so long. It is as McNamara has revealed and as Butler personifies, "because so many who had served in the West's nuclear chain of command (including the time of presidents Kennedy and Johnson) had not revealed their true beliefs regarding the utility of nuclear weapons because of their institutional commitment to the standing NATO policy of potential first use of nuclear weapons against a Warsaw Pact conventional force attack in Europe."

In Europe, a one-time protagonist of the standard NATO view, the former Chancellor of Germany, Helmut Schmidt, who spent much of his political capital in persuading the European electorate to beef up US nuclear forces on European soil, later admitted in 1987 in a BBC interview, "Flexible response [NATO calling for the use of nuclear weapons in response to a Warsaw Pact attack by non nuclear forces] is nonsense. Not out of date, but nonsense ... The Western idea, which was created in the 1950s, that we should be willing to use nuclear weapons first, in order to make up for our so-called conventional deficiency, has never convinced me."

Nevertheless, for all his inhibitions, McNamara makes clear that even he would have gone along with the use of weapons if there was a nuclear attack on the US. Writing about the threat of Fidel Castro to use his Soviet nuclear weapons if the US had launched a conventional attack on Cuba he argues that "no-one should believe that had American troops been attacked with nuclear weapons, the US would have refrained from a nuclear response. And where would it have ended? An utter disaster."

It appears that so embedded in the military chain of command was the notion of replying with nuclear weapons if an attack was launched that not one individual, neither a Butler-type who had his finger on the real button, nor a President Kennedy-type who had a great moral loathing of nuclear weapons, could have avoided or resisted the impetus to do what they had been laboriously drilled to do.

But that is speculation. Never has a former US president gone on the record on this point. The nearest we get to an insight is a remarkable interview conducted by Jonathan Schell of the *Nation* magazine with the former Soviet president, Mikhail Gorbachev. "I recalled that when I was trained in the use of the nuclear button or the nuclear suitcase I once was briefed about a situation in which I would be told of an attack from one direction, and then, while I am thinking over what to do about that, new information comes in – during these very minutes – that another nuclear offensive is coming from another direction. And I am supposed to make decisions!" Gorbachev laughed. "Nevertheless, I never actually pushed the button. Even during training, even though the briefcase was always there with my codes, and sometimes it had to be opened, I never touched the button."

And when Schell pressed him with the most difficult of all questions, "Would you have given the order to use nuclear weapons in retaliation for a nuclear attack?", he replied, "Well, let me tell you right off that this did not concern me, not because I lacked the will or the power, but because I was quite sure that the people in the White House were not idiots."

(Even so, Gorbachev, like most people close to the chain of command, was pre-occupied about how "nuclear weapons might be used without the political leadership actually wanting this, or deciding on it, owing to some failure in the command and control systems.")

This is a very different way of looking at nuclear weapons to the one given me by Zbigniew Brzezinski, the influential former National Security Advisor to President Jimmy Carter. In a long full-page interview he made with me whilst in office (printed in the *International Herald Tribune* and the *Washington Post*), he observed in reply to my question, "could he recommend to the president that he push the button and kill millions of people?" "I certainly think I would without too much hesitation if I thought someone else was launching a nuclear attack on me." To which I said: "Would you still do this knowing that it might make the chance of the regeneration of human society that much more difficult, even impossible?" "Well, first of all that is all baloney," replied Brzezinski. "As far as human society and all that is concerned it sounds great in a rally. The fact of the matter is, and I don't want this to be understood as justifying nuclear weapons, about 10% of humanity [500 million people] would be killed.

Now this is a disaster beyond the range of human comprehension. It is a disaster that is not morally justifiable in whatever fashion. But descriptively and analytically it's not the end of humanity."

He also added in a sentence he asked to be removed from publication according to the rules of a pre-interview agreement: "I actually feel that if I and the society I live in were going to be destroyed that I would want the satisfaction of knowing our enemy's society would soon be destroyed too."[1]

While this admission reflects with almost naïve honesty the darker reaches of the human soul common to many policy makers and military officers, it would be a dreadful mistake to assume that it is or was the dominant mode of thought. The moral revulsion of the use of nuclear weapons at all times during the Cold War ran perhaps equally strongly the other way – and with it an almost rabid urge to get rid of them and the moral dilemmas they posed for unhappy decision makers. How else to explain how the ultra-conservative but bomb-detesting president, Ronald Reagan, came so near to agreeing with the

---

1    After a 25-year delay I have decided that enough time has passed for such an agreement to have lapsed, as is the practice with much US Government secret documentation.

Soviet president, Mikhail Gorbachev, at their summit in Reykjavik in 1988 to get rid of all their nuclear weapons? Only the muscular intervention of their senior staff, who saw that both presidents could be impeached by their legislatures for such extraordinary behaviour, woke both men up to the other realities of power.

The more we examine the nuclear weapons policy the more we discover how boxed in everyone has become. The sheer inbuilt dynamic of the military-industrial complex, the legislatures, academia, public opinion at large and the press, the latter sheltering public opinion for much of the time from the tortured thinking of high-level policy makers, has made it impossible for any one individual, even a president as popular as Reagan, to find he has much room for breaking with the consensus. Only out of office might something individualistic be said and then as McNamara and Butler have found "the public recrimination can be quite poisonous."

McNamara's recounting of the dark 13 days of the Cuban missile crisis sheds some light (but not enough) on how policy making actually works when a decision to use nuclear weapons becomes only a step from reality. (None of the participants has demurred from the view that this was the occasion when the Soviet Union and the US came closest to unleashing their nuclear arsenal.)

The dice with death ended only when the Soviet leader, Nikita Khrushchev, signalled his willingness to remove his newly placed nuclear missiles from Cuba, in exchange for a public pledge from the US (revising its then current policy) that it would not invade Cuba and overthrow the government of Fidel Castro.

The crisis began when the US discovered the Soviet Union had placed nuclear missiles in Cuba and that more were on the high seas en route to Cuba. The US responded by mounting a naval blockade around Cuba. The Soviet ships were a mere 72 hours sailing time away. Richard Neustadt and Graham Allison in their book on the crisis recorded: "If the Russians held their course for a mere 72 hours, we would have had to escalate a step, probably by bombing Cuban sites. In logic, they should then bomb Turkish sites". (One of the triggers for Khrushchev's audacious move was that a few years before the US had put nuclear missiles into Turkey, capable of reaching Russian territory without hardly any warning time.) "Then we ... then they ... then *the third step* is what evidently haunted Kennedy. If Khrushchev's capacity to calculate and control was something like his own, then neither might suffice to guide them both through that third step without holocaust."

It was McNamara who persuaded Kennedy's closest advisors, who met in almost continuous session for 13 days, that they should make it clear to Khrushchev that if a deal were closed on Cuba the US would soon remove its missiles from Turkey. And it was Llewellyn Thompson, the former US ambassador to Moscow, who convinced Kennedy to ignore what Khrushchev later had said more aggressively and concentrate on his private letter which seemed to propose a pledge by Khrushchev to remove the missiles from Cuba in return for the US pledge publicly not to invade Cuba.

Nevertheless, even McNamara with all his abhorrence of nuclear weapons, has to admit if Khrushchev hadn't seized this opportunity for a deal, "a majority of Kennedy's military and civilian advisors (and the inference is including himself) would have recommended launching air attacks on the missile sites in Cuba "which as everyone agrees would have led to a nuclear exchange".

Over the years McNamara, under the influence of his experience, has moved from the position of being able, in his mind, at least to convince himself that nuclear weapons might have to be used (if not first, at least in reply) to where today he regards the actual continuing possession of nuclear weapons as both counterproductive and immoral.

His inference in retrospect seems to be that Cuba was a sideshow, albeit a horrendous one, that grew out of the Cold War confrontations in Europe. And now we know enough to understand that this central confrontation was very much a concocted confrontation. Neither side in fact coveted each other's territory. Stalin's ambitions in Europe were, by all the accounts of a majority of historians, satisfied by the Yalta settlement made with Churchill and Roosevelt. And neither side would have used nuclear weapons first on purpose, whatever their doctrines. (The Soviet Union was in thrall to the naïve doctrine that it could actually win a nuclear war, exhibiting the same thought process as some American neo-conservatives.)

Thus the Cold War, the 50 years of stand-off with nuclear weapons, was essentially a manufactured one, albeit manufactured by a mixture of paranoia, insecurity and ill-informed thinking. Yet not even in the best of times, at the end of the Cold War, could two powerful presidents, Reagan and Gorbachev, do much to unwind the nuclear bomb business, except at the margins.

In retrospect the Cold War years seemed to have passed relatively uneventfully. Although there was the crisis over the Soviet decision to blockade West Berlin and later over Cuba, and although both superpowers mercilessly used small and insecure Asian, African, Middle Eastern and Central American countries as proxy battlegrounds, never a shot in anger was fired between them. To that extent the fear of nuclear war gave both superpowers a self-discipline that they otherwise might have found wanting. Of course such self-discipline could have been formed by a mixture of empathy and diplomacy, but that would have taken a lot more imagination than both sides possessed.

The nuclear arms race continued under its own internal dynamic, the numbers growing, as well as the range and the reach, and the destructive power as well as the number of warheads on each rocket. Despite the attempts under the Strategic Arms Limitation Talks (SALT), which stretched over the life of many administrations, the ceilings negotiated were modest in relation to the growth of technology and firepower. Only under the presidency of Ronald Reagan did SALT metamorphose into START (The Strategic Arms *Reductions* Talks) and for the first time some modest reductions were enacted. Under President Clinton, despite the ending of the Cold War, little effort was made to speed up this process and the greatest window of opportunity for nuclear reductions was to all intents and purposes ignored. Even the move in Congress to win ratification for the Comprehensive Test Ban Treaty, a goal of presidents since Kennedy, that would have worked not just to cap super-power arsenals but those of the would-be new nuclear powers, was defeated, for want of sustained presidential leadership. Only under President George Bush junior was an effort made to dramatically reduce the numbers of nuclear weapons. Yet even this attempt was layered with ambiguity. Bush insisted that the decommissioned nuclear weapons be kept in storage. As for the Russian side, economic circumstances were compelling them to dramatically reduce their numbers anyway. Although both sides had long ago declared their days of enmity were over, although nuclear deterrence as a concept seemed to have been overtaken by events, still the superpowers keep thousands of missiles pointing at each other on hair-trigger alert with all the dangers of acciden-tal or "rogue" launch that has been feared for years. Inertia seems to trump the small, if well argued, disarmament lobby of both sides. Possessing nuclear weapons has become as important as flying the flag. It gives a country status – and this applies as much to France and Britain as it does to the US and Rus-sia – and it seems still to give grossly ill-informed electorates in all countries a false sense of security and self-esteem. In the course of the last couple of years the leaders of the US, Russia, France and the UK have taken decisions that they would never have dared to take in the days of the Cold War when Mutually Assured Destruction (MAD) policies kept both sides in check. Now, prompted by the war-mongering of President George W. Bush on the one hand and the dangers of nuclear proliferation on the other, the political leaders of these four have announced an unprecedented change in their long-established military doctrine. They have said that they now consider that nuclear weapons can be used for war-fighting not just deterrence.

If the progress made in nuclear disarmament between the superpowers was both tenuous and verging on the superficial, even the cosmetic, there were, over the years, substantial positive moves made elsewhere in the globe. In 1986 much of the South Pacific, including Australia, New Zealand and Papua New Guinea made itself into a formal nuclear-free zone. (Later New Zealand went a step further and, to Washington's anger, forbade US battleships, sup-posedly nuclear-armed, from port calls.)

Six years later Ukraine, Belarus and Kazakhstan, all of whom inherited large quantities of nuclear arms when the Soviet Union broke up, forsook what must have been a serious temptation to jump into the new nuclear league of economically underdeveloped countries with modern armaments and agreed to surrender them to Russia for dismantling. In 1993 on the eve of black rule South Africa confessed it had built six nuclear bombs but two years earlier had become the first country ever to abolish a nuclear arsenal. The following year Brazil and Argentina, two neighbouring countries, that at one time competed to develop nuclear weapons, formally announced they had renounced the ef-fort and they finally ratified the 1967 Treaty of Tlatelolco that made South America a nuclear weapon-free zone. The African countries formally did the same.

In May 1995, the Non-Proliferation Treaty signed by 185 Nations, was renewed indefinitely. But what should have been a landmark in arms control
was in reality more a mark of failure, of promises made and broken by the
big nuclear powers, who solemnly undertook to move rapidly toward nuclear
disarmament if the Treaty were renewed, committing signatories to renounce
nuclear weapons. The Treaty was also flawed by a major loophole that any
"rogue" nation could sail through once it had done its secret homework and
was politically prepared to reveal its nuclear bomb potential – all it had to do
was to give six months warning that it was pulling out of the Treaty.

Back in the 1960's President Kennedy had foreseen a world by the end of the
century that would have twenty or thirty nuclear bomb powers. In the event he
was over-pessimistic. Only China moved fairly rapidly to join the nuclear club
and a short while later Israel, with the connivance of the US, its stalwart over-
protector, did the same. Later Pakistan and India made their nuclear tests.

Back in 1982 the American strategic thinker, Kenneth Walz, wrote a study
for the International Institute of Strategic Studies arguing that the world had
less to fear than perhaps it thought from the proliferation of nuclear weapons. "The alternative to nuclear weapons", he said, "for some countries may
be ruinous arms races, with the high attendant risk of becoming engaged in
debilitating conventional wars."

Walz in his study, first drafted for the CIA, takes five arguments of those
who believe that the spread of nuclear weapons is dangerous and shoots holes
through them:

–   Coups – It is true, he concedes, that Third World governments can come
    and go rather quickly. But those that are most coup-prone are the least
    likely to organize the technical and administrative teams necessary to de-
    velop a nuclear bomb. [But what about Pakistan?]
–   Irresponsible leadership – There are or have been he admits leaders like Idi
    Amin (the dictator of Uganda). Yet when confronted with foreign counter-
    vailing pressure these leaders have been "cautious and modest". Egypt and
    Libya have been openly hostile since 1973 and there have been commando
    attacks and air raids, but neither side let the attacks get out of hand. [But
    what about the Iran/Iraq war?]
–   The military – Military governments are in power in most Third World
    countries. Yet military leaders are likely to be more cautious than civil-
    ians.
–   Preventive strikes – The uneven development of new nuclear states would
    suggest that first-comers might decide to strike at their rivals before they
    had a chance to catch up. In practice it is difficult to be sure that the coun-
    try one wants to attack does not have some warheads. Even if it has only
    rudimentary nuclear capability there is the prospect of retaliation.
–   Expense – A nuclear weapons programme is thought to be expensive and
    open-ended. Not at all – only rich countries can afford to consider nuclear
    war and therefore get caught up in arms races to achieve successful first-
    strike capability. But Third World countries as long as they have enough

for simple deterrence will be satisfied with a small arsenal. Moreover, having thus gained security they will run down their expenditure on conventional forces.

In conclusion, he wrote, "the pressure of nuclear weapons makes war less likely."

At the time this was considered very much a minority, if not outrageous, view. Over time as the reality of proliferation became more apparent even such stalwart traditional thinkers as John Mearsheimer began to be won over. Honest enough to take it to its logical conclusion, Mearsheimer was able to argue on the eve of the second Gulf War that even if Iraq did possess weapons of mass destruction the US was so superior in both nuclear and conventional arms that deterrence was working as effectively as it could and there was neither a need for war or indeed for the US to openly brandish its nuclear arsenal.

Yet to many this "free thinking" school of thought appeared to be more a coming to terms with sins and omissions of the past than a creative way of dealing with new dangers. Although all the Western powers and the Soviet Union had been committed to controlling their exports to avoid proliferation there was a great deal of evidence to suggest that they knew their nuclear industries were less that watertight. France was particularly at fault, preparing at one time to build plutonium-producing reactors for anyone who could pay. But even when the Carter Administration successfully persuaded France to ease up on its nuclear promiscuity, industrialists from Germany to Switzerland, to Britain to the US itself, were able to get away with selling critical materials and the knowledge to go with it. As recently as 2003 the US decided to prosecute Boeing for selling rocket knowledge to China – a reminder of what has been going on for decades without rigorous policing. Besides, China had no compunction about aiding Pakistan if it would give its long standing though quiescent enemy, India, pause for thought. Similarly, after the invasion of Afghanistan by Soviet forces and the need to enlist Pakistan in the fight to drive them out, a blind eye was turned by the anti-proliferation Carter Administration to Pakistan's nuclear programme. All attempts to pressure Pakistan were simply abandoned through an annual ritual of giving assurances that all was well in Pakistan's nuclear laboratories. It was not only an ill-conceived policy, it was an unnecessary one. Only in 1990 with the Soviet occupation of Afghanistan defeated did President George Bush senior belatedly cut off military assistance. Even in 2002, after all the lessons learnt, in return for winning Pakistan's support in defeating the Taliban and pursuing Al Qaeda, Washington appeared to be turning another blind eye – to Pakistan's latest acquisition of nuclear-capable rockets from North Korea.

Even on the carrot side great opportunities were missed. Much responsibility needs to be heaped on the shoulders of that most pacific of all American presidents, Jimmy Carter. At that time, when India's prime minister was the near pacifist Moraji Desai, it could have been possible to persuade India to renounce its pursuit of nuclear weapons if Washington had used a little more carrot and a bit less stick in its attempt to pressure India to sign a safeguards agreement on the use of spent nuclear fuel. The quid pro quo would have been for America to step up the pace in negotiating a Comprehensive Test Ban Treaty and to agree to get rid of its nuclear weapons at a faster pace. Yet Carter found himself unable to move faster, partly because of the degree of opposition to such arms control measures in the Senate. It was a missed opportunity of historic proportions. Such a compromise would not only have slowed the American-Soviet arms race. It would have made the Indian and Pakistan nuclear bombs more difficult to develop. Indeed, Desai might have been the strong enough politician to ram through the bureaucracy the policy he believed in – abolition of Indian work on nuclear weapons.

It is to be seen for how long Walz's thesis will hold water. Although a nuclear war between India and Pakistan or between Iran and Israel, unlike a superpower nuclear war, would be limited to a fairly confined geographical area, it would still be totally devastating by any historical standard. The risks of nuclear war, already too high for comfort between the careful and now experienced superpowers, are clearly much more with new powers with immature command and control systems, less discipline and more autonomy among possible "rogue" commanders, and to be honest, certainly in the case of the sub-continent, a popular opinion that often seems rather carefree about the consequences of nuclear war. But then 80% of Indians alive today know nothing about Hiroshima and Nagasaki, or even the Cuban missile crisis.

Perhaps the one would-be nuclear power we don't have to worry about, although Washington worries a lot, is North Korea. For all its isolationism North Korea has no real active enemies. It has Washington on its back, but it is not actually militarily threatened. Indeed, it is the other way round if anything. The US soldiers embedded close to its border are in fact hostages to be quickly killed in any military blow up.

How to stem the tide on proliferation is an extraordinarily difficult question. Japan, thanks to British and French re-cycling policies (again their short term commercial interest has stumped their long-term political sense) has built up a very big store of plutonium, for no good and apparent reason. It does not need it for its present power-producing reactors and the 1970s dream of fusion reactors that would run forever on one fuelling of plutonium has now been relegated to distant academic pastures. What is more, Japan's post World War II Constitution would prohibit such a development, even if public opinion were not as hostile as it is. Yet clearly the senior circles of the military and politics have decided to take out an insurance policy – after all, a pile of plutonium in a highly sophisticated industrial state is almost a virtual arsenal. At the most Japan would need six months to bring it to fruition. As for the enemy – a newly aggressive China, although that seems far-fetched, or a malevolent North Korea, an equally doubtful proposition despite its provocative missile testing over Japan. It defies imagination to conceive of a circumstance in which either country would see the need to stir up Japanese hostility. Nevertheless, there are influential Japanese in both politics and academia who attempt to make a plausible case for Japan becoming a nuclear power. Worst case scenarios always win a larger audience in a time of political and economic uncertainty.

China for its part has been a nuclear weapons state since 1974. If Washington chose to do it it could easily "prove" that China is a "rogue" state. It has designs on both Taiwan (an American "protectorate") and the Spratley islands (if China refuses one day to accept the obligations of the Law of the Sea, which it says it is committed to) and it has, over many years, aided Pakistan's nuclear development which in turn has aided North Korea's. Mao Zedong used to speak with callous equanimity of China's ability with its large population to "absorb" any nuclear attack and claimed that the US's nuclear weapons were the armaments of "a paper tiger".

In reality modern day China is not considered even by the Bush administration as a rogue. Momentous efforts have been made to keep China as a friendly nation, albeit not an ally.

Nevertheless the future is uncertain. The Taiwan Strait is without doubt the world's most dangerous potential flashpoint. It could bring the two nuclear powers nose to nose, if one of the three parties allowed their present self-discipline to lapse, as they did five years ago when the US sent its fleet into the Strait to deter China from firing more warning missiles over Taiwan. It is not so much nuclear deterrence that keeps the two big powers sober; it is the fear of economic disruption that war of any kind would bring. The US is China's largest market and Taiwan is its main source of high technology investment. The better tactic is to keep the present relationship in a state of equilibrium, whilst encouraging the development of human rights in China to reach the state of sophistication of Taiwan. If the "two Chinas" could both be democratic it is reasonable to think that the reasons for mutual hostility would fade into relative insignificance.

Compared with the proliferation on the Indian subcontinent, China and North Korea, the would-be proliferation that has alarmed the Bush administration in Iraq and Iran is relatively small beer. The crisis and war of 2003 made clear that Iraq has no nuclear weapons and that its remaining arsenals of chemical and biological weapons were small and unsophisticated. The UN disarmament process following the first Gulf war in 1991 did its job better than Washington ever imagined.

Whether Iran is or is not building nuclear weapons is an on-going argument among experts. It certainly has every reason to, if one accepts the argument that an underdog who wants to challenge American interests for whatever reason and who feels insecure before America's uncompromising secularisation can easily persuade itself that nuclear weapons are the only thing that could dissuade America from trying an attack.

The US in fact is trying to ride two horses and on both the saddle is slipping. The first is the Nuclear Non-Proliferation Treaty which most countries have signed and wish to adhere to, despite the broken promises of the big nuclear powers to take rapid steps towards nuclear disarmament. At the moment there is not one whit of evidence that Kennedy's gloomy prophecy of twenty or more nuclear powers will turn out to be true. The second is to isolate those regimes it regards as threatening which are trying to pre-empt the striking of American wrath by building a small nuclear arsenal. At the moment the number is small, even on the most pessimistic of scenarios. It can be no more that Iran, North Korea and conceivably Saudi Arabia and Syria. Only if Pakistan were seriously destabilised and fundamentalists came to power would Pakistan become a threat to the West. But, thanks to the war in Afghanistan in 2002, America has already elite troops based in Pakistan who would seize Pakistan's nuclear weapons and disable them in such an eventuality. Indeed the Bush administration has made it clear that it will pre-empt any effort by such countries to build nuclear weapons.

Only North Korea gives it pause because it may have already at least a couple. Since Washington vividly detests being stopped in its tracks it will make sure there are no more North Koreas.

At the time of the first crisis between the US and North Korea in 1994 it became apparent, with its supposed possession of two nuclear weapons and its massive standing army massed close to the border with South Korea, what a formidable deterrent the North possessed. President Bill Clinton decided that the US had to negotiate. Confrontation could lead to a nuclear attack on South Korea's cities and American troops based in the South.

Under an agreement midwifed by former president Jimmy Carter the North agreed to close its plutonium-producing nuclear power plant and seal up the cooling rods from which weapons grade plutonium could be extracted. In return, America with Japan and South Korea agreed to build two modern, non plutonium-producing nuclear power stations to be in production by 2003. Also the US agreed that it would end its economic embargo and help the North with fuel oil, food and electricity. But the deal has been coming apart almost from the day it was signed. All along there have been warnings that if these stumbling blocks were not put right we would end up where we were in 1994, with the threat of nuclear war staring us in the face. For few doubt, even those who are toughest on North Korea, that if it comes to a military conflict and North Korea feels it has everything to lose it will use the two nuclear weapons it supposedly already has. (For a full account of this see my book *Like Water on Stone*, Penguin, 2001.)

It was this threat that persuaded the Republican hardliners in Congress during the days of the Clinton administration to go along with the main elements of the deal, even as they provoked the North with their constant attempts to minimize the commitments the US had made to secure it. There were a number of times when the fuel oil deliveries or the food supplies were seriously slowed. There was the successful effort in Congress to break the promise of ending sanctions, delaying action on this until 1999 when they were finally but only partially lifted. There was the blockage on talking about ways to help the North receive electricity supplies from the South to tide it over until the new reactors were built. Not least, there was the slowdown on the building of new nuclear reactors, with the prospect of them being finally completed five years behind schedule. It had become clear that the earliest date they could be ready is 2008.

All these setbacks have been reason enough in the North's mind for ratcheting up the confrontations. Confrontation, Pyongyang appeared to decide some time ago, is the only way to get results. Whether it is digging an enormous hole that convinced the Americans that the North was about to test nuclear triggers (wrongly as it turned out, after paying a huge sum for the US to be allowed to inspect it), or test-flying a long range rocket over Japan, which was what persuaded Congress to ease the economic embargo.

Still, the 1994 agreement limped along (and even looked as if it might be enlarged to include a restriction on missile sales) until President George Bush junior came into office and made his "Axis of Evil" speech in which Iran, Iraq and North Korea were singled out. Even though the Bush administration did not move at first to discontinue its aid programme (the largest America had in Asia) or to stop work on the building of two nuclear reactors, it did lean on South Korea to slow down its so-called "Sunshine" policy of political reconciliation. It also refused to talk about other sources of electricity supplies, prohibited its ally, South Korea, to honour a promise to send electricity to the North and refused all talk and consideration of a refurbishment of the North's electricity grid despite the growing delays on the new reactors. And it gave the impression that it was in such a confrontational mood of its own that it might well give up on further negotiations with the North. Out of the window went a new deal that Clinton believed he was close to settling that would freeze deployment of missiles with a range of more than 500 kilometres. And out of the window went also the nuclear freeze deal itself that probably stopped the North building 30 nuclear bombs a year in the last few years.

It has come as no surprise to North Korea watchers that Pyongyang decided to up the ante in 2003. Over many years it has discovered that offence is the best defence in dealing with the US. Now, not-so-subtly, it says it is to bring back into use its mothballed plutonium-producing power reactor to make up the shortfall in its energy needs. The US has only two choices – the old ones – either to go to war and risk a nuclear exchange or, for the first time, to honour its side of the 1994 deal and to go full steam ahead, with no ifs and buts, to help the beleaguered North Korean economy to get back on its feet.

Despite the big questions over tactics one can in fact conclude that no Administration has been more committed to stemming the proliferation of nuclear weapons than this one. Compared with the vapid posture of his predecessor, Bill Clinton, who made no serious effort, despite inheriting the end of the Cold War, to strike nuclear disarmament deals with Russia and, after its run-in with North Korea, adopted an easy-going attitude to proliferation, at least the Bush Administration cannot be accused of lacking purpose.

The weakness – and it is the fatal weakness of the Bush Administration – is that it cannot carry the world with it in its chosen approach – military confrontation. With its war with Iraq only Britain and Australia stood shoulder to shoulder on the battlefield, unlike the war of Bush senior when over a dozen countries offered troops. Even if the politicians wanted to be more helpful, public opinion would not allow them, as Prime Minister José María Aznar found in Spain and King Fahd found in Saudi Arabia, as indeed was the case almost everywhere. Public opinion has never been expressed with such singularity of purpose or with such widespread unanimity as it was on this occasion.

The saddle on the Nuclear Non-Proliferation Treaty has more than slipped. It has become undone. For America to carry the world on this issue it has to be convincing. It has to demonstrate that what it is asking of others it is also doing itself. It is not that it need fear further break-out from the NPT – most countries are aware that to become a nuclear power would be on balance a negative asset – but to stymie the efforts of those the US considers are "rogues" it needs to carry out its side of the central bargain of the NPT, which is to begin serious nuclear disarmament itself.

Public opinion in Europe certainly, but also in much of the rest of the world which may not be so well informed, seems to have an intuitive understanding that

a)  war over alleged nuclear weapons capability is hypocritical whilst America is so over-armed;
b)  is doubly hypocritical given the West's long tolerance of exporting the ingredients for making weapons of mass destruction;
c)  is triply hypocritical given the blind eye it turned to Iraq's use of chemical weapons against Iran and the Kurds, and Israel's manufacture of a large nuclear arsenal.

There is also a further point, perhaps too sophisticated for the man or the woman in the street – that neither Iraq, nor Iran, nor North Korea could have logical purpose in actually using a nuclear weapon unless they had their back against the wall in the face of a massive overwhelming attack, and the only country that could actually make such an attack is the US. If America has to fear anything it is an attack from a nuclear suitcase carried into the US by a terrorist with no fixed address, not from a state that would be open to retaliation.

America has no choice but to find a way to become credible again. Moreover, it has no choice but to look with a fresh eye at the arguments of the nuclear dissenters. Their main point is that by possessing nuclear weapons there is a risk they will be used by accident or by a rogue commander. None of the major technological developments of recent years appears to have diminished this risk. Their second argument is that nuclear deterrence is at best an unproved point. The Soviet Union never sought to intrude on Western territory and had no ambitions in that direction. In its own eyes Soviet nuclear weapons were developed only to match America's. Yet America likewise had no active designs on Soviet controlled territory, although it has been quick to assert its interests there and elsewhere in Eastern Europe once the Soviet Union collapsed.

The Indian/Pakistan confrontation also suggests deterrence does not work. Both sides have continued direct conventional fighting – in the Pakistan case using proxy guerrilla forces. Both sides seem prepared to risk nuclear war and have moved several times to the brink, without the heartache or the reticence that seized Kennedy and Khrushchev at the time of the Cuban missile crisis. By developing nuclear weapons both sides have given themselves more severe political and military problems than they had before. India was clearly the superior of the two when both just had conventional forces. Now the playing field has been levelled. Pakistan for its part has introduced a major new element of instability into its already precarious and incendiary body politic.

The only two cases where arguably nuclear weapons appear to work as a deterrent are Israel's vis á vis the Arab world and North Korea's vis á vis the US. Yet Israel was effectively invulnerable to a major conventional attack before it became nuclear armed and its decision to pursue nuclear arms had the counter-productive effect of persuading Iraq and perhaps Iran to try to develop theirs. And North Korea is only in such a strong position because 50,000 American troops are deployed in an essentially static formation so close to its southern border. Even if North Korea develops rockets capable of reaching the US heartland and chose to use them it could not, in the foreseeable future, obliterate more than a handful of small cities or parts of large cities and would know that even if the US didn't launch a retaliatory nuclear strike that it could with conventional means subdue the country and overturn the government and no one, not even China, would come to its aid. It is more deterred by America's conventional power than its nuclear weapons.

The fourth argument of the nuclear disarmers is that, given the above, the continued possession of nuclear weapons must be immoral. General Butler's conclusion is that "nuclear weapons are irrational devices. They were rationalised and accepted as desperate measure in the face of circumstances that were unimaginable....... I have arrived at the conclusion, that it is simply wrong, morally speaking, for any mortal to be invested with the authority to call into question the survival of the planet."

General Charles Horner, who was the allied air forces commander in the first Gulf War and from 1992 to 1994 commander of the US Air Force Space Command, concludes that the moral opprobrium against using nuclear weapons would be such that, "the nuclear weapon is obsolete: "I want to get rid of them all." Even for Israel, where the culture is "eye-for-an-eye", he argues that if the military replied to a chemical Scud attack on Tel Aviv with a nuclear weapon, "they would lose all legitimacy as a nation....they'd be a pariah". Indeed if the US used a nuclear weapon, even a small one, against an Iranian nuclear research bunker, America would effectively make itself an outcast for decades to come. World opinion would regard the act as simply unforgivable, all the more so for being unnecessary with today's sophisticated conventional weapons. America would simply make itself, for all its wealth and power, totally isolated.

But apart from saying nuclear weapons should be got rid of how do these nuclear disarmers think they can actually be got rid of?

Most important is to win the intellectual battle that there are no situations imaginable when they could be useable. Robert O'Neill, the Professor of the History of War at All Souls College, the University of Oxford, is the academic at the forefront of this discussion. They are not much use, he says, in deterring other weapons of mass destruction, biological or chemical. "They destroy a massive area, killing the wrong kinds of people and they do nothing to protect your own forces because chemical and bacteriological weapons will probably be released from sites all over the adversary's country, as were Iraq's missiles in the first Gulf War."

There is a long history of Americas, Soviet and French presidents as looking at how to use nuclear weapons in regional crises. Truman considered using them in Korea as did Eisenhower. The French thought of using them to avoid their catastrophic defeat at Dien Bien Phu in Vietnam. And the US seriously considered using them in the Berlin crisis – as recently as 1980 a US Pentagon study said it would be necessary to "threaten or make use of tactical nuclear weapons" if the Soviets moved their forces into northern Iran.

On the Soviet side Moscow warned the West at the time of the invasion of Suez in 1956 that it was prepared to use nuclear weapons. Georgi Arbatov, at the time Brehznev's adviser on foreign policy, told me that there had been a number of crises when influential advisers had counselled the president to threaten the US with the use of nuclear weapons.

More recently, at the time of the first Gulf war, there was the memorable conversation between Dick Cheney, the Secretary of Defence, and Colin Powell, then Chairman of the Joint Chiefs of Staff. According to Powell's account in his autobiography, "He had a third question and I jotted it down in my notebook simply as 'Prefix 5', my nuclear qualification code. 'Let's not even think about nukes', I said, 'you know we're not going to let that genie loose.' 'Of course not', Cheney said. 'But take a look to be thorough and just out of curiosity.' I told Tom Kelly to gather a handful of people in the most secure cell in the building to work out nuclear strike options. The results unnerved me. To do serious damage to just one armoured division dispersed in the desert would require a considerable number of small tactical nuclear weapons. I showed this analysis to Cheney and then had it destroyed. If I had any doubts about the practicality of nukes on the field of battle, this report clinched them."

The second line of argument must be to elucidate a plausible scenario of reductions. Few disarmers believe the US can go to zero overnight, much as they see zero as their ultimate goal, but all believe there will be no real impetus in the non-proliferation battle unless the big nuclear powers (and that includes France, Britain and China, as well as the US and Russia) show a desire to set the ball rolling. As George Perkovich argued in *Foreign Affairs* (in April 2003) the recent disarmament agreement made by Putin and Bush is riddled with holes: "Because the treaty lacks a schedule of phased reductions, either party could defer cuts until December 31, 2012, at which point violations would be moot because the treaty expires on that day. The treaty also does not require the elimination of a single missile site, submarine missile, warhead, bomber or bomb."

Although the US and Russia have formally de-targeted each other's forces, re-targeting can be programmed in a matter of a few seconds. Nuclear disarmament seems an idealistic, even utopian goal. It is in some ways. Richard Perle talks of the disarming generals as men whose "stars are not on their uniforms but in their eyes". But then to see an end to the Cold War was regarded by an overwhelming majority of experts and politicians as utopian until the moment it happened. France and Germany so recently mortal enemies are now the bedrock of the European Union. There can be profound changes in the way human society works. We are more than halfway there. We have to pound away and believe at some point resistance will suddenly crack. One thing we know from the experience of Reagan and Gorbachev that right at the top of present day power-structures there are probably people who want the same thing as the most idealistic disarmament advocates. (Other senior ex-military men and arms negotiators who have joined the disarmament cause include Paul Nitze, Reagan's hard-line arms negotiator, Field Marshal Lord Carver, former chief of the British Defence Staff and Admiral Andrew Goodpaster, former Supreme Allied Commander in Europe).

It is a question less of convictions than finding the key to the box that holds political society in a straightjacket. The mechanisms of disarmament are profoundly important. The public in the nuclear powers must never be allowed to feel that disarmers want to strip them naked. Unnecessary though more conventional arms may be, it is probably necessary to stress the need to improve those even further, so there can be no question that if a "rogue state" did break out of a universal move led by the big powers to rid themselves of nuclear weapons a conventional force would always be sophisticated enough to deal with it.

Many disarmers have argued that the first steps should be horizontal disarmament – de-alerting weapons, de-mating warheads from delivery vehicles, removing parts from warheads or rockets (or adding parts that spoil their performance or adulterating weapons grade fissile material). As Jonathan Schell puts it, "Vertical disarmament (reducing numbers) makes a catastrophe, should it ever occur, smaller. Horizontal disarmament makes a catastrophe of any size less likely to occur."

This actually happened when George Bush senior was president in 1991. He decided to de-alert all bombers, 450 Minuteman missiles and the missiles in ten Poseidon submarines. Gorbachev, taking the cue, deactivated five hundred land based rockets and six submarines. This wasn't the cosmetic de-alerting talked about today. Silo and submarine crews actually had their launch keys taken away from them.

McNamara, for one, has little time for deploying energy into the horizontal issues. He focuses very tightly on reducing numbers. His aim is zero. Any horizontal deal would enable its owner to fairly quickly re-activate its arsenal. "The risk of nuclear catastrophe" he writes, "derives from the combination of the *magnitude* and the *imminence* of the threat: two many lethal weapons, too little time to decide."

McNamara believes that in the absence of a movement towards zero there will be more and more nuclear states. Moreover, the dangerous stockpiles of the nuclear weapons states will become increasingly at risk of theft. He accepts there will be risks with a nuclear weapons-free world – cheating or a "break-out" by a country or even a terrorist group is possible – but they are less than the risks with a nuclearized world.

Robert O'Neill too has argued against the notion that in a nuclear-free world a cheater would be king, "Well, no king, because using a few nuclear weapons or threatening to use them would be of very limited value. Either the bluff would be called or, if it turns out not to be a bluff, and someone does use them, they would open themselves to unimaginable retaliation by the whole international community, backed by intense public outrage around the world. For the nation that did use nuclear weapons, it would just be another way of committing suicide. We might have to go through an incident like this before the point was driven home, but I think it's better to accept that risk than to accept, as we do now, the continuing risk of the whole planet being blown sky-high."

McNamara sees 100 weapons each for the superpowers, as a first step. After that then there would need to be discussion about security guarantees to be given to smaller states – Britain, France, India, Pakistan, China and Israel – so that they could be persuaded to join the march to zero. There is, he emphasizes, an important "psychological" component to the effort and he likes the way Field Marshal Michael Carver has argued this point – "The most important thing at this moment is to persuade everyone, even those not inclined to accept it, that the target has got to be total elimination. If you start peddling solutions, which are not quite total elimination, but something which comes close to it, you lose the whole force of the argument. Until you've dramatically fixed zero as the target, you'll just get the sort of silly thing you get now. Of course, when you come to actual details and a verification system, you've got to face all these problems; and of course you have to have steps along the way. But don't let's say that a target less than the absolute target would be acceptable."

The passion brought to the discussion by these military men suggests that we have averted accidental nuclear wars by accident more than by clever balance of power politics and that if we roll the dice for much longer and the number of players increases one day for sure the number will come up.

Yet against this passion is arrayed popular inertia on one side and an extraordinarily deeply embedded culture of "nuclear deterrence" on the other, one that has powerful allies not just in the military-industrial complex, as one would expect, but also in the highest levels of academia and the media. As former West German Chancellor Helmut Schmidt (ex nuclear hawk, now a dove) has analysed it, "there is an enormous body of vested interests not only through lobbying in Washington and Moscow but through influence on intellectuals, on people who write books and articles in newspapers or do features on television. *It's very difficult as a reader or as a consumer of television to distinguish by one's own judgement what is led by these interests, and what is led by rational conclusion."*

To break the defences of this world is going to be a highly laborious exercise. If the ending of the Cold War could not do it can anything else do the trick? Can the fear of the raw material for making nuclear weapons being stolen and perhaps passed on to the terrorists?

In the 1960s the late Herman Kahn, arguably the greatest nuclear strategist of all time, pondered pessimistically on the conditions necessary for returning to a nuclear-free world. He thought it would take a US-Soviet nuclear war followed by an immediate pact never to use them again. But Kahn said they must not have time to bury the dead, otherwise the old mistrust and enmity would quickly return.

Perhaps Kahn today would point to a nuclear war between India and Pakistan or the accidental launch of a Russian or Chinese missile on Los Angeles or the use by North Korea of a nuclear missile on South Korea and its American troops.

Perhaps then popular passions would be roused enough for the disarmers to win an audience. But in performances now it is clear they speak to a near empty theatre. We have lived with nuclear weapons for so long that although, apart from a small minority of strategic thinkers, we have not learnt to love the bomb we have not sufficiently learnt to fear it.

Nevertheless, I think Kahn would be amazed to see how little enmity there is today between the old superpower rivals and indeed between both of them and the up and coming superpower, China. Not since 1871-1913 has there been so little active hostility between the big powers. This must be the time to get our grip on the issue of big power nuclear disarmament, for without that there is simply no credibility when dealing with would-be nuclear proliferators in the Third World. Noone is better placed than the human rights community to mobilize discussion on the issue – simply put, to kill millions of people with one bomb must be the worst of all human rights abuses.

# 5  How Far and Fast Can We Push the Frontier of Human Rights Observance?

"We cannot anticipate today what we shall know only tomorrow" wrote the philosopher Karl Popper. Equally prescient is Kierkegaard's remark, "We have to live life forward, but we can only understand it backwards." Any discussion of widening and deepening humanity's observance of human rights must at the onset come to terms with those two observations. Only by having some perspective on how far and fast we have come can we gauge the optimum speed we can hope for in the future.

The history of the evolution of human rights norms is a long – and slow – one. True there has been a spurt over the last sixty years and, as Henry Kissinger argues, even more so over the last decade. "An unprecedented movement has emerged to submit international politics to judicial procedures [and] has spread with extraordinary speed", he recently wrote in a despairing and disparaging tone. It has been brought on in part by popular agitation personified by the rapid growth and influence of Amnesty International and Human Rights Watch, but it truly is the cumulative work of centuries, if not millennia, of political, philosophical and religious thinking, hammered out on the anvil of revolutions, wars and political debate. There is, to mis-quote one of the two most important documents in the human rights canon, the American *Declaration of Independence*, nothing "self-evident" about it.

Let me repeat myself, but somewhat more fully: "We hold these truths to be self-evident, that men are created equal, that they are endowed by their Creator with certain unalienable Rights, that among those are Life, Liberty and the pursuit of Happiness." All of us know, however, that Jefferson's self evident truths about human rights have not seemed self-evident to most of humanity for most of its history. There is no revealed truth on this subject. Indeed Jefferson himself was a contented slave-owner, "happy", to use a keyword in his declaration, to impregnate his female slaves, but not countenancing giving his offspring the rights to be the sons and daughters of an important man.

A UNESCO document of 1949 spoke of "the antiquity and broad acceptance of the conception of human rights," and suggested that the discussion of such rights goes right back to the beginnings of philosophy in both the East and the West. But as Brian Tierney argues in his book *The Idea of Natural Rights*, "few historians would agree with such a broad judgment." Kenneth Minogue has written that the idea of human rights is "as modern as the internal combustion engine." Some have dated it as beginning with Hobbes. Others with Grotius. And Tierney himself has a lot of time for those who say the father of subjective rights was the fourteenth century Franciscan philosopher, William of Ockham. Others argue that the ancient Greeks were the first to start to think about subjective rights. However, there appears to be no elaborated doctrine of natural rights among stoic thinkers. Roman law – the most detailed of all ancient systems – similarly fell short. Many scholars have argued that a doctrine of natural rights was always implicit in Judeo-Christian teaching. But Moses' law was commandment. So was Jesus' and Mohammed's and although St Paul wrote of law written in the hearts of men he certainly did not go so far to say that "all men are endowed by their Creator with certain unalienable rights". Nor can one unearth these ideas in the early history of other cultures. Natural rights theories, for all their worldwide popularity today, are essentially a relatively recent Western invention, dating from around the twelfth century, at the height of the medieval period.

Nevertheless, as Tierney warned us, "it is unprofitable to ask whether the 12th century "discovered" the individual. In all cultures some people are more self-aware and reflective than others. But we can say that twelfth century European civilization was marked, like no other culture, with a new emphasis on personalism and humanism. Not least courtly love literature explored the joys and pain of human lovers. In marriage law, by the end of the twelfth century, the simple consent of the man and the woman, without the need to go to Church, was regarded as sufficient for a valid sacramental marriage. What a human right that was!

When the French Franciscan philosopher, Ockham, arrived on the scene in the 14th century he took this a step further and maintained that the traditional idea of an objective natural law – which existed in Roman law – be transformed into a new theory of subjective natural rights. Natural rights and natural law, he wrote, were derived from human rationality and free will and were independent of Christian revelation. (Today Pope Benedict is an enthusiast of this idea of natural law.)

There were other schools of thought beside his. Gratian used Stoic thought on natural law when he wrote his great canonistic work, the *Decretum* in 1140 and Thomas Aquinas, in turn, used the *Decretum* in his seminal work, *The Summa Theologiae*, written in the thirteenth century. Later in the sixteenth century, the Spanish Dominican monks, in particular Friar Bortolome Las Casas, in their quest to save the South American Indians from the pillage, exploitation and murder of the Spanish Conquistadores, built on Aquinas, elaborating the idea that all individuals were children of God and "made in his image". But they also argued their case independent of Christian revelation, asserting as Ockham did that natural rights and natural law were derived from human rationality and free will. Tragically, all the writings in Spain and all the victories won in the debating halls of Salamanca and Madrid on behalf of the Indians did little to save them from the depredations of the Spanish adventurers.

Until the 16th century it was Catholic medieval theologians who pioneered the thinking on natural rights. After, in the early modern world, it became the preserve of Protestant political theory. It was the 17th century Dutch scholar, Hugo Grotius, the father of modern international law, who straddled the two eras. He was the first to argue that there could be "a common law among nations" and the first Protestant scholar to recognize the importance of Catholic medieval thinking.

When the Enlightenment – the age of reason, independent of, but not necessarily always against, Christian belief – arrived on the European scene late in the seventeenth and early in the eighteenth century, the first wave of great thinkers, most importantly those living in the Netherlands and in Great Britain, regarded Grotius as the founding father of their discipline. One of them, John Locke, was the first political philosopher to argue that government should be underpinned by the popular will and subject to natural law. "Men, by nature all free, equal and independent, no one can be put out of this estate and subjected to the political power of another without his own consent." To be truthful Locke was in part rationalizing what had already happened two years' before – the English "Glorious Revolution" when the Protestant William of Orange overthrew the Catholic king, James II in 1688. In that year was published the "Bill of Rights" marking an end to the King's claims to absolute rule by Divine Right. Three years later came the first Habeas Corpus Act – the demand that all detained alleged criminals must be tried before a court of law.

As the 18th century progressed the centre of gravity of intellectual thought shifted to France – to Rousseau ("Man is born free; and everywhere he is in the chains") and Voltaire ("I know many books that fatigue but not one of which has done real evil"). Voltaire in particular was impressed by the state of English parliamentary democracy and for a time – six years – came to live in London to study it in practice at first hand. Voltaire, who published over one hundred volumes, had two main themes: tolerance in religion and peace and liberty in politics. In one of the greatest tracts ever written on the human rights of freedom of worship, *Traité Sur Tolerance*, he highlighted the Calas affair in Toulouse where a Calvinist father was broken on the wheel for opposing his son's conversion to Catholicism.

In France the ideas of the Enlightenment philosophers, contradictory though they often were, fuelled the agitation against the Ancien Regime. In the American colonies they inspired the rebels who defied the British establishment. But it should never be forgotten that it was the Americans who took the really gigantic first step towards individual freedom and democracy, albeit in resistance to the European country, apart from Austria, that was then the most free and best governed on the continent. The French *Declaration of the Rights of Man*, written in 1789, may have caused more resonance in the subsequent history of Europe, (partly because France was supreme in Europe for most of two centuries, a state which lasted until the fall of Napoleon, and partly perhaps because in every knapsack of Napoleon's soldiers was a copy of *The Rights of Man*) but it was the American *Declaration of Independence* in 1776 that first synthesized the best ideas of the Enlightenment, and did that in the most beautiful prose. Compared with that the French document reads more like a shopping list!

The US Constitution followed thirteen years after the *Declaration of Independence* in 1789, the same year as *The Declaration of the Rights of Man*. As Norman Davies has written, it "contains the clearest and most practical formalities of the ideals of the Enlightenment. They are short, secular, democratic, republican, and rational: firmly grounded in the contract theory of Locke, in English legalism, in Montesquieu's thoughts on the division of powers, in Rousseau's concept of the general will". Most importantly, the Constitution was written in the name of "We, the people of the United States."

French intellectual opinion was enthused by the turn of events in the US – if the Americans could rebel because of a three penny tax on tea had not the French, living under a despised and cruel regime, good reason to throw off their yoke? And Jefferson, who by 1789 had become the American ambassador to France, helped Lafayette with the draft of *The Declaration of the Rights of Man*. It was also the time of Thomas Paine, who as Geoffrey Robertson has noted, was "The first writer to fuse outraged polemic and constitutional philosophy to produce a distinctive literature of human rights." Besides helping fire up the American Revolution with his incendiary pamphlet, "*Common Sense*", he helped Jefferson draft the *Declaration of Independence* and then wrote, in a tavern in London's Islington, the highly influential work *The Rights of Man*. He was prosecuted for sedition and fled to France where he was elected to the National Assembly. Even the English poet Wordsworth, the man of the quiet countryside, got caught up in the fervour. "Bliss was it in that dawn to be alive."

Paine also watched – and suffered imprisonment in the Bastille – as the French ideals were consumed by the Revolution's special brand of terror – the tumbrel and the guillotine which were the chosen instruments of coercion – and fear of that amoral minority, the Jacobins who had hi-jacked the revolution.

In as much as they still believed in human rights the Jacobins limited them to those they called the sans-culottes. The French Revolution turned into Europe's worst ever crisis. It taught Europe a lesson that it should have listened to more carefully – the dangers of replacing one tyranny with another. Nevertheless, its social and political ideas lived on thanks to the influence of French culture which then dominated the Western world. It still has the power to stir the minds of human beings condemned to oppression, injustice and servility – in the modern era in Vietnam under Ho Chi Minh, in China under Mao tse Tung and in Latin America in Che Guevara's time.

Although it is that legacy with its calls for *Liberté, Egalité* and *Fraternité* that echoed through the chanceries and streets of Europe, from Portugal to inner Russia, from Scandinavia to Italy there was also another less remarked upon effort at setting human rights standards – in Hapsburg Austria under the rule of Emperor Joseph. When he obtained sole rule in 1780 he emancipated the serfs and extended religious toleration to all faiths. Children under nine were forbidden to work. Civil marriage and divorce were permitted and capital punishment abolished. Mozart, basking in Vienna's relaxed atmosphere, composed *Don Giovanni*, a tale of sexual seduction. And in Britain too, there was the new cause of abolishing slavery, which happened in 1807. America had to wait until 1865 and the fighting of a civil war until protection from slavery and serfdom was added to the Constitution.

By 1778, the year that both Voltaire and Rousseau died, the Enlightenment was, as Davies, writes, "starting to run out of breath". "It had assured itself a place as a permanent pillar of modern Europe thought", he continues, "yet the rationalism which originally inspired it was losing its force of persuasion. Pure reason was felt to be inadequate to the task of understanding the world and of reading the auguries and upheaval."

The terror in France had something to do with this reaction. "When I hear of natural rights", said Jeremy Bentham, the English philosopher, "I always see in the background a cluster of daggers and picks". He thought natural rights were "nonsense upon stilts." And, according to Robertson, "the force of Bentham's arguments was partly responsible for "natural rights" falling out of fashion in the nineteenth century".

But not entirely. The nineteenth century, especially in England was a time of unprecedented industrial economic development and with it liberal thought. The mid nineteenth century saw the publication of James Mill's essay *On Liberty*, which has become the standard manifesto of human rights. Individual rights, he argued, should only be restricted when they impinge on the rights of others. In a later work he argued for equal rights of men and women. Mill was a prophet of laissez-faire economics, but only if the power of the capitalists were matched by unions of the workers.

Karl Marx was a vociferous critic of *The Rights of Man* – they "are nothing but the rights of egotistic man, of man separated from other men and the community" and "the rights of the restricted individual withdrawn into himself". Later Lenin was to scorn the English and French revolutions as uprisings of the bourgeoisie.

Following the carnage of the First World War, one might have expected a resurgence of concern for human rights. But neither at the Versailles Peace Conference nor in the Charter of the League of Nations did they find a place. It was even decided, under American pressure, not to prosecute war crimes. However, there was for the first time, as I write in the chapter on the UN, a real effort to deal with the complex issue of minority rights in Europe.

Two decades later the issue of human rights was still quiescent. Neither Stalin's show trials and mass executions nor the persecution of the Jews in Germany re-ignited the cause. The dam of apathy was not breached until H. G. Wells, the great science-fiction writer, shortly after the onset of World War II, together with a few socialist friends including A.A. Milne, the writer of Winnie the Pooh, published a declaration of principles on human rights. This was, as Robertson says, the first time since the 18th century revolutions that there was "an attempt to restate human rights in a homely way." Penguin Books quickly followed the declaration up by publishing *H. G. Wells on the Rights of Man*. It was translated into thirty languages and syndicated in newspapers all over the world.

President Franklin Roosevelt was one of its readers. On January 1st, 1942, just after the US entered the war, the Allied powers in a joint declaration pronounced that "complete victory of their enemies is essential ... to preserve human rights and justice in their own hands – as well as in other hands."

The last year of the Second World War saw the writing of the Charter of the United Nations. Article I unambiguously describes the purpose of the UN: "To achieve international cooperation in solving international problems of an economic, social, cultural or humanitarian character, and in promoting and encouraging respect for human rights and for fundamental freedoms for all without distinction as to race, sex, language or religion." This was a momentous turning point for humanity. Although voted on unanimously it probably would not have been that strong a statement if a group of American NGOs, including the American Jewish Congress and the National Association for the Advancement of Coloured People, had not exerted continuous pressure on the US delegation.

In October 1945, the UN Preparatory Commission recommended that the Economic and Social Council (ECOSOC) establish a Commission on Human Rights, charged with drafting an International Bill of Rights. Work began in 1947, beginning with the writing of what was meant to be a "stirring" declaration. The drafters were the US, the Soviet Union, the United Kingdom, France, China, Australia, Chile and Lebanon.

Historians always credit Eleanor Roosevelt, the chairperson, with seeing the document through its many drafts to conclusion. Indeed she was pivotal. But NGOs played a major role, as William Korey has shown. Even less well known is the leading role played by China whose delegate argued that the Declaration could not simply be a reflection of Western philosophy and advised the UN staff to embark on a study of Confucian thought, and the antagonistic attitude not just of the Soviet Union but of Britain as well. (Nevertheless, the Soviet Union was responsible for the Declaration's clear statement on non-discrimination.) Less influential countries too played an important part especially in the drafting committee which contained the representatives of Chile, Lebanon, Egypt, India, Panama, Pakistan, Philippines and Uruguay. As Susan Waltz has precisely put it; "Without the insistence of small states on the applicability of human rights, even in the shadow of colonial tutelage, the Declaration might not have included explicit provisions of universality and its name might have remained (as it was in early drafts) the International Declaration rather than the *Universal Declaration of Human Rights* it became.

Although Saudi Arabia, along with South Africa and the Soviet Union, was to abstain on the December 1948 vote on adopting the Declaration most of the Muslim states happily stood up for it. The Pakistani delegate, speaking on the importance of Article 2, said that he had an "intellectual conviction that freedom [is] indivisible."

In the following years the notion that fundamental freedoms must be widened to include the right to political independence and self determination was central to the debate on the writing of the International Covenant on Civil and Political Rights, a document meant to give binding force to the Declaration. Saudi Arabia, Syria, Lebanon, Iraq, Iran, Pakistan, Egypt and Afghanistan pursued this cause in the face of Western hostility – the US State Department disparagingly called it "the Muslim resolution" When the Covenant entered force in 1976 that right became a provision of international law. But it took the US nearly thirty years to ratify it – the US had effectively abandoned a leadership role in the international human rights project it helped inaugurate.

Nevertheless, from 1948 on the advances in human rights were steady and cumulative. One after another the UN over the years 1948 until the end of the century voted into being a series of conventions on:
- The Right to Self-Determination
- The Prevention of Discrimination
- The Outlawing of War Crimes and Crimes against Humanity, including Genocide
- The Outlawing of Slavery, Servitude and Forced Labour
- The Outlawing of Torture
- On Nationality, Statelessness, Asylum and Refugees
- On Freedom of Information
- On Employment Policy
- On the Political Rights of Women
- On the Rights of the Family, Children and Youth
- On Social Welfare, Progress and Development.

In 1993 at the UN World Conference on Human Rights in Vienna, convened in the optimistic aftermath at the end of the Cold War, 171 governments voted by consensus for a new declaration, the most thoroughly and widely endorsed statement on human rights ever made. Some paragraphs restated the objectives of the 1948 Universal Declaration. Others extended the human rights vision further. The Vienna Declaration states that the universal nature of these rights is beyond question. "All human rights are universal, indivisible, interdependent and interrelated." Thus the entire spectrum of human rights was agreed without division. Unlike in 1948, Saudi Arabia, South Africa and Russia (taking the place of the Soviet Union) voted in favour.

In 1946, under a provision of the UN Charter, the World Court had been established to solve disputes between nations. Later, reflecting the new post-Vienna common consensus on the need to push forward the frontiers of human rights practice, new and important legal institutions were put in place to deal with individual human rights crimes. In the wake of the Yugoslav, Rwandan and Sierra Leonean civil wars of the 1990s the UN established the ad hoc war crimes courts for ex-Yugoslavia, Rwanda and Sierra Leone. In 1998 in a landmark step an overwhelming majority of the world's nations voted to create the International Criminal Court to persecute war crimes and crimes against humanity.

Part of the reason for this stunning pace of advance in international human rights law – a big part – is the energy and determination of Non-Governmental Organisations, most of them not more than 50 years' old. Groups such as Amnesty International and Human Rights Watch have not only captured the popular imagination, they have exerted a massive impact on governments. Amnesty International, uniquely a popular membership driven organisation, (with now well over one million members all over the world) has mastered the art of using the case of the single prisoners, torture victim or disappeared to highlight a general political situation. Perhaps Amnesty's greatest single success was to win UN adoption of the Convention Against Torture and then the subsequent ratification of the treaty by Reagan's America and Thatcher's Britain. It was this that made possible the arrest of General Augusto Pinochet in Britain in 1998.

These astonishing developments reaching into the four corners of the world, which have accelerated by leaps and bounds since the 18th century and even more so since 1945, beg the question – would the understanding that human rights are so important have manifested itself so strongly without its nurturing over centuries in Western culture? I doubt it. But need it be a problem? I don't think so, if it is honestly faced. After all, modern technology is a product of the Western World, even though it borrowed important ideas from the Muslim world ( the repository of Greek mathematics and philosophy during the many centuries when it was obliterated from the Western mind), from the Hindu world (whose mathematicians originated the concept of zero) and from the Chinese (with their multitude of critical inventions from paper to gun power). All over the world today this advanced Western technology is accepted more than willingly.

Even on the philosophical plane, Marxism, a distinctive European concept, has been readily accepted by the most radical – and some would say, in their time, creative – people in the Third World.

Nor should we see human rights as somehow in conflict with the more communitarian values of traditional societies. In its early medieval construct the idea of natural rights was not one of "atomized individualism." And even today in many Western cultures, in southern Europe, Scandinavia and the Latin American countries "atomization" is still limited by a strong communitarian sense. Above all, we should realize that since human beings everywhere prefer life to death, freedom to servitude, sufficiency of food to starvation and dignity to humiliation it is not surprising that the language of human rights that evolved in Western culture has won a universal audience.

If it is so that the West is the fountain head of modern human rights law and practice, then it is confronted with two international dilemmas for the future. How does it avoid becoming a parternalist patronizer as it chivies, cajoles and even punishes those not in the West and mainly in the Third World and Russia for their human rights failings? And, second, how does it resolve its own tensions between the US on the one hand and Europe on the other, the former whose Realpolitik pushes it continuously into compromising on its traditional human rights?

Needless to say those fault lines are not as clear cut as I've made it sound. There is a very strong constituency within the United States for a more coherent, less compromised and tougher policy on human rights. As for the Third World and Russia, there are both strong personalities and movements that are as vociferous about implementing human rights law as any in the West.

Ask the democrats in Hong Kong or Taiwan whether or not they feel the urge for democracy is an implant or a natural home-grown thing and you'll, often as not, get the answer that it is home grown. In part that reflects a cultural adaption that has been welcoming to human rights norms as these countries have stormed ahead economically and educationally. But some will also remind the inquirer of Mo Tzu, initially an advocate of Confucius, who later (470-391BC) rejected Confucianism because of its over emphasis on filial objections and hierarchy. Instead he stressed the importance of administering justice impartially and the need for universal love. India, soon to be the world's most populous nation and one day its major economic power, has been democratic for as long as nearly any living Indian can remember. Although introduced by the British colonialists Indians have adopted it as warmly and effectively as they have cricket! For most Indians today it is something they imbibe with their mother's milk. Latin America, Chile and Costa Rica have over a century and a half of experience in practicing democracy, although in Chile's case it was briefly interrupted by the coup of General Pinochet. It was the Africans at the Vienna Conference on Human Rights who pushed some doubting Asian countries to sign on for a reaffirmation of the values of the Universal Declaration of Human Rights and thus engineered a unanimous vote for the document.

In the Islamic world there is a strong tradition of the importance of law in international relations. The Islamic scholar Farhad Malekian argues that the Koran "constitutes the main source of Islamic law" and that it "contains a large number of provisions governing the humanitarian law of armed conflicts and this law was consolidated fourteen centuries ago when there was scarcely a sign of the humanitarian law of armed conflicts in the practices of most nations." The Koran together with the Islamic philosophy of law based on Shari'a (divine law) inspired the Universal Islamic Declaration of Human Rights, agreed in 1981 by an overwhelming majority of Muslim nations.

But while notions of international law and human rights observance are moving apace in the Third World – and arguably nowhere faster than in China – the tensions between old Europe and new America appear to be widening. Yale Law School professor Jed Rubenfeld puts this down to the immediate aftermath of World War II, the experience of which was different on either side of the Atlantic. For Americans winning the war was a victory for nationalism – "that is to say, for our nation and our kind of nationalism." Whereas Europe reacted against the excesses of nationalism and the perversion of democracy that in Germany had precipitated the war.

Thus for post-war Europeans the point of international law was to address the problem of nationalism – to put checks on popular sovereignty, the will of the crowd. But in the US the belief was that internationalism and the multilatarism that it promoted in the aftermath of World War II "were for the rest of the world not for us. What Europe would recognize as international law we already had. The notion that US practices – such as capital punishment – held constitutional under our bill of rights might be said to violate international law was, from this point of view, not a conceptual possibility".

This view was partly triumphalism, partly parochialism, partly the influence of racist white southerners during the early post war years, but it was also something more fundamental, deep down in the American psyche. It delayed for thirty years the US ratifying the anti-genocide and other principal human rights conventions. And at the present time it accounts for the hostility towards the International Criminal Court.

Today, continues Rubenfeld, there is also another consideration that separates the political cultures of America and Europe. Europe has tended to believe that its judges are somehow apolitical, which leads it to "invest courts the full jurisdiction over individual rights, without acknowledging that judicial decisions about the meaning of rights are highly political." Thus Europe finds it easier to bow before the rulings of an international tribunal, whether a European one or a world-wide one. Americans, in contrast, feel that constitutional interpretation is too interwoven with judges' political biases and therefore electoral politics, for decisions to be handed over to a body that is not US voter-dependent.

These reservations have grown as the international system has become more powerful in recent years. Although the unilateralism of the Bush Administration has widened the divide, the signs were there in the proceeding Clinton administration. Recall how the US (and the UK) put the UN Charter on one side when they decided to bomb Belgrade when majority opinion in the Security Council considered it illegal.

Anne-Marie Slaughter of Princeton and president of the American Society of International Law has taken issue with Rubenfeld's arguments. She believes that "Rubenfeld's account of both European and American constitutionalism is historically inaccurate and politically naïve."

Most European governments put parliament above the law, she argues, and even when, as with the European Court of Justice, judges hold immense powers, their terms are for no more than 12 years, rather than life as in the US system.

Rubenfeld also ignores, she says, that Article VI of the US Constitution declares that "treaties are the law of the land," and so trump state laws. And today, she continues, the US must continue to believe in the extension of international law because it serves all nations' long term interests. As long as a new body of rules are created bottom-up and ratified by democratic legislatures

Americans should have no problem with them. "If other nations no longer believe that the US will honor those rules, they will no longer agree to bind themselves, and then we will slide from coalitions of the willing to chaos." As the political scientist, John Ikenberry, has argued, the US should continue on that path because it is the only way the US can reassure its allies that it is willing to restrain its own power in the service of common goals, thereby increasing that power by diminishing the incentive of either allies or enemies to find a way to balance against the US, which would lead to more self-conscious and antagonistic power blocs.

It must be the hope that when Bush steps down that a newly elected President would return the US back towards a truer interpretation of its own long tradition, not least by doing a somersault on its attitude towards the International Criminal Court.

Once the US, Russia, China and India sign up for the ICC (and if the US did the others would probably follow), we will have in place all the instruments the international community needs for a better practice of human rights. The real need in the first part of the twenty-first century is consolidation, not expansion, for honest application to make these institutions work, not subterfuge and sabotage. If we look at the last sixty years in the light of history we see clearly that it has been, by far and away, the most rapid period of advance in the history of human rights. Now the job is to make it all work.

Take, for example, the World Court (the International Court of Justice) – a grossly underutilized institution. In recent years both the US and France have withdrawn their automatic consent to be made a party to any case in the court. China and Russia have never given theirs. Britain is the only member of the Security Council to accept automatically the Court's jurisdiction.

The Court, which arbitrates disputes between nations, lost favour in America when in 1984 Nicaragua took the US to the Court for mining the harbour of its principal port. On the other hand, more recently Nigeria has demonstrated – at its own considerable cost – its respect for the Court. President Olusegun Obasanjo of Nigeria decided to take to it the charged dispute over who owns the oil-rich Bakassi peninsular, Cameroon or Nigeria. Although Obasanjo was pressured by his minister of defence to threaten Cameroon with military action and popular opinion was nationalistic, Obasanjo did not budge. The Court ruled in Cameroon's favour and Nigeria has implemented its decision.

The International Criminal Court, meant to deal with future war crimes and crimes against humanity, is openly being undercut by the US which has used all manner of threats to weaken its reach, particularly in the hypothetical direction of the US itself. Nevertheless, the fact that the Court now exists even though the US, Russia, China and India have not signed up, is recognition that, for the first time since Nuremberg and the trials of the Nazi leaders, the idea of individual personal responsibility for gross atrocities is becoming a given in international life. As the East Timorese resistance leader and Nobel Peace Prize laureate, Jose Ramos-Horta, commented,"In this day and age, you cannot kill hundreds of people, destroy a whole country, and then just get fired."

Yet this is what happened in Indonesia after the mass murders in East Timor in 1999. Next time round the ICC presence may ensure it doesn't happen.

Professor Anne-Marie Slaughter has suggested that the ICC needs to be backed up by orders of the Security Council when the world community is faced by particularly notorious dictators, malevolent governments or movements. Then it can become an alternative instrument to waging all out war. "In Iraq, for instance, instead of debating a decade of sanctions and ultimately the deployment of military force, the Security Council could have authorized an international prosecutor to investigate Saddam Hussein's war crimes. Once an indictment has been issued, the Security Council could determine that in the interests of international peace and security, a national or international force should be authorized to arrest an indicated suspect. When the individual resists the arresting authorities could be authorized to use force."

This, surely, is a better alternative than full frontal, nation to nation war, with the inevitable killing of the innocent. Killing innocents to save innocents is an unacceptable moral choice, when their only crime is to be ruled by a tyrant.

Some writers on human rights have taken this argument a step further – they have devised the notion of "humanitarian intervention" – that when human rights are being abrogated on a large scale outside nations have a right to set on one side Article 2 (4) of the UN Charter – "All members shall refrain in their international relations from the threat or use of force against the integrity or political independence of any state" and Article 2 (7) which prohibits intervention in matters essentially within the domestic jurisdiction of any state.

This in fact was done in 1999, when it was widely believed in the West that Serbia was about to massacre the people of the province of Kosovo. NATO mounted a large-scale bombing of Belgrade that supposedly brought Serbia to the negotiating table. But in fact, as is now widely accepted, the bombing did not forestall ethnic cleaning, it appeared to precipitate it. Moreover, in a bitter twist the "peace agreement" that ended the war demanded much less from Serbia's president, Slobodan Milosevic, than the diplomatic effort at Rambouillet that proceeded the decision to go to war.

War is war, even if it is launched in a "good" cause, and human rights is too often the loser, however stringent the control exercised by democratically elected politicians of their fighting machine.

Nearly all these crises that provoke the debate about humanitarian intervention can be seen coming, sometimes many years beforehand. I have argued at length in my book *Like Water on Stone* what is needed is pre-emption. As Pierre Sané, the former Secretary-General of Amnesty, has put it, "Why should we be forced to choose between intervention and inaction?" If the international community can be encouraged to move with economic carrots, with meditation and with the careful deployment of UN peacekeepers before a crisis moves to its boiling point, much can be achieved. This surely is the true lesson of the failures of Yugoslavia and Rwanda.

We have come a long way, very fast, on human rights in the course of the lifetime of a single generation. For that we should be thankful. But it is important, looking to the future, to remember where it all came from. Most of the philosophers who tackled this subject saw the advance of natural rights and later civil and human rights as essentially a non-violent enterprise. Indeed, most of them argued, or at least inferred, that to pursue these ideas by the sword was an immense contradiction.

It is important that we be on our guard so that, as with the French Revolution, our good ideas are not hijacked by latter day Jacobins and twisted and distorted so that we can no longer recognize ourselves in the mirror. As Martin Luther King once said, "The means and the ends must cohere." "We will never have peace in the world", he preached in a famous sermon, "until men everywhere recognize that ends are not cut off from means, because the means represents the ideal in the making, and the end in process. And ultimately you can't reach your good ends through evil means, because the means represents the seed and the end the tree".

# 6  Can Human Rights Be Pursued by Making War?

Human rights, of a kind, have been around for a long time. A citizen of ancient Rome, if condemned to die, could choose to be beheaded. A non-citizen would be tortured to death, or crucified.

In more recent times, England's *Bill of Rights* in 1689, the American *Declaration of Independence* in 1776 and the French *Declaration of the Rights of Man* in 1789 have been seminal influences on modern institutions. Lord Acton believed that the "*Declaration of the Rights of Man* made by the revolutionary movement in France had a more powerful impact on European history than all Napoleon's armies". (Yet we must not overlook that the French Revolution's ideals were played out in the Reign of Terror to the roll of tumbrils carrying ever more victims to the guillotine.)

In post-war history two watersheds stand out in contemporary political events. The first was the United Nations' *Universal Declaration of Human Rights*, codified in 1948 under the influence of its presiding genius Eleanor Roosevelt. The second, perhaps more controversial, was the determination of a US president – Jimmy Carter in the late 1970s – to make the issue one of the central points of his presidency.

I have no reason to quibble with what Mr. Carter told me in Vienna in 1993: "There is no way that Amnesty International, for all its wonderful work, can play the same role as the president of the United States can play." What was missing, however, from the end of that sentence were the words "if he wants to". That certainly applied to Carter himself, who was, to say the least, inconsistent in the application of his human rights norms. Even in his final speech as president before the Democratic party congress he almost exclusively lambasted the Soviet Union for its falling short, ignoring the many parts of the world where the US gave tacit support to unsavory regimes for geopolitical reasons. But he did lay down, particularly within the Democratic party, precepts by which the actions of future presidents could be judged and which could be used by organisations like Amnesty International to hold the politicians to account.

Nothing perhaps illustrates more sharply the gap in thinking between those who try to integrate human rights into everyday geopolitical thinking and those such as Amnesty who stand apart from day-to-day political compromise and insist on an untarnished standard, than the debate over the bombing of Yugoslavia in 1999. NATO claimed it was a crusade to forestall the ethnic cleansing of the Albanian people of the province of Kosovo. But in fact the bombing turned out to be nothing less than the precipitating event in the ethnic cleansing, which, contrary to NATO propaganda, did not occur on a massive scale until after the bombs began to drop.

Amnesty, although critical of the bombing at the time, did not issue its blockbusting press release until thirteen months after the event. It had taken that long for its thorough checking processes to be completed. But once its then Secretary-General, Pierre Sané, had taken the final decision to go public in May 2000, it became quickly apparent this was the essence of Amnesty's long tradition: to stand apart from governments, even democratic ones, and to question means as well as ends. On 7 June the Amnesty press release went out, with a copy sent simultaneously to the US State Department, the foreign ministries of Britain, Germany and France and NATO headquarters in Brussels. The *New York Times'* Steven Erlanger began his despatch: "In an extensive report that has infuriated NATO leaders Amnesty International said that NATO violated international law in its bombing over Yugoslavia by hitting targets where civilians were sure to be killed. Amnesty accused NATO of war crimes, of 'breaking the rules of war', said that those responsible 'must be brought to justice' and asked the UN criminal tribunal on the former Yugoslavia to investigate these allegations."

Ironically, this perhaps showed that the Pentagon generals who had waged a bureaucratic war against President Clinton to water down and, in the end, oppose the creation (which initially he had strongly favored) of a permanent International Criminal Court for trying war crimes had focused their attention in the right direction. Their intuitive alarmism, which many at the time thought was overdone, turned out to be essentially correct. The human rights lobby has the wind in its sails and is going about its business in a way that is pushing its ship forward at a fast rate of knots. Over the last decade, it has won world-wide ratification of the Genocide and Torture Conventions, the creation of a UN High Commissioner for Human Rights, the establishment of ad hoc War Crimes Tribunals for ex-Yugoslavia, Rwanda and Sierra Leone, the arrest and detention in Britain of General Pinochet of Chile and, most important, a permanent International Criminal Court for the prosecution of crimes against humanity.

The reasons the Pentagon gave to President Clinton for opposing an International Criminal Court – that other nations would not allow the US to write into the treaty language that would in effect give cast-iron guarantees that US troops could never be arraigned before it – now can be seen as prescient. Guantánamo and Abu Ghraib prisons and the use of rendition and torture suggest that a case could be made for a prosecution of the US by the Court. It will be deeply ironic if the human rights cause to which an American president in the 1970s gave so much of a fillip should progress to the point where it is hoisting the US with its own petard. (For a fuller and profound discussion of the growth and extension of the norms of international jurisprudence, see "Judging War Crimes" by William Pfaff, in *Survival*, 42/I, Spring 2000).

But that, indeed, is what Amnesty is up to. Case by case, the logic of its own mandate is leading it more and more into a head-on clash with the liberal democracies. Contrary to the current widespread opinion, given voice to by such diverse personalities as David Holbrooke, Clinton's ambassador to the UN, the Canadian writer, Michael Ignatieff and the Oxford don, Timothy Garton Ash, the pursuit of human rights is not particularly well served by military action. To quote Michael Ignatieff: "The military campaign in Kosovo depends for its legitimacy on what fifty years of human rights has done to our moral instincts, weakening the presumption of state sovereignty, strengthening the presumption in favor of intervention when massacre and deportation become state policy."

But war is war, even if it is launched in a "good" cause, and human rights is too often the loser, however stringent the control exercised by democratically elected politicians of their fighting machine. The war in Afghanistan has provided yet one more example. While anger at the atrocities of Osama bin Laden's Al Qaeda movement appeared to move a large majority of humanity, it remains clear that America and Britain's decision to go to war with arguably the poorest country in the world is not the best answer to ending this particular kind of terrorism. As Amnesty's new Secretary-General, Irene Khan, told European Union policy makers, "Human rights do not need to be sacrificed to obtain security." The US and the rest of the international community should have decided at the outset to pursue bin Laden with the same perseverance as Israel showed hunting down the Nazi exterminator-in-chief, Adolf Eichmann, to bring him to trial before the International Criminal Court, with quiet police work, following the accepted precepts of international law, not noisy war work.

Indeed, if the preservation of human rights is really the first and paramount purpose of policy, the whole approach to the kind of political impasses that lead to war becomes very different. Simply put, one avoids the recourse to war and leaders are compelled to search for alternative ways of dealing with the situation. Naive? Although the issue has not been exclusively human rights, one can see an example of how such an approach could work out in practice with US policy towards North Korea, an uncompromising dictatorship.

In this case Clinton had to find an alternative to war because the US feared if it chose the military option North Korea might well retaliate against a US/South Korean ground invasion with the two or three nuclear weapons it is supposed to possess. Apart from the devastation this would cause in South Korea, it might lead to the loss of over 50,000 American troops.

There have been any number of reasons why since 1994 America could have decided to get tough with a country that gave many indications that it had serious ambitions not just to build a nuclear bomb but to develop a long-distance missile to deliver it. Even today North Korea is the arch-demon for those who advocate the necessity of building an anti-missile shield to "protect" the US from nuclear attack from a "rogue" country.

Yet, contrary to many of its basic instincts, the Clinton administration used the soft glove rather than the mailed fist. Indeed, North Korea became the main recipient of US aid in Asia. The US supplied free much of the country's fuel oil needs and a good part of its food requirements. At the same time South Korea and Japan were building, free of charge, a state-of-the-art light-water reactor capable of supplying most of North Korea's electricity needs for years to come.

In retrospect, it seems amazing that debate in Washington in 1994 was almost dominated by those discussing the best way of bombing North Korea. US intelligence had discovered that North Korea was about to remove spent nuclear rods from a cooling pond to recover plutonium, sufficient to make four or six nuclear bombs to add to its supposed (but never proved) stockpile of two or three. Former Secretary of State Henry Kissinger, former National Security Advisor Brent Scowcroft and former CIA chief Robert Gates loudly went public with calls for battle. The saving grace was that they ended up shooting each other in the foot. Gates and Scowcroft argued that the US should immediately bomb the North Korean reprocessing plant before the cooling rods could be transferred to it. This, they said, would minimize the risk of radioactive fallout. Kissinger advocated immediate tough sanctions and unspecified "military action". But his timetable miraculously allowed time – a short three months while the rods cooled – both for a conference of the nuclear-haves and for sanctions to work. Military action should occur, he said, only if North Korea re-fuelled its reactor or started to reprocess its plutonium from the cooling rods. However, this seemed to ignore Scowcroft's and Gates' point about the dangers of an aerial bombardment on reprocessing facilities. Nor did any of them appear to worry that North Korea might use the two or three nuclear bombs they said the country already had to repulse an American attack.

In fact, the three of them talked themselves into the ground and made it easier for ex-president Jimmy Carter to journey to Pyongyang on a peace mission and pave the way for a deal with Kim Il Sung to accept a nuclear freeze. In return, the US would be committed to working with South Korea and Japan to build two conventional power-producing nuclear reactors.

Since then there have been all manner of ups and downs in the US-North Korean relationship. Congress nearly sabotaged the agreement fashioned in the wake of Carter's visit by reneging on White House commitments to begin liberalizing the US's trade and investment and ending sanctions. Kim Il Sung died, to be succeeded by his son, Kim Jong Il, who took the best part of five years to show he was firmly in the saddle. In 1998, when North Korea test-fired a long-range rocket over Japan, it seemed that Pyongyang was determined to play out its role as the world's number one agent provocateur. Later in 1998, US intelligence spotted a massive hole being dug suitable for exploding secret triggers for a nuclear weapon. In the end, for a payment, the US was allowed to inspect the hole and found that a hole was all it was.

Not without a great deal of political contortion, the Clinton Administration managed in the end to convince Pyongyang of its good faith. North Korea, for its part, reciprocated by drawing in its horns, albeit often at the last moment.

Meanwhile, the South Korean president, Kim Dae Jung – an ex-Amnesty prisoner of conscience – pursued his so-called "sunshine policy" with the North. Despite immense opposition from the old guard, he succeeded in sustaining it to where the temperature of the Cold War between North and South began to rise so the waters were unfrozen enough for a highly successful summit to take place in June 2000. At the end of 2000 Secretary of State Madeleine Albright broke more of the ice with her visit to Pyongyang.

The North Korean peace was one of President Clinton's rare positive foreign policy achievements. The Pentagon's influence for once was stymied by North Korea's supposed possession of nuclear weapons and, this time, willy-nilly, other less confrontational means had to be tried. Seven years of carrot rather than stick did not produce the end of narrow-minded, dictatorial communism in North Korea, but it has averted war and the immense human suffering and dislocation that is its inevitable corollary. (For a fuller discussion see "International Law, Universal Rights, the Global Dilemma", by Richard Reoch in Jonathan Power (ed.), *Vision of Hope – 50 Years of the United Nations*, Regency Press, 1995).

The North Korean example, for all its inadequacies, is a parable of our times. It demonstrates that progress can often be made by engagement in moving nations out of their entrenched positions. Endless confrontation can be endlessly counterproductive. There is no conclusive evidence that isolating or cornering a nation succeeds in moderating its behavior. Yet President George W. Bush, seemingly mindlessly, decided to end the Clinton approach to North Korea. Seven years later all he has to show for it is an end to the implementation of the Carter-Clinton deal, a ratcheting up of North Korea's nuclear bomb-making abilities and further missile tests.

Carl Bildt, the former prime minister of Sweden, made this point more effectively than most in an icily ironic essay on Yugoslavia and the Kosovo war penned for *Prospect*. (Bildt, for a time the UN Secretary-General's special envoy for the Balkans, is a man of political leanings, if elections are anything to go by, too far to the right for most of his countrymen.)

"The Baby Bombers", as the editor headlined the piece, was a wake-up call for the baby-boomers, now in the higher reaches of Western political power, "who have never learnt about war and power the hard way" and who, with their "smart wars – high rhetoric, high altitude and high technology; smart bombs for smart politicians", believe there is a "third way in war".

Bildt wrote of meeting Gerd Schmueckle, a retired German general who was wounded six times on the Russian front during the Second World War, but then served in the highest positions inside NATO. Perhaps, said the general, it is a question of generations. While the war veterans are losing their hair and teeth, the new generation suddenly has a different attitude towards war. For Schmueckle, war was associated with horror beyond imagination, leaving deep psychological scars on individuals and nations. Bombs, he said, "do not create peace: instead they breed hatred for years, perhaps for generations."

A decade on we can see the truth of this in Yugoslavia. The bombing did not forestall ethnic cleansing, it appeared to precipitate it. And it has bequeathed a cauldron of mutual hatred and a political potage in Kosovo that no amount of NATO and UN policing and Western economic aid can clear up, even if it were forthcoming in something like the quantities promised – another example of the war-time rhetoric that misled the public.

Aficionados of Carl Bildt had the chance to pursue his thinking, one year after the bombing, in *Survival*, the quarterly journal of the International Institute for Strategic Studies. This is a much more lengthy discourse on the limits of force, and looks not just at Kosovo but at Bosnia before the conflict. Its essence is to challenge what has now achieved the status of conventional wisdom – the idea of the supremacy of air power.

Bildt argues that the Dayton agreement that brought an end to the fighting in Bosnia was "far more a victory for diplomacy than for force". He certainly doesn't deny that the NATO air operation, initiated on 30 September 1995, "had a significant psychological impact during its first few days", but the political momentum that led to the accord came about primarily because of a new diplomatic approach. "The essential diplomatic innovation was the willingness of the US to accept some of the core demands of the Bosnian Serbs; demands that the US previously had refused even to contemplate. In particular the Bosnian Serbs had consistently demanded a separate Republika Srpska inside a weak Bosnian framework."

After Dayton, there was an unforgivable lull in Western diplomatic activity. Neither the European Union nor the US were willing to launch any serious diplomatic initiatives to head off the brewing crisis in Kosovo. Albanian opinion inside Kosovo, once more fluid and open to diplomatic options, was allowed to harden, leading to the birth of an armed insurrection and driving the population into the embrace of the Kosovo Liberation Army. The West, misreading the lesson of Bosnia, tried to head off Serbian repression with the threat of air power. Thus when diplomacy failed – and the Rambouillet agreement demanded much more from Slobodan Milosevic than the "peace agreement" which ended the war – the West had little choice but to make good its threats.

The air operation, however, could not prevent a major humanitarian disaster. Whether it triggered it, Bildt, more cautious than I, just says "will remain a subject of debate". But he adds scathingly that "despite all the talk about a revolution in military affairs, Kosovo brutally demonstrated that the axe remains the superior short-range precision-guided weapon when it comes to one man killing another; there is very little that increasingly long-range and high-tech weaponry can do about it." Tragically, the painful lesson is now being learnt once more by the Americans and British in Iraq and Afghanistan.

Perhaps we can suggest the direction of an alternative way with a question: what would it have taken to draw Milosevic's sting in the early days of the crisis in Yugoslavia – a move to offer Yugoslavia, as has recently been offered to its successor states, a chance of entering the European Union if the peace were kept? Or perhaps it would have been sufficient to offer post-communist Yugoslavia massive amounts of aid to effect a transition to modern capitalism, as long as human rights were respected. (Sums which now, in retrospect, would seem modest compared with what the West has subsequently had to spend via the UN, NATO and the humanitarian relief agencies.)

Or what would it have taken to persuade the Hutu-run government of Rwanda to shelve its contingency plans for massacring the minority Tutsis? Even if every member of the Hutu elite had to be bribed with ten Mercedes each it would have been peanuts compared with what was spent in feeding the fleeing refugees both inside and outside the country. More seriously, a programme instituted even as belatedly as the early 1990s (there had been many earlier smaller-scale pogroms from 1959 on to give warning aplenty of what was to come) to deal with the underlying issues of land-shortage and lack of agricultural development together with the ill-training of the institutions of government, in particular local administration, the courts, the police and the army, would have cost a significant amount, but then again nothing compared with later sweat, guilt and even expenditure.

A fuller perspective of this tragic land would also take into account two points: (1) while tens of thousands of Hutu participated in the genocide of 1994, millions did not; (2) with a thirty-five-year exception, between 1959 and 1994, the Tutsis have been oppressors of the Hutu majority for centuries.

As a foreword to Amnesty's yearbook for 2000 Pierre Sané penned an essay with the provocative title, "Soldiers in the Name of Human Rights". It was an intellectual's demolition job on the modern-day crusader school of thought. "Are invasion and bombardment by foreign forces justifiable in the name of human rights? And have external military interventions succeeded in winning respect for human rights?" he asked. His reply in five lines is this: "Amnesty International has long refused to take a position on whether or not armed forces should be deployed in human rights crises. Instead, we argue that human rights crises can, and should, be prevented. They are never inevitable. If government decisions to intervene are motivated by the quest for *justice,* why do they allow situations to deteriorate to such unspeakable *injustice?*"

Sané points to Yugoslavia. The NATO governments which bombed Belgrade are the same governments that were willing to deal with Slobodan Milosevic's government during the break-up of the original Yugoslavia and were unwilling to address repeated warnings about the growing human rights crisis in Kosovo.

As long ago as 1993 Amnesty was arguing in public: "If action is not taken soon to break the cycle of unchecked abuses and escalating tensions in Kosovo, the world may again find itself staring impotently at a new conflagration."

A similar argument, continues Sané, can be made for the West's other great preoccupation during the 1990s – the dictatorial regime of Saddam Hussein, defeated and driven back after an attempted invasion of neighbouring Kuwait. It was Amnesty which called for international pressure on Iraq in the mid-1980s, especially after the 1988 chemical weapons attack by Saddam Hussein's troops on the town of Halabja which killed an estimated 5,000 unarmed Kurdish civilians. Amnesty also drew attention at this time to Saddam's notorious conduct towards his political enemies, incarcerating and torturing their children. Yet Western governments were then foursquare behind Iraq as it fought a First World War-type conflict of attrition with its neighbour Iran, whom the US could not forgive either for its fundamentalist stridency or for taking hostage the diplomats of the US embassy a few years earlier. The West simply turned a blind eye to Saddam's human rights violations, while it sold him increasingly sophisticated weapons of war.

Sané is also right to question the rhetoric of Western governments. When they do intervene they say they are motivated by *"universal values"*. "But why", asks Sané, "is the international community so selective in its actions?" The imposition of UN sanctions on Libya or Saddam Hussein's Iraq stands in marked contrast to the non-imposition of sanctions on Israel for refusing to comply with UN Security Council resolutions or invading neighbouring Lebanon. The actions over Kosovo and East Timor beg the question of why little or nothing was done in Rwanda or Chechnya or today in the Sudan.

This begs another question. If the motivation of governments is "peace", as they often claim, why do they fuel conflicts by supplying arms as they did for many years to the Taliban of Afghanistan or allowing their nationals to trade in arms? Despite the recent rapid increase in wars in Africa, arms exports to the region doubled last year, mainly small arms such as assault rifles and submachine guns that have been virtually ignored by those who seek controls on nuclear, chemical and biological weapons, yet which appear to be the weapons that cause most of the damage in most of the wars. In the case of East Timor, two of the major powers who argued for international intervention – the US and the UK – were also the major suppliers of arms to the Indonesian government, whose security forces were responsible for widespread and systematic violations of human rights in East Timor.

The history of the last few years has demonstrated vividly that those who seek to do good by military intervention find, more often than not, that it is a double-edged sword. Failure is more likely than success.

In Somalia, twelve years after a UN military intervention – in which, in fact, the US army acted as an autonomous agent – there is no functioning government and no judiciary. Continued fighting, especially in the south, imperils hundreds of thousands of people already suffering famine. The UN forces themselves committed serious human rights abuses. And the unsuccessful attempts of the US Rangers to arrest one of the guerrilla leaders diverted them from the ostensible purpose of their mission. They killed and arbitrarily detained hundreds of Somali civilians, including children.

In Afghanistan it has proved to be enormously difficult to establish a government that is seen to fairly represent all the tribes of this war-torn country. In Iraq, according to a UN report issued in July 2006, over a 100 civilians were dying each day in the preceding months, more than any other months since the fall of Baghdad three years ago.

This is not to argue against intervention in every situation. We can see how disastrous it was in Rwanda when the UN pulled out its forces as the mass killings began, and up to a million people died in the ensuing genocide. Yet, if we have our wits about us and not just our reactive impulses, we will observe that none of the human rights tragedies of recent years were unpredictable or unavoidable. The international community needs to deploy its influence before things explode. A year before the genocide in Rwanda, the UN Special Rapporteur on Extrajudicial, Summary or Arbitrary Executions warned of what was to come. Amnesty, for its part, repeatedly exposed the Indonesian government's gross violations of human rights, not just in East Timor, but also in Aceh, Irian Jaya and the rest of Indonesia. As Sané concludes his argument: "We fear now that our pleas for action on other countries are similarly being downplayed. When some human rights catastrophe explodes, will we again be expected to see only military intervention as the option?"

All of which brings us back to the main point: prevention. Prevention work may be less newsworthy and more difficult to justify to the public than intervention in times of crisis. It requires the sustained investment of significant resources without the emotive media images of hardship and suffering. It's the hard day-to-day slog of human rights vigilance – using diplomatic measures to persuade governments to ratify human rights treaties and implement them at home. It means ensuring there is no impunity and that every time someone's rights are violated, the incident is investigated and those responsible brought to justice. Not least, it means speeding up the work of the International Criminal Court.

It also means that governments must be prepared to condemn violations of human rights by their allies as well as their foes. It demands a halt to the sale of arms to human rights violators. It means ensuring that economic sanctions do not hurt the wrong people – as in Iraq, where it is estimated that 40,000 children a year died because of the tight sanctions on essential foods, medicines and hospital equipment.

Why should we be forced to choose between two types of failure when the successful course of action is known? The best we can do is to ensure that whatever route is chosen, we do what we can to contain the suffering and let the powerful know our anger. Prevention of human rights crises is the correct course. The problem is not lack of early warning, but lack of early action. Only by protecting human rights everywhere, every day, will we render the debate over humanitarian action obsolete.

Nevertheless, we live in a world which, on balance, despite all its many wars, poverty, refugees, weapons development, arms sales and human rights abuses, is actually changing for the better at a rate quite unprecedented in human history. What is needed at this time is men and women with the necessary insight to seize the moment: to take the rising tide and push the boats even further out.

The signs are mostly, though not in every case, propitious, which ever way one looks at it, political, military, economic or social. Is such a conclusion naive? Won't historians be able a hundred years hence to look at the end of the twentieth century much as we now look at the end of the nineteenth and say, "Unfortunately the peace and prosperity of that moment was but an interlude before the bloodiest century in mankind's history?" Will they conclude, as Aldous Huxley did, that "Every road towards a better state of society is blocked, sooner or later, by war, by threats of war, preparations for war. That is the truth, the odious and unacceptable truth."?

The pessimists now have grist for their mill: in 2002 President Bush announced he wanted the largest rise in the military budget since the end of the Cold War build-up under Reagan, and every year the budget is increased even further; the conundrum of how best to contain and restrain Iran and North Korea remains imperfectly answered; civil wars that target civilians more than soldiers are being fought all over the place; Israel and Palestine are at war; nuclear weapons are proliferating in states that don't have the secure control systems of the old nuclear powers; and the American plan to build a national missile defence, even if it meant abrogating unilaterally the Anti-Ballistic Missile Treaty, worked to aggravate relations with not only Russia but with China too.

Yet, despite these ominous developments, including the terrorism of the Al Qaeda movement, the big picture is good, arguably far better and more inherently stable than it was in 1899. Major war, involving the most powerful industrialized states, those capable of massive destruction far and wide, is much less likely than it has ever been. Unlike in previous ages neither economic, religious nor ideological forces point us or push us in the direction of all out war. War, pace Lenin, in the age of nuclear and high-tech weapons, is a loss-making enterprise. Virulent religious strife, once the cause of so much bloodshed in Europe, is now limited to former Yugoslavia – and even there, with the fall of Milosevic, his subsequent arrest and transfer to The Hague for trial before the United Nations International Criminal Tribunal for former Yugoslavia, an end to it may be in sight. Communism in Europe is practically dead and the credo of the West, democracy, does not lend itself to wars of conversion. War, moreover, has lost most of its glamour. Honour and heroism, the old virtues for every war from the time of the *Iliad* to General Douglas MacArthur, got lost in the jungles of Vietnam. President Clinton, a draft-dodger, came to power by defeating two Second World War heroes.

The state is no longer made by war for the purpose of making war. The modern industrial state is, *par excellence,* an economic institution. Democracy, not so long ago an uncertain, precarious achievement, is today deeply embedded in all the most advanced economies. And democracies do not seem to go to war with each other either. Elections, increasing political and economic transparency, the separation of powers, the media constantly on the watch, the urge of young men to make money not war and, in Europe, not least, the formation of the single currency, make serious all-out war a remote possibility.

But this sense of common security is, of course, confined to Europe, North America and Japan – and, it should be added, South America, which, for all its historic tendencies towards bravado, is, over the last two centuries, the continent that has gone to war least.

In the Middle East, all the old-time ingredients of war-making are present – financial greed over a scarce resource and religious fervor, combined with the new-time ingredients of modern weapons. Still, combative though many of the countries in the region tend to be, they lack the capacity to wage major all-out war in the World War sense. (Even Osama bin Laden's movement used only old-fashioned truck bombing and airplane hijacking to make its terrible points.) Outside the Western world only China and Russia could do that. And it is these two states that hold in their hands the peace of the twenty-first century, to make it or break it.

Russia, potentially dangerous, claims a sphere of influence in the territory of the former Soviet Union; China in the South China Sea. Yet neither are in any real sense preparing for major war. Both are essentially inwardly preoccupied and neither are committed, as were their orthodox communist predecessors, to the violent overthrow of present-day political, military and economic arrangements.

"The practice of war, once the prerogative of the strong, instead is increasingly the tactic of the weak," argues Michael Mandelbaum. His argument, as I have mentioned in an earlier chapter, is that "the great chess game of international politics is finished, or at least suspended. A pawn is now just a pawn, not a sentry standing guard against an attack on a king." We'll still have our Kashmirs, Iraqs and Sudans but, over time, they are becoming less numerous and the stakes for the rest of the world are lower. That doesn't mean that this new century won't have some bad wars. Doubtless, there will still be plenty of those. But major war, involving a clash of the best-armed gladiators, with convulsions on a scale that twice consumed the young men and the innocents of the twentieth century, could be in abeyance.

Nevertheless, even if the point about large-scale inter-state war is accepted, many would argue – I have even heard Pierre Sané make this point – that the number of ethnic wars is on the increase. The media certainly work on the assumption that tribal and nationalist fighting is rising on a frightening scale. But they are wrong. The modern era of ethnic warfare peaked in the early 1990s.

Every year for the past sixteen years, the authoritative Stockholm International Peace Research Institute (SIPRI) has monitored the course of world conflicts; nearly every year since the end of the Cold War the number has fallen, from thirty-two in 1991 down to seventeen last year. Even in Africa since 2000 there has been a constant decline in the number of conflicts – in 2005 there were only three, the lowest figure for the region in the post Cold War period.

Confirmation for the analysis made by SIPRI comes from a major study carried out by the Minority at Risk Project at the University of Maryland. Professor Ted Gurr, the project leader, wrote in *Foreign Affairs* in early 2000: "The brutality of the conflicts in Kosovo, East Timor and Rwanda obscures the larger shift from confrontation towards accommodation. But the trends are there, a sharp decline in new ethnic wars, the settlement of many old ones, and a pro-active effort by states and the international organizations to recognize group rights and to channel ethnic disputes into conventional politics."

It was only a few years ago that US Secretary of State Warren Christopher, commenting on the outbreak of ethnic strife in countries such as Somalia, Zaire and ex-Yugoslavia, asked, "Where will it end? Will it end with 5,000 countries?" It was a gross misjudgement. Two-thirds of all the campaigns of ethnic protest and rebellion of the last seventeen years began between 1989 and 1993. Since 1993 the number of wars of self-determination has been halved. During the 1990s sixteen separatist wars were settled by peace agreements and ten others were checked by cease-fires and negotiation.

Governments and media have been culpable in cultivating a weary cynicism about the inexorable growth in ethnic conflict. They have misled us. Concerted efforts by a great many people and organizations, from UN agencies to Amnesty International, from Medecins Sans Frontieres to religious groups, from Sweden's small, private Transnational Foundation for Peace and Future Research to the large intergovernmental Organization for Security and Cooperation in Europe, have helped bring about a sea-change.

The list of countries where the problems of ethnic conflict looked until quite recently potentially ominous but which are now vastly improved is a long one. Baltic nationalists have moderated their treatment of Russians. Hungarians in Slovakia and Romania are no longer under threat. Croatia's new moderate government is respecting minorities. Likewise, conflicts between the central government and India's Mizo people, the Gaguaz minority in Moldova and the Chakma tribal group in Bangladesh's Chittagong Hills have all diminished. Nationalists willing to continue fighting for total independence, such as the rebel leaders in Chechnya and Aceh are increasingly few and far between. Central governments, for their part, appear to be becoming more flexible and sensible about devolving power. One of democratic Russia's most important but least-noted achievements has been its peacefully-arrived-at power-sharing agreements with Tatarstan, Bashkiria and forty other regions. It is important to know that the large majority of these conflicts were brought to successful conclusion without outside military intervention.

A list almost as long can still be made for ethnic disputes unsolved. But what we have learnt in the last few years is that the pool of ethnic conflicts is not infinite; that the ultra-pessimism of just a few years ago was misplaced; and that human beings can settle for less, as long as the dominant party recognizes the underdog's integrity and gives it enough room for manoeuvre.

Side by side with these developments over war and conflict has been the remarkable spread of democracy in recent years. Every December the New York-based Freedom House publishes its annual survey of democratic trends. In 2005 it concluded that "There were major gains in liberty in every year since the end of the Cold War and there now exists the largest number of politically free countries in the history of mankind." Contrary to popular Western belief, there are more people in the Third World living under democratic governance than there are in the West. What is more, thanks to transformation in Nigeria and Indonesia, the majority of the world's Muslims are now living in countries that practice democracy. This end-of-century survey finds that only 35 per cent of the peoples of the world live in countries that are not free – and the overwhelming proportion of those are in China. Two-thirds of the world's countries have achieved democratic rule.

Yet still the argument continues: is the glass half-full or half-empty? That, in fact, it's nearly full seems to be ignored by most of our active political class, who seem to believe they thrive personally if they can paint the world blacker than it is, with only the prowess of their own country able to sort it out.

Democracy has been throughout the last century a slow, uncertain but, in the end, steady cumulative process and now in the new century it is a hard thing for anyone to block, at least for any length of time. While one can worry, and sometimes despair, about the homogenized uniformity brought about by many aspects of globalization, one can only rejoice in this phenomenon.

At the beginning of the twentieth century there were only 55 sovereign polities. (There are now 192.) Not one enjoyed fully competitive multiparty politics with universal suffrage. A mere 12.5 per cent of mankind lived under a form of government that could be described as somewhat democratic, although suffrage was generally limited to males. Even as recently as mid-century there were only 22 functioning democracies and a further 21 restricted democracies. They accounted for a mere 12 per cent of the globe's population. Meanwhile, totalitarian communism had spread to govern one-third of the world's people.

But the last quarter of a century in particular has seen this tremendous acceleration in democracy's spread. One doesn't have to be too gullible an optimist to imagine that the first two decades of this century could well see the dawn of a near-totally democratic world. To say democracy and its handmaiden liberty are now only Western constructs is as foolish as saying that rice is only an Asian food or that the concept of zero and the decimal system should have remained in India where they were invented. Any long view of history, with rather more time-span than the life of McDonalds, will realize that the cultures of the world have been cross-fertilizing each other for thousands of years.

Of course, democracy has had some high moments before, but then regressed; as in pre-war Europe with the rise of fascism and subsequently the spread of communism. In Iran, in the early twentieth century, democracy was the constitutional order but then the monarchy reasserted itself and since then Iran has never known real democracy. Even today, an elected parliament and president are circumscribed by the independent, and constitutionally superior, power of the chief religious leader. In Egypt in 1923 there was universal suffrage and a parliament with considerable power. But it didn't last long and, as was made abundantly clear in the country's recent controlled elections, Egypt shows little sign of being able to shed the military's totalitarian grip.

There is a powerful, if pessimistic, school of thought that argues that democracy will never take real root in the Muslim world. Yet we can see a significant and widespread pro-democracy ferment in much of the Muslim world and important steps towards democratic reform under way in many Islamic countries. Six out of 42 predominantly Muslim states now have democratically elected governments: Albania, Bangladesh, Indonesia, Mali and Turkey. In fact, if one takes into account these five Muslim democracies, add in Nigeria, where half the population is Muslim, and the Muslims who live in Europe, the Americas and India, a majority of the world's 1.15 billion Muslims live under democratically elected governments.

In several Arab states, the passing away of old monarchs has led to reform. In Morocco, under the new king, there is a much greater tolerance of opposition parties. In Jordan, under its new king, press laws have been relaxed and there have been competitive elections at the municipal level. In Lebanon, although still under Syrian influence, there have been relatively pluralistic elections. In Kuwait the national legislature (no longer elected by exclusively male suffrage) has wide legislative authority and the emir's decrees are subject to its approval.

Qatar, an oil-rich state on the Persian Gulf, may itself have progressed only to the point at which it allows open elections at the municipal level. But it is the home of the Al-Jazira television station, which has become a major source for the spread of the idea of openness and democratic practice. It includes regular debates on theology, democracy and human rights and allows wide-ranging interviews with dissidents and political exiles from throughout the Arab world.

In 1984 Iran's representative at the UN said that the Universal Declaration of Human Rights "represented a secular understanding of the Judaeo-Christian tradition". Saudi Arabia abstained in the vote on it in 1948. The Saudi delegate to the UN said that the provision for religious liberty in the Declaration violated Islamic law. But he was answered by the delegate from Pakistan, who argued that Islam supported freedom of conscience. And today the delegate of Iran to the UN can be heard speaking of the desirability of democracy for his country and the full observance of human rights.

Islam, as Christianity before it, is evolving at a rapid pace. Many Muslims today, including a number of its most informed religious leaders, argue that many so-called "traditional" Islamic practices, the forms of punishment and the attitude to women and non-Muslim minorities, are not Islamic at all, or at least not mandated in all circumstances. Most Muslims understand their religion's essentials as a message of tolerance, compassion and social justice.

It came as no surprise that at the UN Conference on Human Rights in 1993, meant to review and renew the commitments made in 1948, the Islamic world was split. In the end, however, there was an overwhelming endorsement of resolutions that reaffirmed the validity of the original Declaration (in the drafting of which a number of Third World countries, including India, Chile, Cuba, Lebanon and Panama, had played an active and influential role), and indeed extended its scope. Even China and Saudi Arabia felt compelled to cast their vote in favour of the consensus. The African and Latin American countries in particular had fought hard for such a meeting of minds. The universality of human rights was reaffirmed. The final declaration states that "The universal nature of these rights is beyond question. All human rights are universal, indivisible, interdependent and interrelated." Thus, the entire spectrum of human rights was endorsed without division, an amazing, if under-reported, step forward for mankind.

The Vienna Declaration also stated that "the human person is the central subject of development". Human rights were reaffirmed as including not just civil and political rights, but the broader range of economic, social and cultural rights, together with the right to development. The first set of human rights was seen as guaranteeing freedom from fear; the second set dealt with freedom from want. Even up to the middle of the Vienna Conference, the US was arguing that social and economic rights were not so important.

Yet the progress we have witnessed in the last fifty years in civil and political rights has come about, in part, because of advances in economic, social and cultural rights. The two have a symbiotic relationship. The swift advance of political rights is so much easier where the standard of living is rapidly rising. The rise of authoritarianism is more likely where there are either great disparities in incomes or a general, widespread economic malaise. Contrariwise, democracy is more likely to provide the climate for economic advance and steps towards a more benign distribution of income.

Proponents of so-called "Asian values" – the former Prime Minister Mahathir bin Muhammad of Malaysia or ex-Prime Minister Lee Kuan Yew of Singapore – dispute this. They attribute growth in south-east Asia to the Confucian virtues of obedience, order and respect for authority. "The exuberance of democracy leads to indiscipline and disorderly conduct which are inimical to development," says Mr. Lee. (It was only a generation ago that observers of the Confucian ethic blamed it for much of Asia's economic backwardness.) They claim that the suspension or limiting of human rights is a sacrifice of the few for the benefit of the many.

Yet anyone who has visited Japan will know it's perfectly possible for Asian societies to embrace modernity without discarding the virtues of respect, order and obedience. Besides, if one looks at the Western world with a broader view than focusing on, say, San Francisco, there are a lot of so-called Confucian values at work in the West. Family values are certainly enormously strong in Italy and Spain. Collective obligations are taken more seriously than possibly anywhere else in the world in Scandinavia. (And you can see how both strands in European culture have been transported to parts of America.)

Democracies, in fact, tend to make economic reform more feasible. Political checks and balances, together with open debate on the costs and benefits of government policy, give the public both a sense of involvement and a stake in reform. One reason India has never been overwhelmed by unexpected famine as China and Ethiopia have is the free press. In India the press has always alerted the central government to what was going on in the distant countryside long before the cautious bureaucrats got round to filing their grey reports. (And when India under Indira Gandhi introduced a state of emergency suspending parliament, the electorate, mainly uneducated peasants, took the first opportunity to throw her out.) India now seems poised to become the greatest economic success among the larger Asian developing countries, overtaking China.

All countries in the end come up against the reality that nearly all the world's richest countries are free, and nearly all the poorest are not. If dictatorship made countries rich, then Africa and Latin America would, by now, be economic heavyweights. (The fact that countries such as China and South Korea progressed rapidly on the economic front under dictatorship probably owed itself to the Confucian work ethic rather than the dictatorship. But even that seems to work better – as in Hong Kong and modern-day South Korea – if there is room for democracy.) A study made by Surjit Bhalla, formerly of the World Bank, examined ninety countries over the period 1973-90. It found that civil and political freedoms do promote growth. Other things being equal – in particular economic freedom – an improvement of one point in civil and political freedom raises annual growth by approximately a full percentage point.

In the long run even the most apolitical capitalist learns to appreciate a political structure that will protect his property, both material and intellectual. A dictatorship, however benign, is always more vulnerable than a democracy. It can be more easily overthrown and its policy simply reversed. Democracy and the freedoms that usually go with it – an independent judiciary, freedom of expression, the enforcement of contracts and the inbuilt pressures of free trade – give the businessman what he wants for the long run, while offering the educated classes an outlet for their opinions and the workers a safety valve for their grievances.

All this suggests we are moving towards a more democratic and less violent world. It would be a sad irony if this movement was slowed by those who argue, in the name of democracy and human rights, that military intervention is the way to make it all go faster. It is simply not true, as wars from Vietnam to Iraq attest. Force in this regard is usually shortsighted and quite counter-productive. Both the neo-conservatives with their agenda of the imposition of democracy by force and the liberals who have a misguided sense about the use of force in situations of human rights abuses are bereft of the common sense that comes from an honest look at the history of conflict. We cannot pursue human rights by the application of force and the sooner that lesson is drawn the faster will the cause of human rights and democracy progress. What we can do is anticipate situations of abuse and move to head them off by a clever mixture of non-violent intervention, astute diplomacy, political and economic pressure (but the latter only aimed at the leadership not the masses) and, when absolutely necessary, the deployment of UN-mandated peacekeeping troops.

# 7 Does the United Nations Have What it Takes?

"On the last day of the war" – the great European war of 1914-18 – wrote Gilbert Seldes, a newspaper correspondent accredited to the American army press section, "the fields still green, the sun shining brightly, four members of the press section drove into terrain which a few hours before had been a battlefield."

"In that scene of peace and beauty the torn and twisted bodies of human beings seemed so shockingly out of place; yesterday they were a commonplace of war; today they were murdered men. As we stood silent in the un-harvested fields and uncovered our heads, the same thought came to us all. Without questioning each other's feelings, we there pledged ourselves to tell the world, or the many who would read our newspapers, the 'true facts' about the war, so that there would be no more wars."

The American president, Woodrow Wilson, charged with much the same fervour, determined that the destruction and grief brought upon the most enlightened and loveliest lands on earth must never happen again. "There was a wide realization," wrote Shirley Hazzard, "that civilized society could not materially or spiritually survive another such onslaught of self-inflicted wounds."

Yet, war has continued, the Second World War more horrific than the first, ending in the so far one and only use of nuclear weapons. Now near sixty years later humanity stands once again dangerously close to the threshold of a nuclear strike, initiated by perhaps North Korea or Israel, Pakistan or India, conceivably once again by the US itself, as it has threatened to against Iran.

Although Woodrow Wilson was so seized by his mission that he appointed himself the American representative to draft the Covenant of the League of Nations he failed to convince his European allies to forgo the imposition of crippling reparations upon Germany that bled the Germany economy dry, bred the resentments and nurtured the ultra nationalism that enabled Hitler's spectacular, largely democratic, rise to power.

Nevertheless, there is another rarely told side of the history of the last century. The truth is that over the last 100 years states have committed themselves to a far more just, humane and peaceable world than their practice often suggests. Dorothy Jones, in her carefully researched book, *Codes of Peace*, argues that there is a "hidden history" of the last century, "the record of un-noticed breakthroughs in treaty-making when the great warrior states have adopted apparently minor stipulations that, in fact, represent agreement to significant restraints on their sovereignty."

The League itself rests in a perpetual historical cloud because of its failure to deal with Germany. But it did resolve the Aaland Island dispute between Finland and Sweden (which mattered more at the time than say, the Falklands did in 1982) and helped keep the peace among Albania, Yugoslavia and Greece (1921), Greece and Italy (1923), Iraq and Turkey (1924-25), Greece and Bulgaria (1925), and Colombia and Peru (1932-35). Most notably, throughout an extraordinarily tense situation in 1935, an international military force kept order during the plebiscite that returned the Saar to Germany. (To gauge the passions involved, think of returning Ulster to Eire today.)

As one reads the debate and discussions at the Paris peace conference and immediately afterwards it becomes apparent that the great issues that so preoccupy us today – sovereignty, human rights and the protection of minorities – were regularly atop the agenda then. In the final treaty recurring phrases spelt out responsibility towards vulnerable groups: "Poland undertakes to put no hindrance in the way of ..."; "Austria undertakes to assure full and complete protection of ..."

Still, the League failed and Hitler succeeded. The League's sophisticated mechanisms for arbitration and, if necessary, for collectively resisting aggression, were never applied as intended because the support of the public was not there. The US Senate, humiliating Wilson, never gave its consent for American membership. One Republican senator, sitting in on one of Wilson's sessions at Versailles, said that he felt "as if I had been wandering with Alice in Wonderland and had had tea with the Mad Hatter."

In fact, however, the Senate would have voted to ratify the League treaty if Wilson had been prepared to compromise on Article 10, which would have mandated League members to take part in any military action against aggression. Wilson, over-obsessed with his notion of an American model of world government, refused to accept the proposed "reservation" that would say that Congress possessed the sole constitutional power to authorize the use of force.

The victors-to-be of World War II had two main thoughts about the UN. (The Charter was actually drafted during the war years.) First, that it should be steered, even controlled, by a cabal of big powers – the US, Britain, the Soviet Union, France and China. "Those whom war hath joined together, let not peace put asunder", said the US Secretary of State, James Byrnes. And second, returning to Wilson's foiled plan for the League, that it would have enough fire power to impose its will on an errant world. Article 42 of the Charter says, "The Security Council ... may take such action by air, sea, or land forces as may be necessary to maintain or restore international peace and security." In 1947, the UN's Military Staff Committee prepared a proposal which the Big Five briefly agreed to, on the strength and size of a UN force: Air force: 700 bombers, 500 fighters, 250 others. Naval force: 3 battleships, 6 carriers, 12 cruisers, 33 destroyers, 64 frigates, 24 minesweepers and 14 submarines. Army: 15 divisions – 450,000 men. Not enough for a world war, but certainly enough for a Saddam Hussein.

The British delegation to the discussion drew up a list of possible areas for the deployment of this UN force, one that would not look out-of-place today:

a)  The Balkans: Yugoslavia, Albania, Bulgaria and Romania.
b)  The Middle East: Syria, Lebanon, Palestine, Jordan, Iraq, Saudi Arabia and Egypt.
c)  Southeast Asia: Burma, Thailand, Malaya, Vietnam and Dutch East Timor.

We can ponder a while what the world would have looked like if the Cold War had not intervened and this forward thinking had not been rapidly shelved. Would there have been a Suez crisis? The post-independence Congolese civil war? The Vietnam War? Numerous Middle Eastern wars? The Falklands war? The Yugoslav wars? There is an interesting footnote worth recounting. After the UN had failed in Yugoslavia with its now traditional use of blue-helmeted peacekeepers that use their weapons only in self-defense, the United Nations agreed to NATO intervening in a more robust way. In early August 1993 we were treated to an astonishing, if under reported, development. The US and its European allies decided to put a joint fighter-bomber contingent numbering 50 planes on standby in southern Italy, prepared to attack Serbian gun positions. After bitter wrangling with Washington, the Europeans and the Canadians won agreement that the force could not be activated by command from President Bill Clinton but only by the Security Council and Secretary-General Boutros Boutros-Ghali, essentially making him for some days commander-in-chief of a powerful, state-of-the-art fighting force. (As we know, the moment passed and when NATO did get involved later it was with its usual command structure.)

It is quite obvious that the essential dilemma of the UN as a political instrument and before it the League of Nations is this question of an almighty force. It runs like a thread through nearly a hundred years of history. It is not just the Americans who have shied away from going all the way. At various times countries from all the four corners have given it short shrift. "Peacekeeping" with lightly armed troops was the compromise, which worked well when both sides had arrived at the point (often after a lot of fighting) when they wanted a neutral middleman, as the Middle East or in Cyprus (where it averted a Bosnian type Christian /Muslim war), but less well when things were still on the boil, as in the Congo in the early 1960s and Rwanda in 1994.

The question now is will the UN membership continue to support from time to time the deployment of such an almighty force for the purpose of imposing peace in areas of terrible conflict and ending its inevitable corollary, the gross abuse of human rights? It can be American-led as it was in Korea in 1950, Iraq in 1991 or, on a smaller scale, Australian-led as it was in East Timor in 1998 and British-led as it was in Sierra Leone in 2001 or Italian-led as in the Lebanon in 2006/7. This is not quite how the founding fathers of the UN saw it, but if America has the largest and fleetest-of-foot military machine is not this a proper way to make use of it, assuming, as has been the case in the past, the Big Five approve it or, at least, don't cast their vote against it?

A more robust UN has its dangers – it will inevitably devalue the old time Hammarskjöld – conceived compromise of peacekeeping, a tool fashioned out of necessity when more ambitious plans were necessarily frozen by the imperatives of the Cold War. Brian Urquhart, who for many years was the head of UN peacekeeping and for a brief period ran the now mythical UN campaign in the Congo in the early 1960s, wrote in his autobiography of many of the tensions implicit in that quite terrifying peace-keeping operation that left Urquhart himself beaten unconscious and Secretary-General Hammarskjöld killed in an air crash as they sought to mediate. Many of the soldiers, Urquhart recounts, from Swedes to Indians to Ethiopians wanted to use force. The Swedes, at one point, even took off to start bombing in retaliation for the murder of an Italian airman, only to be thwarted by bad weather.

Urquhart and his boss, the American Ralph Bunche, gradually persuaded them of the virtue of restraint. "They simply did not want to understand either the principle involved or the bottomless morass into which they would sink if they descended from the high ground of the non-violent international peacekeeping force. The moment the UN starts killing people it becomes part of the conflict it is supposed to be controlling and therefore part of the problem. It loses the one quality which distinguishes it from and sets it above the people it is dealing with."

Bold words and with a sizeable element of truth, as Bunche and Urquhart and their successors demonstrated in a large number of successful and largely forgotten or barely noticed peace keeping interventions – in the Lebanon, in Sinai, in Cyprus and Namibia, in El Salvador and Iran/Iraq, in Cambodia and Macedonia, and, more recently, in Liberia and the Congo once again.

Yet even in the Congo the secession of the province of Katanga, a major cause of the civil war, was finally ended when U Thant, Hammarskjöld's successor, in response to a series of attacks on UN soldiers, authorized military action to remove the mercenaries and gendarmes who guarded the secessionist stronghold in Katanga. There was a dose of impatient pragmatism here. Once confronted by the highly professional Indian UN soldiers it took only a couple of days to send them running. Urqhuart himself in his regular post-retirement writings in the *New York Review of Books* has argued for the UN to sponsor an "enforcement" arm to do what peacekeepers are not able to.

It might seem that this chapter is now heading in the dangerous direction (for the author at least) of arguing for armed might as the UN's solution to its alleged impotence. On the contrary, armed intervention must be the last resort, for often it can bring on – as in the Kosovo imbroglio with the ill-thought out NATO bombing of Belgrade – the very situation it is trying to avoid. Besides, it can be an easy option, a substitute for the hard long-term grind of preventive action, which many of those who in recent years argue for "humanitarian intervention" seem to give short shrift to. (I argue this at length in the previous chapter.) Moreover, it overlooks or at least devalues the role that the UN Security Council and the secretary-general play, and did even during the worst years of the Cold War as interlocutors, arbitrators and "fixers".

The UN is everybody's kicking boy, but it's interesting how in a crisis – and Iraq and the Lebanon are but the latest examples – the big powers can run to it to chew the cud and find a solution short of war. When the antagonists have talked themselves into a corner they can as a last resort let the UN and its procedures find an exit.

One such instance was the 1954 crisis over the capture of 17 American airmen by China. Just as in the later Iranian hostage taking, American opinion became extremely agitated. There was even some wild talk about the use of nuclear weapons. The UN was asked to intervene and Hammarskjöld went to Beijing to talk to Premier Chou Enlai. It took six months of negotiating. But the men were released. President Dwight Eisenhower has a whole chapter in his book on the incident but the central role of the secretary-general is almost totally ignored.

It is the same in Robert Kennedy's book on the Cuban missile crisis. There is only a passing reference to U Thant's letter to Soviet premier Nikita Khrushchev, written in the face of a strong protest by the Soviet ambassador to the UN. Yet it was U Thant's letter that elicited a crucial response from the Soviet leader indicating there was room for compromise. In Suez in 1956, the Lebanon in 1958, in the Congo in 1969 and the 1973 Middle East war it was the UN that provided an escape hatch for the big powers who had put themselves at the height of the Cold War on a collision course. In the wake of the Yom Kippur war, although both the US and the Soviet Union had agreed in principle to a cease-fire, there was no way of implementing it. The situation looked exceedingly dangerous. Egypt was calling for Soviet help. President Richard Nixon put the US on a nuclear alert. It was fast footwork at the UN, principally by a group of Third World countries, that helped break the impasse. They pushed for a UN force to go in – and by the standards of the slow-moving UN bureaucracy of today it did the impossible by starting to arrive on the ground the next day.

If the UN has been a force, a peacemaker and an interlocutor, today it must also seriously consider the need to become a coloniser. Haiti, Somalia, Afghanistan, Sierra Leone, the Congo and Rwanda present what one historian called "a caricature of civilization." In all these six countries, torrid personal ambition and gross administrative incompetence combined with ruthless application of the most sordid and undisciplined forms of violence have destroyed any semblance of normal life or ordinary discourse. They all stand in danger of becoming the shelterers of tomorrow's terrorist networks.

In 1992 the US and the UN went into Somalia, supposedly to end a devastating famine. But by 1994 they had fled in an ignominious retreat, hounded out by Somalia's competing warlords. In arguably the most serious felony of the Clinton Administration Washington blamed the death of 18 American Rangers – one of whom was filmed by television being dragged dead through the streets of Mogadishu – on flaws in the UN command. The truth was that all UN military operations in Somalia were under US military command. The great, quite counterproductive, firefight that climaxed the hunting down of a faction leader was initiated by Special Operations Command in Florida. The obfuscations spewed out on orders of the White House effectively sank the raised expectations and hopes of the post Cold War UN in the eyes of American Congressional and public opinion, a mood which endured during the years of the presidency of George W. Bush. (Nevertheless, US public opinion at large is not as hostile towards the UN as that inside the Washington beltway. A poll carried out in 2002 by the Chicago Council on Foreign Relations found that 77% of Americans believe that the UN needs to be strengthened. The same proportion supports having UN members each committing 1000 soldiers to a rapid deployment force for crisis management.)

The Irish journalist Edward O'Loghlin writes that Somalia now "bears a growing resemblance to the post-apocalyptic world of the Australian Mad Max movies, where outlaw bands scout the wasteland in weird jury-rigged vehicles to scavenge the debris of civilization, killing the weak for the contents of their gasoline tanks." (And this in a country, one of the few in the world, where everybody is of one race and religion and speaks the same language.)

The raw truth is that the only time any of these countries, with the exception of Afghanistan, built up any kind of economic and social infrastructure was when they were occupied. There's not much of the Italian and British legacy to be seen in Somalia these days, but not that long ago Mogadishu was a city of fine buildings with functioning hospitals and schools and a judicial system that worked.

It started to fall apart in the days of its post-independence dictator, Mohammed Siad Barre. Part of the problem was his mercurial despotism and part was the undisciplined rivalry of the US and the Soviet Union, which sought to control the Horn of Africa and its strategic outlook on the entrance to the Red Sea. The rivalry's only measurable legacy was an enormous stockpile of destructive weapons.

Somalia, 1992, showed the weakness of trying to sort a post-colonial mess with just a veneer of military might. The British did not rule India, nor the French Indo-China, nor the Dutch Indonesia nor the Japanese Korea and Taiwan with an armed veneer. They administrated their fiefdoms down to the small town hospital, school and courtroom. One can cavil about the unjustness of one nation ruling another – and indeed it had many unpleasant, arrogant and even racist features – but sometimes it propels a society out of its ruts.

Afghanistan and Somalia will not become quiet developing countries unless the international community deploys itself to the country's four corners for many decades to come. Neither will a post-invasion Iraq escape its past unless a decade or two of hard work goes into putting it on its political feet. (At least it can pay for itself and who said the "UN-colonizers" have to be westerners? They could be South Koreans, Malaysians or Indians). As for Haiti, Clinton again bumbled his way in and, before he left office, more or less out. Did he never read Wordsworth's *Ode to Toussaint L'Ouverture*, leader of the slave revolt and father of Haitian independence, "Thy friends are exultations, agonies? And love, and man's unconquerable mind."?

Another serious question is why didn't the UN come more into its own when the Cold War wound down towards the end of the 1980s? One only has to recall the article written in *Pravda* in 1987 by the Soviet president, Mikhail Gorbachev, followed by his speech to the UN a year later, to be reminded of how high were the hopes at that time. As Anthony Parsons, the former UK ambassador to the UN, has written, these proposals "altered previous policy [towards the UN] through 180 degrees", challenging in effect the US to follow the Soviet lead. President George Bush, nervous though he was as to whether Gorbachev was as true as he looked, rose to the challenge.

The harmony between the superpowers at the UN, by the standard of what had preceded it, was astonishing. The years between 1990 and 1993 were the longest period without use of the veto in the history of the UN. In quick succession the Security Council in July 1987 demanded a cease-fire in the Iran-Iraq war (the first time ever that the five permanent members of the Security Council had jointly drafted a mandatory resolution) and a cease-fire was secured in 1988. In November 1990 the Security Council authorized the use of force to reverse Iraq's invasion of Kuwait. In the following year it unanimously set the terms of the Gulf War cease-fire. In December 1992 it authorized the use of force in Somalia to end what was fast becoming a humanitarian disaster. At the same time the two superpowers began to withdraw their support from the opposing antagonists in long-running disputes, as varied as Afghanistan, Namibia, Cambodia and El Salvador. In the latter three, UN peacekeepers and observers went in to facilitate the transition from war to peace and elections.

Parsons has argued that it was the complex problems of Angola and Bosnia that brought this unprecedented state of harmony to a crashing halt. I would put Somalia first on the list, argue that Angola, although a failure, was never that central to anyone's concern and that Bosnia could not but be difficult given that ex-Yugoslavia was by common consent the most intractable of all the ethnic conflicts then erupting. Unfortunately the wars of ex-Yugoslavia simply came too early for the new "consensus" at the Security Council to have put down roots deep enough where the UN could have been in a position with its own standing intervention force to immediately swing into action. The Somalia debacle of 1993-94 when the US deployed what should have become, if it hadn't been so trigger happy, a prototype of armed intervention mandated by the Security Council, further queered the pitch. Moreover, one should add, to fill out the picture, that the degree of harmony at the UN could not but be affected by the counterproductive way the Western group of seven nations had failed to respond in a positive way to the gathering Russian economic crisis in the crucial period 1991-92 when the economic reformers were in power in Moscow, thus allowing anti-western forces in the Russian Duma the opportunity to build up too much of a head of steam. Neither did it help that a powerful Republican Senator, Jesse Helms was using his position as chairman of the Senate's Foreign Relations committee both to squeeze the UN financially and to hold up the ratification of the latest big nuclear disarmament treaty, START 2, to the point where it allowed his obscurantist counterparts in the Duma the chance to assault it and sideline it for many years. President Bill Clinton, as inexperienced in foreign policy as his predecessor George Bush was experienced, seemed to flounder before the Republican onslaught in Congress rather than give the lead that events demanded. Indeed, he compounded the worsening relationship by pursuing with extraordinary vigor his peculiar election-driven vision of a NATO expanded right up to Russia's frontiers and for a while bowing before Congress' push to abrogate the Anti-Ballistic Missile Treaty, one of Moscow's sacred cows. The astonishing level of good will between the erstwhile Cold War enemies that was so manifest at the time of Bush and Gorbachev all but evaporated on Clinton's watch, save for the tenuous personal closeness that Clinton fought hard to maintain with the alcoholic, manic depressive, Russian president, Boris Yeltsin. Much was lost in this painful process. Many opportunities were forgone, not least on re-building the UN to live out the hopes of its Charter.

Fashioning the political purpose of the UN is one thing, but directing the energies of its myriad agencies and their varied and disparate purposes is quite another. At one level the UN family seems quite huge, spread out from Nairobi to Tokyo, from New York to Geneva. At another, adding it all together and comparing it with, say, the British National Health Service, it is rather modest both in budget and the number of its personnel. Yet rightly it is constantly pilloried for its extravagances, its procedures, its opaque conferences, and its seeming inability, despite millions of hours of the time of over-paid bureaucrats, to capture the world's imagination with its endeavour.

Over the years much of the energetic idealism necessary to make it work well has been systematically bled out of the organisation. This began during the tenure of its first secretary-general, the Norwegian labour leader, Trygve Lie, when he allowed the US government to weed out dozens of top American staff (and some others) as part of the McCarthy purges. The process was continued by Hammarskjöld, indeed did not cease until 1986, and left the organisation bereft of significant numbers of its most talented bureaucrats. Their places were too often filled by third class appointees, at salaries way out of line with what they could ever earn at home. If Joseph Stiglitz' quip about the International Monetary Fund and the World Bank being stuffed by "third class minds from first class universities" has the ring of truth, then it is as nothing compared to what could be said about most UN agencies.

In the late 1960s Robert Jackson, one of the true high fliers within the UN system, once described it as "probably the most complex organization in the world". It is a multilayered, sprawling octopus, with multiple governing bodies. (Most agencies such as the Food and Agriculture Organization, the World Health Organization, the IMF and International Atomic Energy Agency are autonomous.) "Who controls this machine?" Jackson asked. "The evidence suggests that governments do not, and also that the machine is incapable of intelligently controlling itself. This is not because it lacks intelligent and capable officials, but because it is organized in a way that makes managerial direction impossible. As a result it is becoming slower and more unwieldy, like some prehistoric monster."

Jackson compared the UN as it had become with the wartime United Nations Relief and Rehabilitation Administration that he directed, that moved supplies "on a scale and at a rate unsurpassed by any military organization in World War II, as well as dealing with over 8 million displaced persons. But the polycentric structure of competing autonomies UN agencies, created by "accidents of history" was "inimical to efficiency."

Jackson argued, as have Brian Urquhart and Erskine Childers in their later reports for Sweden's Dag Hammarskjöld Foundation, that the UN has to both centralise policymaking and de-centralise its application. The Economic and Social Council should be gradually reinforced to serve as "a one-world parliament for economic and social progress", not a "parlement", however, as Michael Howard once jibed. A UN director general, equal in rank to the secretary-general, should be appointed to oversee all this.

Rosemary Righter in her sharp but thorough dissection of the UN in her book, *Utopia Lost*, argues that the UN has created its own "microclimate". "Diplomats can work for hours to reach agreement on whether the 'debt situation' should be described as something to be debated in a 'spirit of shared responsibility' or 'responsibilities' and emerge feeling that they have made a vital contribution to international dialogue." If occasionally overstated, she does illuminate in chapter after chapter why it is impossible to fashion substantial reform of the UN and why a suggestion like Jackson's will never find a real constituency.

Even if we limit our focus to the twin specialized UN agencies, the IMF and the World Bank, whose resources dwarf those of the rest of the UN put together and are shielded by statute from control by the General Assembly, we find many of the same kind of criticisms being made as of the rest of the UN although it is apparent that the quality of their staff, their ability for self-criticism, their intellectual mobility and their day-to-day speed of action are generally of a higher order. Still, at the end of the day, they have been a lightening rod for much serious criticism, especially from the US, but more recently by informed academics and Non-Governmental Organisations. In President Ronald Reagan's day the Bank was considered by the Administration to be too "Socialist". In more recent years the criticism has turned towards the inability of the Bank to reach down to the rural grass roots where much poverty is concentrated and the IMF's mistaken stringencies towards Third World economies in crisis, added to their troubles, rather than alleviating them. In particular, there is Joseph Stiglitz' (the former World Bank chief economist and Nobel prize winner for economics) searing attacks on the IMF for compounding the great Asian crisis of 1997, almost causing what he called "a global meltdown."

If one of the lessons of the constant carping and criticism of the UN that accompanies nearly all its activities, as Professors Adam Roberts and Benedict Kingsbury argue in their book, *United Nations, Divided World*, is not to evaluate the UN "by standards unrelated to its actual capacities" – which means accepting that the UN is a multilateral organization incorporating many traditions other than our own – we still need to find a way to make it work much better. Otherwise, sooner or later, it will grind itself to a very slow march. Although an older generation may have a kind of sympathetic tolerance for its well-meaningness, younger people who have little historical memory of its *raison d'être* will look on it with increasing indifference.

A reading of the meticulous report, "Of the Actions Which the UN Took At The Time of the Genocide in Rwanda", commissioned by the Secretary-General and headed by Ingvar Carlsson, the former prime minister of Sweden, reveals much of what is wrong. Of course, it blames Security Council members for averting their eyes to what was unfolding, and explains in excruciating detail how opportunity after opportunity was missed for heading off the holocaust that was to come. Yet unless someone, somewhere, has a magic wand for improving the state of mind of governments that hold the reins of responsibility in the Security Council there are no lessons to be learnt here, or at least not that can readily be applied. But one other line of criticism does stand out: the weakness of the UN secretariat and the secretary-general himself. In paragraph after paragraph the criticism mounts up in biting detail. The peacekeeping department "did not brief the secretary-general" about a key cable warning of what was likely to happen from the UN's force commander in Rwanda, General Dallaire of Canada, and "the Security Council was not informed." "The Inquiry believes that the secretary-general could have done more to argue the case for reinforcement in the Security Council". "The analysis of developments after the genocide began to show an institutional weakness in the analytical capacity of the UN." "Several members of the Security Council have complained that the quality of information from the Secretariat was not good enough." And so on.

The recent incumbent of the secretary-generalship, Kofi Annan, who was at that time the head of the UN peacekeeping department, has admitted and apologised for his falling short. No one doubted his sincerity, but surely it is right to ask if the higher echelons of the UN are staffed with people of sufficient intellectual and administrative competence, not to mention analytical ability?

The UN if it is to work needs remarkably clever people in its secretariat and it needs as its secretary-general someone way out of the ordinary. It is a mantra of the enthusiasts of UN that it once was led by such a man, Dag Hammar-skjöld. Yet we have to remember he was appointed at the age of 40 only because he was considered to be the archetypical faceless, obsessive, bureaucrat. And by the time he died, although he matured into a man with a strong and independent sense of mission, he was widely considered an autocrat, who had alienated key members of the Security Council, the Russians and French in particular, and who in his private journal, "Markings", argues Shirley Hazzard, wrote "less an account of the moral progress of an intensely private soul than a self-conscious and at times histrionic rendering of such journey". Even his biographer and admirer Brian Urquhart feels that despite his many accomplishments the appreciation of him is overstated and that in his last years there were alarming elements in his sense of destiny.

The UN will probably continue to decline in influence and effectiveness unless two or three important things are done and to a great extent they depend on each other. First, a secretary-general of proven experience in world affairs and the art of governance must be elected who as a first order of business would reorder the permanent civil service to be recruited by competitive international examination. (These days there are plenty of well-educated high fliers all over the Third World who can hold their own against the best in the West.) Second, a person of recognised world stature needs to be appointed secretary-general. There should be no notion of someone "growing into the job". At the time of the last stepping down of Secretary-General Boutros Boutros-Ghali, it was suggested that Mikhail Gorbachev would be a good candidate. If unrealistic, the general line of thinking was probably correct (as argued in my column of July 8, 1996 in the *Los Angeles Times,* the *Statesman of India*, and *Moscow Times*). Certainly what is needed is that type, someone with "a nice smile but iron teeth."

Thirdly, America must resume its rightful place as the driving force of the Security Council. Only when America wills it (as it did not with Rwanda or as it does today with the Sudan) do things tend to happen. (Even the negotiations that led to the creation of the International Criminal Court only came to life when President Bill Clinton threw his weight behind them, albeit he felt compelled later to pull back when the Pentagon bested him when his guard was down at the height of the Monica Lewinsky affair.) Perhaps, once Iraq is out of the way, the US could conceive of resuscitating the Military Staff Committee, considered to be one of the great innovations of the Charter, to give the Security Council the necessary staff work and contingency planning for enforcement action. Perhaps too it could support the UN developing the capacity for "peace-enforcement action" with an elite standby force recruited from armies around the world. (This was a suggestion of candidate Clinton and later, elected president, the National Security Council considered placing American troops under UN "operational control".) Perhaps too, and even more important, it could become more innovative in pre-empting potential conflicts with artful diplomacy, a clamp down on arms supplies, the interposition of on-the-ground peace negotiators following the Norwegian model, and a more ready preparedness to seize and bring warlords and the politicians who support them to trial at the International Criminal Court before they have got up an overpowering head of steam. The pursuit of human rights has to be fought on all these fronts.

Finally, India, Japan, South Africa, Indonesia and Brazil (all democracies) have to join the veto wielding inner group on the Security Council. (A first step would be to give them permanent membership without a veto. In that way they at least become part of the so-called sixth veto, the right of Security Council members to defeat a resolution by denying it the nine votes needed for passage.) One day one of them, or even Russia, China or a unified European Union (taking over the seats of Britain and France) may have the vision, the energy and the application to demand the systematic overhaul that an organisation as complex as the UN needs and give it dynamic leadership. But for now we have to admit that America is the only Security Council member that gives the UN regular critical attention and that the machine ("*ce machin*", said Charles de Gaulle disparagingly) only jumps to life when and if the US, for better or worse, is energised and engaged.

Perhaps some of us in a fit of realpolitik were tempted to conclude that there was only a chance of this coming to pass if America had got its way on Iraq. Others concluded, probably rightly, that the war with Iraq showed that the world is going dangerously backwards. I think both conclusions are a misinterpretation of what went on in the great debates at the UN Security Council. The continued and feverish debating managed to delay war by many months. It also gave time for anybody who could read a newspaper, even the more conservative ones, to realize that Washington and London had only a paucity of evidence to prove that Iraq was the threat they said it was and that the supposed connections with Al Qaeda were tenuous at best. It allowed public opinion in Europe to move from its long-standing stance of deferring to Washington's judgment on matters concerning life and death to becoming independently minded in a way it never had before. It made Mexico and Canada, the United States' near neighbours and most important trading partners, realize that there are some overriding matters that simply push aside economic self-interest. It made the Africans, who held 20% of the votes on the Security Council and who desperately need more American aid, realize that on some critical issues principles and judgment have to come first. And, not least, it made Russia that has been tempted to develop a condominium of power with the US over Europe's head, realize that its only hope for a stable future lay with allying itself with the major European powers and looking for its anchoring point inside the European Union.

It also made the UN more relevant, not less. The US and the UK may have pushed it aside to the anger of many international lawyers. (Two of the British government's most senior legal advisers resigned in protest.) But the UN as an institution can hold its head high. It didn't try to compromise its principles based on its Charter as it did at the time of the misguided Kosovo adventure. Moreover, George Bush with his instinctive abhorrence of the UN does not reflect a majority of American public opinion and before long there may be an American president elected who will not ride rough shod over it and a Congress that is better educated in the limits of strong arm tactics.

Perhaps one day the divisions that overtook the debate at the UN on going to war with Iraq will come to be seen like a bad dream. We will have woken up to the fact – and America too – that we all need the UN to have a future that works.

# 8 Can We Feed All the People?

Food security is the *sine qua non* of human existence. Without food nothing happens, no economic endeavour, no science or engineering, no music or literature, not even procreation. Food security as defined by the UN's Food and Agricultural Organisation (FAO), "essentially means a state of affairs where all people at all times have access to safe and nutritious food to maintain a healthy and active life."

Since 1974, the time of the great World Food Conference, there has been immense progress made on the journey towards providing food security for all, even if we have rather miserably failed in fulfilling the ambition of the Conference's final declaration that "within a decade no child will go to bed hungry, no family will fear for its next day's bread, and no human being's future and capacities will be stunted by malnutrition."

Progress, yes, of impressive proportions, but it has been uneven, both within and among countries. There remain an unacceptable large number of countries with food availability levels that leave too many of their peoples with inadequate nourishment.

World per caput food supplies are impressively above what they were 30 years ago. The developed countries have continued to improve and diversify their agriculture while the majority of developing countries has also progressed, significantly improving its nutrition. Nevertheless the progress in reducing hunger has slowed to a crawl. Six million children under the age of five die from hunger or malnutrition every year. Today there are about 840 million people undernourished out of a world population total of 6.5 billion, and the numbers are rising. 75% of the hungry live in the very rural areas that grow food and a disproportionate number of them are women.

What gains are being made in reducing these numbers are the result of rapid progress in a few large countries during the 1990s, China in particular. China has reduced the number of malnourished in the last decade by around 74 million. Other significant countries have also made significant if lesser inroads on malnutrition including Indonesia, India, Nigeria, Peru, Vietnam and Thailand. Yet in 47 countries progress has stalled with a combined increase of those suffering from malnutrition of 96 million people. Even India and China, despite their present day high growth rates have seen their efforts slow.

Latin America and the Caribbean have shown that it is possible to get the numbers of hungry sharply down, with Peru under the administration of President Toledo making noticeable progress. Africa is also starting to make progress.

Most hunger is concentrated in Africa. In the 46% of its countries the undernourished have an average deficit of 300 kilocalories per person per day. By contrast only in 16% of the countries of Asia and the Pacific do the undernourished have such high shortfalls. Indeed, given expected trends, the number of hungry in this region will be cut by half by 2015. And by then in India and China, reason FAO experts, based on expected trends and plans set afoot to turn back the failed policies of recent years, only 7% of the people will be undernourished.

Even in Africa the situation is not uniformly grim. Most of the recent sharp increase in hungry people was because of the ongoing warfare in the Congo where the number of undernourished tripled at least. West Africa has significantly reduced its number of hungry people.

For the world as a whole there are in the foreseeable future no major constraints that will inhibit further increases in food production. There will continue to be, if poor people could only afford it, enough food for everyone. But poverty remains widespread and poverty remains the principal reason why under-nutrition persists. In the majority of developing countries increasing food production remains the quickest and most satisfactory way of diminishing poverty since the majority of poor depend primarily on agriculture for both employment and income.

We should never overlook the lesson of the 1943 Bengal famine that claimed the lives of between two and three million people. There was no overall shortage of food in Bengal but an economic boom pushed prices beyond the reach of the poor, a phenomenon that on a world scale today effectively keeps available food out of the hands and mouths of those most desperate for it.

What is under-nutrition? There is in fact no ideal or universal dietary pattern. Human societies the world over meet both their essential nutritional requirements and the pleasure of eating in varied and diverse ways. Nutritional requirements also vary between individuals, between sexes and according to age and the level of physical activity. Moreover, the digestion and absorption of vital nutrients depends on good health and the degree of well-being. Infections, particularly those that accelerate the passage of food through the digestive system, can reduce the body's capacity to absorb nutrients and can lead to a deleterious loss of water and body salts.

No single food, except breast milk, provides all the nutrients required. Variety, indeed, is not only the spice of life, but its basic essential. We need carbohydrates, fats, proteins, vitamins and minerals, together with water and dietary fibre. We need them in the right proportions and we need them regularly. They are critical both to vital body processes and to providing the energy for living.

Over 800 million people, mostly residing in the developing world, are chronically undernourished, eating too little to give the body its basic ingredients. Over 200 million children suffer from protein-energy malnutrition and every year 6 million children under five die, victims of hunger and an inadequate diet.

Even in the womb the unborn child can suffer from malnutrition. And in early life children are particularly susceptible to an inadequate diet. Vitamin A deficiency can lead to an early death and is a major cause of infant blindness. Iodine deficiency leads to slow growth, retarded mental development and goitre. Iron deficiency leads to anaemia, a leading cause of maternal mortality and for children it impedes learning and reduces productivity. Calcium deficiency provokes osteoporosis, where joints become fragile and brittle. And inadequate Vitamin C can lead to scurvy and an increasing likelihood of a number of non-communicative diseases, such as cardiovascular ailments, strokes, hypertension and diabetes.

Children are particularly vulnerable to the debilitating effects of under-nutrition. Not only are they underfed they may also have to work long hours at menial jobs to supplement the family's meagre income. Infection from one of the innumerable diseases they are prey to can push children very quickly from a state of marginal under-nourishment to one of acute malnutrition.

Women too, although often working longer hours than men, are more prone to under-nourishment – the men are often served first and receive the most nourishment. Girls, moreover, are likely to marry early, suffer from too many closely spaced pregnancies and then repeat the cycle of deprivation by giving birth to low-weight babies, many of whom die in infancy.

The elderly, refugees and AIDs sufferers are all particularly at risk, living off inadequate diets, often bereft of family support and too weak or impoverished to either grow their own food or buy it from the market.

What are the chances of improving world food security in the decade ahead? In part to answer this we need to examine the progress made since the World Food Conference of 1974. The 1970's as a whole was a decade of improvement for many developing countries with a faster rate of growth in food supply than in the 1960s or the subsequent decade of the 1980s.

The 1970s, however, was the decade when disparities between developing countries became more pronounced. While per caput food supplies remained at very low levels in South Asia and fell in sub-Saharan Africa, they increased substantially in the Near East and North Africa, Latin America, the Caribbean and East Asia. But significant parts of this increase came, not from indigenous production, but from a sharp increase in imports from the developed countries (often subsidised as part of the effort to aid their farmers, more often the richer ones), unfortunately financed by borrowing.

The progress in raising per caput food supplies continued up to about the mid 1980s and at a slower rate thereafter. In East Asia, and by the late 1980s in South Asia, progress was only upward. Both India and Pakistan broke out of the 2,000-2,200 calories per caput range to over 2,300. Indeed Asia, with 70% of the developing world's population, pulled up the average for the world at large. However, in Latin America and the Caribbean progress came to a halt and was only modest in the near East and Africa. In Africa there were further setbacks.

The debt crisis of the 1980s also cut short the previous rapid increase in food imports by many countries. Moreover, the slackening of import demand and the resultant declines in international prices, exacerbated by subsidized exports by the developed countries, reduced in the developing countries both the production incentives and the stimulus to invest in building capacity for future production increases in their own agricultural sectors.

In the 1990s Asia and the Pacific continued their remarkable progress. North Africa and the Near East are now within striking distance of the calories per caput of high income countries. Latin America and the Caribbean have begun to recover from the "lost decade" of the 1980s. Sub-Saharan Africa, however, has fallen further behind.

The 1990s, despite the advances made, were beset by a range of new uncertainties, all of which work to undermine the progress still being made towards world food security.

Despite the ending of the Cold War and the rapid spread of democracy more and more small states are emerging, requiring new forms of extra-national arrangements and development assistance. The prevalence of ethnic and religious conflict disrupts food production and severely hinders distribution and adequate consumption. The tragedy of civil war in ex-Yugoslavia, Rwanda, Somalia, Afghanistan, the Sudan, the Congo and elsewhere has increased the number of refugees, made famine more likely and dramatically reduced the standard of nutrition. Conversely, growing hunger, exacerbated by land shortage, slow progress on land reform and lack of resources, has deepened ethnic and political tension, often contributing to war, violence and political instability.

Food security, even without war, is being threatened all the time, by population growth most of all, but also by widening poverty, deforestation, environmental degradation, over fishing, migrant and refugee movement, climate change, water scarcity, concentrated resource ownership and management, and disease.

New challenges also arise as greater numbers of people gravitate towards often overcrowded towns and cities. Twenty years ago 80% of the population of the developing world lived in the countryside. Now it is approaching less than 60%. In Africa in the early 1970s only one city in sub-Saharan Africa had more than half a million inhabitants. Today, over 10% of the region's population live in cities of more than a million people and this trend is accelerating all over the developing world.

This is profoundly changing both the nature of work and the role of agriculture in the economy. For example, in sub-Saharan Africa the steady exit of men from the land is putting added emphasis on women's often traditional role as the principal cultivator. Women now produce three quarters of the region's food, yet agricultural advice and services are still often male-orientated.

Women in rural areas are particularly vulnerable to poverty. The number of rural women living in poverty in the developing countries has increased by almost 50% over the past 20 years to an awesome 565 million – 374 million of them in Asia, 130 million in Africa, 43 million in Latin America and the Caribbean and 18 million in the Near East and North Africa. This is not just the consequence of over-rapid population growth. There has clearly been a sharp jump in the number of female-headed households. In fact, while poverty among rural men has increased over the last twenty years by 3% among women it has increased by 48%.

A study of 74 developing countries found that one in five households is headed by a woman; they are either widowed, divorced, separated or abandoned.

The magnitude of the problem depends partly on the influence of culture and partly on the state of social instability as a consequence of war, civil disturbance or over rapid urbanization. In most of the Middle East, North Africa, much of Asia and the western Sahel of Africa the proportion of households headed by women is well under 20%. Indeed in Asia where it is only 9% most single women are widows without dependants. In sharp contrast, in Central America, the Caribbean, Southern Africa and Vietnam it is over 30% and here the number of relatively young mothers on their own with children is worryingly high.

Throughout the Third World women are not, as widely perceived, merely mothers and housewives but they are often a critical contributor to the family's food supply. In Africa in many cases women are expected to produce or purchase nearly all the food eaten at home. In North Africa and the Middle East women tend the flocks and work in the family fields. In Asia women both work alongside their husbands on the farm and work outside to earn sufficient to supplement the diet by labouring for richer farmers or in small businesses. In Latin America and the Caribbean women harvest and process food crops, raise livestock or go out to work.

In short, women by their labour outside the house are vital elements in sustaining life in the poorest areas. Indeed, the poorer the family the more important the woman's contribution becomes. There is much evidence that poor women spend a greater proportion of what they earn on food than do their husbands. Of course, in many, probably most, families the excessive weight of responsibility of being the lone parent leads to children being less well fed and less well looked after.

But whether a woman is alone or with a man, despite the fact that she is a critical element of production in the rural economy, she is to all intents and purposes given second or third rank by social custom. What is more, she is often ignored by those institutions, government and private, that are supposedly working to improve the output of the rural economy.

Why do women get such a raw deal? The answer is as intellectually straightforward as it is socially complicated – men's control over productive resources is much greater than women's.

First and foremost, women's access to land is severely constrained by both legal and customary forces. Yet in the rural economy without land of one's own one has no assured access to the means of production. Men usually own the land. Men have the say who in the family can have access to it. Any attempt by government or outsiders to modify this age-old tradition is a most charged and complicated business.

Many Third World countries have passed statues legally affirming a woman's basic right to own land. In practice, however, female control of land is non-existent. Even land reform programmes, redistributing land from rich to poor, and resettlement schemes invariably give title to the male heads of households. In Islamic law, for example, women's land rights are clear-cut. But in day-to-day life custom, the threat of divorce or other social sanctions all contribute to pressuring women to cede practical control of "their" land to the men.

In Africa under customary land systems married women often have the right to a certain number of fields themselves, giving them a degree of independence. However, the understanding is clear – a woman must also contribute labour to her husband's fields and livestock, as well as see to the day-to-day tasks of family life.

Women badly need productivity-enhancing tools and methods to break out of poverty. Yet ninety percent of the time, probably more, new technology, training and credit are targeted on "households" with an implicit orientation towards its "head", the man. Rarely, when men receive resources and technological training, does it "trickle across" to their wives.

Project designers, banking officials and extension staff all too readily assume that women cannot afford to buy improved seeds, fertilizer, irrigation systems and the like. Nor can they repay loans if they are advanced to purchase such items.

Only very recently, as food production has steadily fallen in Africa and the precariousness of family food production has been highlighted in Asia and Latin America, has any research been focused on how to improve the quality and quantity of the kind of crops and animal rearing that women tend to concentrate on.

Belatedly, there is now some recognition, by no means on a wide enough scale, that women have specific problems with new varieties of crops. Women look at a crop from a different perspective than men, weighing not just the question of yield but its qualities for processing the storage. Women, conscious of the manifold demands on their time, are more interested in their ability to phase the cycle of cultivation so that it harmonizes better with their other responsibilities.

Women, too, feel more comfortable with female extension agents. Yet despite the evidence of their value in motivating women farmers, very few exist and the number of girls recruited into agricultural training remains abysmally low.

Likewise, the impediments to women receiving credit are only at this late date being given serious attention. Commercial banks and credit societies alike have long been reticent about advancing loans to women because of their lack of land, cattle or other types of collateral.

These attitudes are more based on prejudice than fact. The repayment records of the rural poor, especially of poor women, are often much superior to that of better off borrowers.

More difficult to overcome is the perception by some aid agencies and credit administrations that it is the male farmer who makes the important cropping decisions and that it is to him the loans should be made.

If the question of attaining universal food security were simply a matter of curtailing universal population growth at least it would be conceptually easy. But simple arithmetic, dividing the world's food supply by the world's population, leaves us with a theoretical state of abundance, while many in reality remain hungry. It is the distribution of food and, in particular, the purchasing power of the poor that determine per caput consumption.

Nevertheless, it is useful to look in some detail at the question of the global population-food supply balance, particularly when the issue of the capacity of the earth to support its ever growing population is under discussion.

Only 30 years ago the population of the world was 3 billion. In 1992 it was 5.5 billion. In May 2006, it was 6.5 billion. Every year the world's population increases by some 9.3 million. Population growth, however, is now slowing. Last year, for the first time, the UN's Population Division reported that it projects future fertility levels in a majority of developing countries, at some point in the century, will likely fall to below 2.1 children per woman, the level needed to ensure the long-term replacement of people. Nevertheless, world population will be around 8.5 million by 2050, getting on for three times as much as it was in the early 1960s.

Even with this historically unprecedented rate of population growth agricultural production has more than kept up. Per caput calorie consumption today is about 18% more than it was 30 years ago, despite the ever increasing amounts of cereals diverted to animals. Indeed, if only one third of the cereals fed to animals were channelled instead to human beings the world's average calorie intake per person per day would jump from 2,700 to 3,000, not much less than the actual increase which occurred over the last 30 years (a rise from 2,300 calories per person to 2,700). In short, the improvement in agricultural productivity is quite remarkable.

That is the good news. The lack of purchasing power of the poor to buy food and the lack of growth in agricultural productivity in a number of countries in the world is the bad news. So too, some argue, is the evidence that world agricultural growth has been slowing down. The growth fell from 3% per annum in the 1960s to 2.3% in the 1970s, to 2% in more recent years. This led some observers to suggest that production constraints are tightening and that world agriculture has now reached an ominous turning point.

The FAO, while acknowledging the mid-1980s as a turning point, came to a rather different conclusion. The first important point to recognise is that the proportion of the world's populace which is well fed today is much greater than in the past. In fact, it is obvious that the "well-fed" part of the world that consumes well over 50% of food output does not require the growth rates of the past since its diet is already more than satisfactory, at least in quantity terms. Added to this is what we have already observed: the growth of the world's population is at last slowing down. We should not be surprised, then, that production in the main cereal exporting countries has been cut in response to stagnant export demands and the need to control the growth of stocks.

Thus to have a fruitful discussion on the question of the "turning point" it is necessary to look at the developing countries, themselves a very diverse crowd when it comes to agricultural production,

The best way to examine the developing countries' vulnerability to food insecurity is to look at the share of the agricultural labour force in the total labour force.

Of the 91 developing countries 31 (making up 19% of the population of the developing countries) have a relatively low dependence on agriculture for both employment and income generation. They can be said to be less vulnerable to variations in the growth rate of per caput agricultural production.

The majority of 62 countries, however, are potentially vulnerable. Nevertheless, for this group per caput agricultural growth rates have been higher in recent years than in earlier periods. The so-called "turning point" does not exist for them, although what we do have is worrying enough – the persistence of low and totally inadequate growth rates in countries that are desperate to improve their production.

Clarifying the debatable issue of the so-called "turning point" enables a clearer discussion on the equally debated issue whether or not land and water resources are becoming so environmentally degraded that the onward momentum of continuously growing yields is coming under increasing challenge.

If there were a problem of truly serious proportions then there would have been a rise in prices. In fact, during the 1980s, prices tended to decline. Of course, in a number of places serious degradation of land and water resources is under way but there are yet no signs that they are having a serious impact on the global market place.

What is the likely future? Can we identify areas of progress and pinpoint what has to be done?

By the year 2010 the world's population may be 7 billion, with well over 90% of the increment occurring in the developing countries.

On the broad economic front developed countries are likely to continue as they have in the past. The prospects for the former centrally-planned economics of Eastern Europe is uncertain, with some countries doing well and others limping along.

Among the developing countries, Asia will do well and Latin America and the Caribbean, The Near East and North Africa will experience a modest recovery. Sub-Saharan Africa is beginning to recover reasonably well but per caput income will only grow modestly because of high population growth.

However, the growth rate in agriculture on a world average will be lower in the period to 2010 compared with that in the past. As explained above, this decrease is natural for the developed countries and as developing countries become more prosperous they too will contribute to this slowing trend. On the other hand if those now on minimal or insufficient diets could better their circumstances world output would expand rather faster.

The likelihood is that chronic under-nutrition will decline in the Near East, North Africa, East Asia, Latin America and the Caribbean. There will also be further progress in South Asia although there could still be some 240 million undernourished people in the region by the year 2010. Chronic under nutrition will continue in Sub-Saharan Africa affecting some 300 million people (35% of the population), but it has begun to decline.

All in all, however, nutritional progress will continue for the overwhelming majority of the inhabitants of the developing world. From an average of 2,500 calories per person per day in 1990-92 it will increase to just over 2,700 calories in the year 2010. The Near East, North Africa, East Asia (including China), Latin America and the Caribbean will be near or above the 3,000 calories mark. South Asia too will continue to make significant progress.

A more detailed breakdown of production and demand is necessary for understanding all the complex factors involved and if we are to understand the long-term trends.

In the developed countries there is limited scope for further growth in per caput consumption. Moreover, policy reforms underway will make it difficult for them to expand exports with the aid of subsidies, as they have in the past. The developing countries, likewise, will not expand their demand as rapidly as they have in the recent past, although there will be a number of important exceptions and the slowdown will be rather less dramatic. But the gradual progress in recent years towards higher consumption levels in some countries, combined with the overall lower growth rate of population, will reduce demand. East Asia in particular and to a lesser extent the Near East and North Africa, having been the regions with the highest growth rates of per caput demand over the last 20 years, will now be the "pioneers" in lower growth rates. At the other extreme sub-Saharan Africa badly needs a higher growth rate than in the past.

Nevertheless, despite the general slowdown, it will not be long before the developing countries as a whole turn from being net agricultural exporters to being net importers.

Even though these imports – mainly cereals and livestock products – will be financed by export earnings from other agricultural exports and, increasingly, manufactures, it will still impose a heavy burden on their trade balances.

Looking ahead to the year 2010 and beyond there is widespread concern that the continued wear and tear of population growth, raised consumer expectations, pressure on finite land and water resources and the degradation of the environment will make it difficult to continue sustaining world food security.

Yet there are a number of reasons for not being overly pessimistic. First, there will be a more efficient use of food in the developed regions. Second, that the most populous region in the world, East Asia, will not need to maintain by then the very fast growth in consumption presently apparent and, third, the countries and peoples with low consumption are unlikely to break quickly out of their poverty and thus improve their food intake very dramatically.

As one would expect, projections after the year 2010 are more difficult to make. UN population projections country by country are available only to 2025. Moreover, although developing countries as they get richer eat more meat and less grain they will not necessarily follow the pattern of changeover witnessed in the developed countries, tending not to be so carnivorous.

The best estimates of agricultural production in the post 2010 world suggest the following:

- For the world as a whole, a continuing of the trend towards a slowdown. This would happen even if sub-Saharan Africa achieves a sustained recovery and even if the better-off developing regions increase per caput food consumption.
- There will be no obstacle to growing the food required.
- South Asia, the most populous region with food problems, will in all likelihood be able to improve its nutritional levels, even though its agricultural growth rates will be less than in the past.
- The demands placed on the developed countries for agricultural exports can be met even with a production growth rate lower than in the past.

If the overall picture might seem a positive one the micro is much less so. Many countries are coming face to face with the daunting issues of limited water supply, a decreasing diversity of life, a fast depletion of one main source of protein, fish, and deforestation. As Barbara Ward wrote so eloquently, "Man inhabits two worlds. One is the natural world of plants and animals, of soils and airs and waters which preceded him by billions of years and of which he is part. The other is the world of social institutions and artefacts he builds for himself, using his tools and engines, his science and his dreams to fashion an environment obedient to human purpose and direction." We have not yet learned to use the techniques of the second world to get the best out of the first.

Most of the world's water is salt or frozen or underground. Only one-hundredth of 1% is actually suitable and accessible for human use. It is farming that absorbs some 65% of the global water supply, far dwarfing other uses.

For many water is abundant, available night and day at the turn of a tap. But in reality water is a finite resource even for the most affluent, and for the poor it is strictly limited, often polluted and what is potable is in very short supply.

Water is randomly distributed. Nearly a third of the peoples of the developing countries have no access to safe drinking water, a major contributory factor to the high ratios of disease and mortality.

The pressure on scarce and valuable water supplies is increasing by the year, as both population and economic wealth increase. In parts of a number of countries the water table is sinking, water supplies are becoming more polluted and lack of pure water is becoming a real constraint on future well-being.

As population growth continues its upward climb many countries have less water available per person. By the year 2000 Latin America's per caput water resources had fallen by nearly three quarters since 1950. Under Beijing the water table is falling by 2 metres every year.

Water is becoming a political issue as countries argue over common rivers and lakes, fiercely debating the rights and wrongs of their respective water requirements and the responsibilities for their stretch of water.

The Euphrates, one of the world's great rivers, fought over since Biblical times, is now the object of a bitter dispute between Turkey, where it rises, and Iraq whose territory it traverses.

In many parts of the world agriculture cannot thrive without irrigation. In the Middle East irrigated lands have supported great civilisations since time immemorial. And today 33% of the world's food comes from irrigated land.

Yet irrigation is faltering – 60% of it never reaches the crops. Bad management, bureaucratic interference, lack of involvement of users, poor construction and interrupted water supplies all make their negative impact.

Moreover, dams silt up or accumulate pollutants and become the ideal habitat for vectors of waterborne diseases.

The diversity of life – mammals, birds, fish and plants – are essential to the survival of humanity. Yet natural habitats are being destroyed, degraded and depleted at a rapid rate. Many wild species once prevalent now no longer exist. 3,000 million years of natural evolution including 12,000 years of domestication and selection are being challenged by human rapacity on the one hand and by science and changing human needs on the other hand. There is a danger that we are losing irreplaceable genetic material and thus perhaps narrowing the choices of future generations.

Already, in recent years alone, the "knowledge bank" of traditional indigenous peoples has been severely reduced. Also the number of varieties of common grains has been reduced from thousands to tens. In India, for example, there will soon be only 30-50 varieties of rice; not so long ago there were 30,000. While the varieties lost may not seem at this time of increased intensification the truth is the lost varieties may well contain genes that could be used in future years to develop varieties that are more productive or pest resistant.

The spread of intensive agriculture and high yielding varieties to large parts of the developing world has accelerated and widened a process once confined to the developed world. Yet we know now that many of the varieties being lost contain valuable genes that modern science could take advantage of.

It is a similar story with fish, an important part of the diet for people all over the world, in particular in Asia where it provides nearly 30% of the region's animal protein. It is in fact their main source of dietary protein. However, in Latin America it is only 8%.

Some 60% of the world's fish harvest is caught – mainly from the sea – by developing countries where 100 million people depend on fishing and related industries for their livelihood.

In 2000 the total fish captured was the highest ever, although it has dropped back a little since. In the mid 1990s the world fish catch fell mainly because of the influence of the El Nino ocean current on the catches of Peruvian anchoveta, although recently it seems to have stabilised, apart from the North Pacific where it is declining.

Today, over 70% of the world's marine fish stocks are in trouble – from the Northwest Atlantic to the Black Sea to the Western Central Pacific. There are regular disputes between countries, clashes between fleets and the smaller, poorer, artisan fishermen of the developing countries are being squeezed out of business by large-scale commercial fleets. Moreover, uneconomical high government subsidies to the fleets of many developed countries are leading to too many boats chasing too few fish.

Fortunately, aquaculture – fish farming in ponds – has exhibited a large increase in production in recent years, growing at an average rate of 5% a year, and is widely viewed as the best way of maintaining and increasing supplies of fish.

Started by the Chinese 3,000 years ago it is now a big business in many parts of the world; in others like Africa it is a useful ancillary food supply for villagers who developed the potential of their local ponds. Today over half of all freshwater fish production comes for aquaculture.

Forests cover an area the size of North and South America combined and they are essential not just for providing raw materials and food but for the environmental well-being of the planet.

They produce oxygen and absorb carbon dioxide. They help anchor the soil and they shelter it from the direct impact of heavy rain. Water vapour released from foliage is a vital part of the hydrological cycle.

Forests are being lost at a fast rate, mainly to agriculture, especially the tropical moist deciduous forests. 60% of tropical rain forests were destroyed during the 1980s and few were replanted. Europe is the only part of the world where there has been any significant increase in forest and woodland but in many of the industrialised countries forests have been damaged by airborne pollutants.

This poses great dangers – not just to the fragility of the soil and the loss of future earnings from timber and wood products – but also for wild animals and wild plants, often an important source of protein and the folk medicines still used by three quarters of the world's people. Active ingredients culled from the forest contributed each year to an estimated $100,000 million worth of modern drugs while genes from forest plants are used to raise agricultural yields around the world.

The importance of forests in protecting soils and regulating water supplies is crucial. Once denuded of its forests the land exposed can be easily threatened. Wind erosion can strip 150 tons of topsoil from a single hectare in just one hour. Water erosion may wash away 25,000 million tons of soil every year. It is estimated that the deforestation of the Himalayas contributes to the flooding of nearly 5 million hectares every year.

Forests are right at the centre of the debate over global warming. Certainly, if global warming persists, it will confirm that the loss of our forests has been a major influence in the increase of carbon dioxide in the earth's atmosphere (which along with water vapour, methane and nitrous oxide forms the principal "greenhouse gases").

Agriculture depends on climate more than any other human activity and changes in temperature and concentrations of carbon dioxide will have far reaching effects.

Overall, global warming is expected to add to the difficulty of increasing food production, even though higher concentrations of carbon dioxide can in certain situations exhibit a benign influence, for example, a fertilizing effect under optimal growing conditions.

Overall, global warming, if it persists, is likely to accentuate the existing imbalance in world food production between developed and developing countries. For the latter, weather and climate would become more unpredictable, making farming more difficult.

Agricultural zones could shift even by hundreds of kilometres in latitude and by hundreds of metres in altitude on hills and mountains. Poorer farmers might find it difficult to adapt. Diseases and pests could increase and biological diversity would be under renewed threat. Moreover, since coastal plains are among the most productive and highly populated of the earth's surface, there would be a real danger to hundreds of millions of people from a rise in the sea-level.

❖ ❖ ❖

To what extent will environmental constraints on developing countries' natural resources impinge on the prospects for increasing food supplies? And can such progress be achieved while ensuring that the gains made and the potential for further gains are maintained for future generations, the very essence of sustainability?

The FAO has compiled a resources/person ratio. It spans a wide range from, at the low end, countries like Egypt, Mauritius and Rwanda, which show virtually zero reserves for further expansion. At the other extreme are Argentina and The Central African Republic with large resources.

Population growth is tipping most countries towards membership of the first group. It is wrong to be over-alarmed. The evidence confirms that there is no apparent close relationship between resource/person ratios and per caput food supplies. In real life the truth is that many land-abundant countries have low per caput food supplies and those with the most severe land scarcities are those nutritionally better off. (Admittedly many of them are large cereal importers.)

This doesn't mean that it will always be like this. Just because the latter group are such large cereal importers their nutritional well-being is dependent on there being enough productive land elsewhere. Indeed, this point throws into relief a wider issue – resource/person ratios only indicate one of many factors that determine food supply.

There is now available sufficient evidence to show that the productive potential of at least part of the world's land and water resources is being degraded by agricultural activity. Soil erosion, water-logging and salinization are all taking their toll. Moreover, agricultural activity also endangers biodiversity and the pollution of both surface and ground water.

For many farmers there is what can be fairly described as a "caring" relationship vis á vis the natural resources they use. The farmer, witnessing any decline in his resources, is conscious of the increased value of what remains. This tends to lead partly to their more efficient use and partly to improving their productive potential.

Yet, if this may be the norm, too often this caring relationship breaks down as farmers and other economic actors destroy rather than conserve. One reason for this is poverty. Poverty shortens time-horizons as people desperate to feed their families take shortcuts with their farming methods, discounting tomorrow to fill hungry stomachs today.

But this is far from a complete explanation. In many regions of dire poverty – for example the Machokos district of Kenya – there is a sense of the need to maintain sustainable exploitation of resources. Moreover, in many cases it is the non-poor who do the worst exploiting and this occurs, often more so, in situations where poverty is on the decline. This can happen, for example, when non-agricultural job opportunities start to open up and people abandon the maintenance of terraces and irrigation channels.

It is important, then, not just to focus on poverty but on other influences – on the institutions governing access to resources; the inequality of the access to land; government policies which distort or neglect incentives against conservation-orientated technologies. Examples of this latter factor vary from pricing fertilizer too high thus perhaps compelling farmers to "mine" the land, to giving tax and financial incentives to logging operations which end up making available new land that is not suitable for sustainable farming.

One must also take into account the impact of the consumption habits of the peoples of the developed countries. Their day-to-day decisions on what they buy can end up making a deleterious impact on the environment of the poorer countries. Most of the livestock output produce in concentrate-feeding systems is consumed by better off people. But the cereals and oilseeds required for the feeds may in fact cause degradation in far-off places.

Farmers themselves, in the developed countries, too often use excessive amounts of fertilizers and other agrochemicals. Livestock operations often produce toxic effluents. Again, this highlights that it is not only poverty that is associated with resource degradation.

Any balanced discussion on the environment recognises that because the day-to-day existence of the poor is so precarious the consequences of bad farming techniques can have a profound and devastating impact. Thus it is right to focus primarily on the developing countries. But this can be no excuse for ignoring resource degradation elsewhere, for if the food-exporting developed countries don't nurture their habitat it will reduce the global production potential, pushing up prices and making food more expensive for poorer consumers.

In the short run, since by no stretch of the imagination can resource problems be put to rights quickly, the world will have to live with a trade-off between more production on the one hand and conservation on the other.

Nevertheless, there are certain, very useful, things that can be done over the next few years. For example:
- It is not necessary for tropical forests to be depleted.
- The adverse impact of fertilizers and pesticides could be minimised if users follow the FAO's Integrated Plant Nutrition Systems and Integrated Pest Management.
- Water use is dismally inefficient. There is great scope for savings.

If there is a degree of success, as anticipated, in improving the food-security of poorer peoples then it is likely that these people, as they become less hungry, will devote more care and attention to the maintenance of their milieu.

This is Malcolm Muggeridge writing about the Soviet Union in 1945:

> "Famine is something quite peculiar. It concentrates all effort and thought and feeling on one thing. It makes everyone a frustrated glutton. In a famished town, as in a cheap restaurant, there is always the flavour of food in the air. Everybody

brooding on food makes a smell which hangs about them like the smell of gravy and cabbage about a dirty table-cloth. Somehow famine goes beyond hunger and puts in each face a kind of lewdness; a kind of grey unwholesome longing. People's white gums and mouldering flesh suggest rather a consuming disease like leprosy than appetite. They seem diseased, even evil, rather than pathetic. Their eyes are greedy and restless, and linger greedily it sometimes seems, on one another's bodies. Their skin gets unnaturally dry and their breath parched and stale like dry air, in a cellar."

It is easy – too easy – to understand the realities of hunger in our TV age. Over decades, reports of famine in the Sahel, in Ethiopia, Bangladesh and India have more than put the rest of the world in the picture: children with extended stomachs, old shrivelled faces and people dying of starvation on the streets. But hunger is not limited to these emaciated people, who are the first to die in a famine. They are only the tip of the iceberg. "The lack of any of the constituents of a balanced diet causes premature death. In the last decade more people died from famine than were killed in war. But these numbers are smaller when compared with the number whose diet is inadequate to maintain health." So wrote Lord Boyd Orr, the first Secretary-General of the FAO in 1952.

Much has changed since then. The Green Revolution has transformed agriculture all over the world. The majority of the vast increase in the world's population has been fed, contrary to expectations. Yet there still remains 800 million people, mostly in the developing world, who are chronically undernourished, eating too little to meet even their minimal energy requirements.

Studies show that the size of the family affects the amount of food available for children. The worst forms of protein-calorie deficiency are found in families with more than four children. The vicious circle of hunger and overpopulation is apparent: hunger creates higher mortality in children and this means that larger families are needed. Thus these children are poorly fed and have a low chance of living. It is not so much overpopulation that causes hunger, but rather hunger causes overpopulation.

For a larger proportion of the population hunger is a life-long experience. Chronic hunger induces depression and apathy. Those who are affected by it quickly lose their appetite, their motivation and their energy for work.

In its analysis of the world food crisis, prepared for the World Food Conference in 1974 the Society of German Scientists stated that: "The lethargy and shyness for hard work which is something to be observed in the tropics cannot be traced back to the climate or lack of will to work. It is a self-preserving check that it is caused by insufficient nutrition. These people are consequently less capable of performing as a work force, are liable to have accidents at work and are threatened by illness. The result for both individuals and the collective societies of a number of developing countries is a viscous circle of under nourishment, inadequate work performance and growing poverty."

The decisive factor is not the quantity of available food but its distribution. If the fight against famine is to be successful, then people must study the distribution mechanism; in other words, which part of the population is undernourished and why they are so must be understood. Poverty is the prime cause of hunger and malnutrition and the group most affected are the landless poor and such isolated groups as pastoral nomads and small fishing communities.

Wherever there are poor it is usually true that it is the women, the children and sick who suffer the most from under-nutrition. The men get first call on the scarce food and the others have to wait their turn.

Most of the widespread hunger in a world of plenty is a consequence of grinding poverty. A small 5 to 10% is due to exceptional occurrences, such as drought, floods, earthquakes, war or social and economic disruption. Last year most of this latter kind of hunger was concentrated in Africa, mainly in the south.

Africa receives a good portion of the food aid distributed but Asia in total receives more, mainly because of the ongoing precariousness of food production in North Korea and Afghanistan. Elsewhere Central America has been in desperate need, partly because of drought and partly because of the collapse (since reversed) of coffee prices. Likewise many countries in the Commonwealth of Independent States faced severe food shortages because of economic decline.

Food aid is an imperative for some countries; nevertheless its importance is often exaggerated. Nearly 90% of the cereals imported by the hardest hit countries – 88 low income food-deficit countries – are bought on the open market. Food is only 5% of the total aid given by the countries of the OECD.

Food aid is not merely used in a time of crisis, a bad harvest, a flood, earthquake or war, but also to boost development. Then, for example, it is given in lieu of wages as food for work on such projects as soil conservation and reforestation.

The danger of food aid is if a project is poorly designed it can undercut the motivation of the recipient to grow crops themselves or, on a wider scale, depress the market so that domestic trade between surplus and deficit regions no longer takes place. But well designed programmes which reach those most in need, take local dietary habits into account and promote local food production are important tools of development.

Another way of aiding the hungry is by means of a government price subsidy. These have been extensive in developing countries because they are administratively convenient, especially where private channels exist. However, they can be costly and the non-poor can end up benefiting as well as the poor. This can be got round as, for example, in Egypt where subsidies are concentrated on items such as coarse flour which only the very poor tend to buy.

Another alternative to a general subsidy is rationing. Ration schemes are designed to ensure access to a regular supply of staples at an affordable price. But ration schemes need infrastructure and distribution networks which many rural areas, where the poor are concentrated, don't have. Thus in India, Pakistan

and Bangladesh, where rationing has been tried, the benefits have disproportionately favoured urban consumers.

Land reform is one of the most powerful means of ensuring food security for
the largest number of people.

The equity case rests on three considerations a) the landless and small owners are usually poorer than large landowners b) often total employment and
production per hectare increases as farm size decreases and c) it tilts the scales
more in favour of the poor being able to have access to credit and political
power.

In East Asia in the late 1940s and 1950s sweeping land reforms in Japan, the
Republic of Korea and Taiwan profoundly stimulated production and resulted
in a much more balanced distribution of income.

In Latin America, despite major land reforms in a number of countries, the
results have not been so impressive. After the land was redistributed other
inputs were generally not provided on terms the new landowners could afford
and production credit loans tended to dry up. Furthermore, resident farm labourers, the highest status worker in Latin American agriculture, were usually
apportioned the land while the *campesinos* that had no access to land rarely
obtained property – thus lessening the income distribution effects of reform.
Moreover, these new landowners were less willing than the former landlords
to hire landless *campesinos* at the going wage.

Governments also often compromised the income effects of land reform by
turning the domestic terms of trade against agriculture or spending for the
reform in a profligate manner. Thus the resulting inflation tended to eat away
at the incomes of both the rural and urban poor.

In their book *Land Reform and Democratic Development*, the two wise men of
land reform, Roy Prosterman and Jeffrey Reidinger, identify three causes of
revolutionary violence in Third World countries. The first is when expectations
are unchanged but the actuality worsens. A good example would be Ethiopia in
1974, when poor rains caused the peasantry severe crop failures but the landlords tried to continue collecting a normal year's rent. This was the undoing of
the emperor, Haile Selassie.

The second cause is when the expectations and the actuality remain the
same but the gap between classes and the level of opposition to authority that
it generates can no longer be managed by the government. This may come
about either through a relative change in power or when the tools of authority,
the military and the police, are crumbling. The collapse of the Russian Army
in 1917 and the return home of the peasant soldiers, weapons in hand, was a
critical element in the revolution.

Third is the traditional cause: The revolution of rising expectations, which
increase while actuality remains the same. This is the situation in the Philippines.

In sum, it is not poverty alone so much as it is *blameable* poverty that seems to serve as the trigger of violence. A large number of the most violent 20th century conflicts have occurred where a substantial part of the population was blocked from earning a secure living from the land it tilled. This was an important ingredient not just in the Russian revolution, but it the Mexican revolution, the Spanish civil war and the Irish struggle for independence. Since World War II, land protests have played a catalytic role in successful resolutions in China, Bolivia, Vietnam, Cuba, Algeria, Ethiopia and Zimbabwe, and it was of substantial significance in the toppling of the shah of Iran.

Land reform movements also have triggered violent upheavals in Kenya, Guatemala, El Salvador, and Indonesia and the Philippines. Other reform programs have taken place without violence: in Japan, Egypt, Taiwan and South Korea. (One of the most vigorous, that of Japan, was carried out by the US occupation administration headed by General Douglas MacArthur.)

The Philippines is crying out for land reform. So are India, Pakistan, Bangladesh and many parts of Latin America. If these countries can come to grips with this it could be done at miniscule cost compared with that of military repression. Moreover, there would be four major consequences: 1) avoiding civil conflicts that might involve millions of casualties; 2) avoiding 100 million or more deaths from hunger; 3) avoiding twice the number of births as now seems likely, as the essential conditions for voluntary family planning are created; and 4) avoiding a takeover by Marxist regimes, Maoist peasant movements, as in India and Nepal, or reactionary despots.

Whether there is land reform or not, need for it or not, the farmer, by the very nature of his work, will always need credit. And the smaller the farmer the more crucial the need.

Agriculture with its long time lapse between planting and harvest demands that the farmer finds a way to bridge the interval. Facilitation of access to credit is now widely recognised as a crucial instrument in the alleviation of poverty.

In recent years, however, the climate for subsidized credit has changed. With the current emphasis on privatization, long-standing government-subsidised credit systems have been eroded.

In many poorer rural communities informal finance plays an important role in rural development, often working more efficiently and equitably than the formal system.

It is a great mistake to assume that just because a region or village is poor there is not a potential for savings. Surprisingly, large amounts of savings can be mobilised if a reliable or effective system for doing so exists. Indeed, a large proportion, even the entire seasonal lending required for agricultural production, can be financed with funds mobilized in the rural areas. What is needed is a national financial system that is capable of transferring such savings from surplus to deficit areas.

The Green Revolution was a phenomenon that started in the 1960s – the doubling of yields of rice, wheat and maize, particularly in Asia but in some developing countries elsewhere. It was, in essence, nothing more than a technological package comprising high-yielding varieties, irrigation, fertilizer, pesticides and, not least, management skills.

It was a major technological achievement and its effects are still continuing, moving into other crops, other regions, even including some areas of Africa. Indeed, the commercial farmers of Zimbabwe launched a Green Revolution for maize in 1960, five years ahead of the Green Revolution in India, and then went on to introduce a second Green Revolution for smallholders in the early 1980s. Sadly, the success was thrown away by the incoherent Marxist regime of Robert Mugabe.

The Green Revolution was never a simple runaway success. It had inbuilt problems almost from the start. The reliance on genetically homogeneous seed, often produced and marketed commercially, led to older varieties, which possessed greater genetic variability, being abandoned. Thus, the new varieties were more vulnerable to attacks by pests and diseases, requiring control methods that initially relied on agrochemicals. Many of these were not environmentally benign. Some, in fact, constituted a serious risk to human health.

Another problem was that the Green Revolution required sophisticated irrigation management, demanding skills and a socio-economic environment that were new to many farmers and even to the policy makers. The resultant salinisation, alkalisation and water-logging were a particular problem in South Asia, often reversing the yield advances that had been made. Unfortunately, the research base for counteracting these negative trends was not adequately developed.

The Green Revolution is also criticised for the advantage it gave to better-off farmers who had access to capital and skills, strengthening their position in society, often at the cost of disadvantaging poorer groups. Moreover, the long-established rôle of women in traditional farming systems was often challenged by a technology that was orientated towards men.

There have been, it is now clear, both winners and losers. On the one hand, the Green Revolution averted a major food crisis in Asia and became the foundation stone for rapid economic growth in China, South East Asia and South Asia. It also inspired the subsequent development of more environmentally-benign methods, for example, pest control in rice. It lowered the price of wheat and rice in the world market place, thus making available cheaper food, not least for the huge number of urban poor in the developing countries. Against this, many rural poor, including large numbers of women, have found their means of making a livelihood squeezed even further. (It is important to note that many of the critical academic studies overstate the arguments on this.) Moreover, the fact is there were alternative pathways to improving food security for several billions of poor people that would have caused less negative social and environmental disturbances.

The new Green Revolution holds even brighter prospects than the first. With rice, some farmers in South East Asia are now producing yields similar to those achieved on research stations. But for other crops there are large yield gaps between research stations and farmers. For example, most dry land farmers achieve yields less than 50% of research stations and sometimes as little as 1%. Thus, the potential exists for rapid yield increases, once the right incentives are in place, not least access to markets and the chance to sell surplus production.

Similarly, there is a large gap between research station and farmer with paddy rice production. The International Rice Research Institute aims to raise yields from 3.5 ton/hectare/year to fifteen.

Some observers emphasise the limits that there are for ever-increasing yields. In the irrigated rice and wheat areas of Asia experimental yields appear to have reached a plateau. Indeed, they have been static for a decade or more. The challenge to break through this ceiling has become a major challenge for research institutions, concentrating on (a) production of crop varieties with enhanced tolerance or resistance to moisture stress and soil nutrient constraints, (b) overcoming micronutrient deficiencies and (c) improving soil conditions under intensive crop production.

Much future progress is going to depend on the humdrum work of research that has a 10 to 15 year time frame. It needs to concentrate on the energy front on renewable resources, mainly biomass, solar and wind energy and how to integrate the management of energy with other inputs, water fertilizer, pesticides and mechanization. It needs to safeguard the marginal areas, improving some for high potential agriculture and conserving others where the environment is simply too adverse. For example, using the minimal tillage techniques that have transformed dry land crop production in parts of the USA. There needs to be more research, too, on how to reduce the cost of external inputs or else reduce the need for them. For example, as with the use of expensive, imported phosphate fertilizers. It would be, in fact, often possible to use domestically produced, low-grade phosphate rock if cheap methods could be found for treating them. Alternatively, it may be possible to genetically transfer to other crops the ability of pigeon peas to release bound phosphates in the soil.

On another plane it is also clear that new tools of biotechnology, including genetic engineering, are now becoming widely available with quite remarkable consequences – despite a Luddite retinence to their adoption in Western Europe – and that there remain many crop, livestock and fish breeds that have not been subject to much biotechnology research work.

One very important objective of the ongoing Green Revolution is to narrow the present yield gaps between farmer and research station but without degrading the natural resource base. Biotechnology offers the prospects for progress on both those fronts.

Biotechnology offers particularly promising results in the effort to build genetic resistance to pest and disease into crops and animal breeds, which are at the moment significant yield-depressing problems. The alternative – agrochemicals – is both expensive and often disturbing to the resource base and to the farmers whose low level of education often prevents them having a proper understanding of both environmental and health risks.

At present much of the advanced work – and controversy – on biotechnology is focused on the needs of developed country farmers. That work needs to be broadened to include tropical farmers. Also, it is important to redefine the role of the farmers to encourage them to be both the curators and selectors of genetic material so that there is an incentive to retain the large genetic diversity of the present pools.

On the livestock and fishing front there is much evidence to suggest that modern science is a long way from having realised the genetic potential of producing species, even though recent advances for chickens, dairy cows, pigs and Atlantic salmon have been remarkable.

In fish species and for some types of livestock current research appears to be at the lower end of steeply rising productivity curves. In tropical aquaculture genetic improvements in carp and tilapia over the last 10 years have led to yield gains of from one-third to one-half. Thus, as farmers move from monoculture to mixed farming, including fish ponds, they can avoid many of the problems of the earlier Green Revolution with its emphasis on monoculture.

Genetic enhancement and biotechnology alone, however, cannot solve the food deficit problem. Evidence from the recent drought in Southern Africa showed that about two third's of the yield increases obtained from improved sorghum varieties based on materials from the International Crops Research Institute for the Semi-Arid Tropics could be traced back to better management at the farm level. Good extension work is at least as important as the genetic material itself and this is also a more sure-footed way of making certain poorer farmers benefit as much as more successful ones. The lessons from the Green Revolution have taught practitioners that scientific advances alone cannot solve the food security problem of developing countries. Suitable socioeconomic and institutional enabling environments are necessary, in particular creating access to credit and markets. Sustainable progress also demands broader popular participation so that the farmers themselves can adapt the new techniques and tools to their traditional technological, social, cultural and economic settings.

It is in fact true that those countries with the best record on achieving all-round food security, including the poor, have given political priority to agriculture, developing incentives and supporting research, extension and training.

This is why if progress is to accelerate the world community has to give priority to make the second Green Revolution advance on a broad front. For developing countries this means: Revitalising their national agricultural extension, training and research facilities with a particular emphasis on creating capabilities for reaching the poor and ill fed, in particular women. It means making these extension and research systems sensitive to environmentally sustainable agriculture. It means close co-operation with the international agricultural research systems which in turn must develop a clearer focus on poverty alleviation and on new scientific methods, in particular biotechnology, biological and weed control and integrated pest management.

On the international level it means developing a consensus among all the stakeholders involved in both recipient and donor countries to ensure that high priority be given to food security. This means not just aid to sound national agricultural policies but also the creation of more open access to markets and fair and predictable prices for produce.

For the future it is not possible to give more than a working hypothesis of the incremental annual investments needed to generate the quantity and quality of increases in food production necessary to bring about adequate food security. The available evidence suggests that incremental gross investments of some $16 billion per year above the average for 1987-92 will be needed in primary production. In other words, apart from sub-Saharan Africa, little additional net investment. Added to this an extra $8 billion gross investment in the post-harvest and marketing chain and an additional $10 billion in working capital. Most of this investment should originate in the private sector. However, some public investment will be needed to provide improved rural access, markets and social support. Urban bias is so pronounced a shift of resources of $7 billion per year out of total annual infrastructure, investments, although modest, could make a significant impact in rural areas, adding some 25% in current rural infrastructure investments and services, much of it going into research and extension. One third of this total should come from existing assistance.

None of this, of course, will benefit those who are hungry today. The only practical way of helping the hungry in the short term is to increase targeted food assistance through a variety of programmes – for schools, for mothers and infants, for displaced persons or food-for-work projects. Only a small amount of food relative to world supplies is necessary (30 million tons of cereals out of 2 billion), but it is the organisation, logistics and targeting that is the demanding part. For that which is needed is political commitment at home and, for the poorest countries with no surplus of their own to redistribute, from abroad. The chronic food deficits of those poorest countries are a major challenge. Food aid is only a palliative. What is needed are priority investment programmes. Contrary to the popular view, in many case conditions can be created which would stimulate a relatively quick increase in output. Above all what are required are policy changes which improve farm-level profitability.

Then with better incentives in place farmers will do more to use intensifying, sustainable production technologies or novel approaches to storage, processing and marketing.

Emergency food assistance needs to be integrated with such policies, so that it doesn't have a counterproductive impact. Food-for-work programmes are particularly valuable because they can be used to build new transport links, markets and irrigation infrastructure.

Foreign aid will always play an important part in such projects as the poorest countries have both very low domestic savings ratios and a low creditworthiness in international bond and loan markets.

Beyond meeting the needs of the poorest and hungriest is the on-going work of attracting sufficient capital, principally private, to ensure the increases in food production necessary for improved well-being are secured.

The impetus of the Green Revolution has to be maintained and for this to happen much of the perceived inferiority of agriculture as a destination for investment needs to be rethought. Anti-agricultural bias can, if not rectified, become a heavy drag on both the well-being and economic progress of the whole society.

Such a change of attitudes will also give developing countries the room for manoeuvre and confidence to move towards greater economic maturity and independence, irrespective of the mood and policies within the international donor community.

Workable decisions which incorporate the consensus of the stakeholders, both private and public, both within the country and without and which are capable of successful implementation are absolutely essential to progress. The decisions have to be far-sighted and the consensus has to be durable, for the commitments once made must be adhered to. Agriculture, by its very nature cannot operate successfully on anything less. Moreover, only then will the hoped for private investment be forthcoming.

Food security, because it is so fundamental to human life, has to be given the priority it deserves, particularly so for the very poorest who depend on agriculture exclusively for their barest existence.

There is food in abundance in global terms. But the serious shortfalls in important corners of the world demand that we must all be aware of the needs outstanding and the sheer urgency of the quest to improve productivity and techniques of cultivation. Moreover, those wealthy enough to think of food more as a pleasure and pastime than as a nutritional necessity have to have due regard for the pressures that may be generated by the excesses of their demand. The least they can do is help to bring agricultural knowledge to those who desperately need it. We live in a world where traditional boundaries and pre-jet and television age distances mean less and less. Other people's failures and setbacks have a way of impinging on all our societies. At the simplest level many of the more fortunate feel a great sense of unease when other societies suffer so much misfortune. At a more tragic level there is always the danger that such poverty can produce political turbulence, even war that can disturb everyone's political and economic interests. The security of the food supply of the poor in the long run is as much in all our self-interest as it is in theirs.

# 9   How Far Can Human Development Progress?

When Mahbub ul Haq died in New York in July 1998 the traffic did not stop, nor did the United Nations, for which he had done so much, lower its flag. But all over the world, people who have been touched by the special wisdom of this astonishing man felt their hearts miss a beat. He left behind one of the great ideas of the 20th century.

When he died he was preparing to join Mikhail Gorbachev, the former president of the Soviet Union, in San Francisco in a private seminar with some of the world's most influential minds. Simply put, Haq was the greatest living expert on measuring human progress.

Formerly Pakistan's minister of finance, for seven years he was the creator and continuing intellectual force behind *The Human Development Report*, published annually by the United Nations Development Programme. In his years in ministerial office he became convinced that amid the jargon of modern government, finance and accounting, we lose sight of the main direction we are going in.

Too often we attempt to measure progress by statistical aggregates and technical prowess. We overlook that the main goal of life is to ensure survival and, beyond that, to enable the pursuit of well-being, achievement and, as the American constitution (not without a great debate at the time) so aptly puts it, of happiness. (The opposition wanted the pursuit of wealth.)

This debate reaches back in European thought at least to the time of Aristotle. "Wealth is evidently not the good we are seeking, for it is merely useful and for the sake of something else", he wrote. Even the 19th century philosophers of political economy never were gross national product absolutists after the fashion of today. Adam Smith, David Ricardo, Karl Marx and John Stuart Mill, from very different perspectives, all saw the creation of wealth as only one part of a complicated, organic whole.

Haq was convinced that the contemporary obsession with increased income per head blinded both observers and participants to the tremendous advances that could be made in social wellbeing, even in quite poor countries, with only a modest rise in incomes. He produced sophisticated tables in which countries were not ranked by income per head but on yardsticks which he considered more telling – longevity, knowledge and a decent standard of living. In these early tables Japan came out on top, followed by Canada, Norway, Switzerland and Sweden. Later, he factored in the status of women and produced an even more accurate profile of wellbeing. Sweden and Norway came out on top with Denmark not far behind, and Japan fell to 17th place.

Then he did the same exercise for Third World countries. Barbados came out first, followed by Hong Kong, Cyprus, Uruguay, Singapore, Taiwan, Trinidad and Tobago, Malaysia and South Korea. They, quite poor until relatively recently, had dramatically lowered infant mortality rates that used to be at present day African rates and assured life spans, only two generations ago 50 years or less, that today are up to the levels of the richest countries.

Haq's two favourites were Malaysia and South Korea. Malaysia, instead of being traumatised by the race riots of 1969, used the bitter experience to formulate a 20-year plan to raise growth and human development, reduce poverty and racial discrimination and improve education and health standards.

South Korea, likewise, surged from rags to well-being in a single generation. In 1945 only 13 percent of adults had any formal schooling. By 1950 the average years of schooling for all reached 9.9 years, higher than for the industrialised countries.

The challenge, argued Haq, which these countries met, is to combine high levels of human development, low employment and rapid economic growth, creating a virtuous circle in which productivity rises and triggers an increase in real wages which, in turn, attracts more investment in human capital, in education, and in access to social services.

Amidst the jargon of modern government, finance and accounting, it is all too easy to lose one's way. Too often we attempt to measure progress by statistical aggregates and technical prowess; we overlook that the main goal of life is to ensure survival and to enable everyone to realize their full potential for well-being and achievement.

National income figures give us only the bare bones of a society's progress. They neither reveal the real beneficiaries nor the composition of that income. Neither do they value the things that human beings consider important for themselves but have little or no market value for other people or for those beholden to statistical aggregates – better nutrition and health services, greater access to knowledge, more secure livelihoods, better working conditions, security against crime and physical violence, satisfying leisure hours and a sense of participating in the economic, cultural, religious and political activities of their communities. Of course, people also want higher incomes. But income is never the sum total of human life. For most people health, security and love are the three important things in life, and how many people can put their hands on their heart and can say they are sure that in their own lives these three things are eternally spoken for?

Today many governments have found, after many decades of stressing the pursuit of high growth rates, that they have failed to reduce the social and economic deprivation of a substantial number of their people. Even some of the advanced industrialised nations, which have focused too absolutely on the pursuit of wealth, now find that they are besieged by violence, homelessness, drugs, AIDS and the breakdown of the family.

At the same time we have become aware that a number of low-income countries have achieved high levels of human development by a judicious use of their scare resources to ensure a basic level well-being throughout their societies. Few outsiders looked at China, Taiwan and South Korea twenty or thirty years ago and anticipated their present fast growth rate. The present income of a country may offer little guidance to its future growth prospect if it is nurturing its resources by investing in its people, as these three countries did in the early years of their decision to modernize and develop economically.

Not least, we should be aware of how misleading aggregate figures can be. Income is a means not an end. It may be used for essential medicines or narcotics, for sitting in a luxury car in a traffic jam or for a high-speed train link, for parks and green spaces or for extra wide thoroughfares and multi-storey car parks. Everyone in any country that has experienced rapid economic growth, whether it be a mature economy like the United States or Sweden or an up and coming one like Taiwan or Brazil knows from their own bitter experience that it doesn't tell you that much about a society. It gives a kind of useful bench mark of aggregate economic momentum. But, beyond that, the more one looks at it the more misleading it can become.

The human development idea is distinctive from other concepts of growth and development. Economic growth is regarded as necessary but not sufficient for human development. Present day theories of human capital formation and human resource development regard human beings primarily as a means rather than as ends. But human beings are more than the suppliers of capital goods for commodity production. They are the ultimate end and beneficiaries of this process.

The question of how to measure progress defined in this way demands some ingenuity, given the lack of detailed statistics that would make a comprehensive look possible. Perhaps if we had too many indicators it would produce too perplexing a picture and even distract policymakers from the salient trends. This is why the UNDP concentrates on only three yardsticks of well-being which are regarded as the essentials of human life – longevity, knowledge and a decent standard of living.

To measure longevity the UNDP uses life expectancy at birth – not just because a long life is a common aspiration of mankind everywhere, but for it to be realized one must assume adequate nutrition and good health.

To measure knowledge it uses a crude measure, adult literacy figures combined with the number of years of schooling, aware that they are only the first step in the ladder of knowledge, but nevertheless the most essential one, without which further learning and education is not possible.

To measure decent living standards is even more difficult. Ideally, we need information on land holdings, credit availability, income and other resources.

These figures are not available so the UNDP falls back on per capita income, adjusting it to reflect the purchasing power in different societies. The figure is refined by using the logarithm of real GDP to emphasize that greater wealth on its own does not ensure a decent living.

Even with these reservations there remains the problem of averages, which conceal wide variations, especially income differentials which can grow to enormous heights.

These three yardsticks are combined to give what is called the Human Development Index. For each of its components the HDI looks at the data to find the current minimum value – for, say, life expectancy, which is 42 years in Sierra Leone – and the maximum desirable value, which is 81 years in Japan. For each component, the difference between its maximum and the minimum forms the denominator of a ratio.

In its numerator, the difference between the actual value of the component from its minimum is represented. The simple mean of these ratios gives the HDI index.

The HDI allows us to compare easily various countries. For instance, Oman has a per capita income two and a half times that of Costa Rica, but its literacy rate is one-third that of Costa Rica, its average life expectancy is nine years less and its child mortality two and a quarter times higher. Once this information is aggregated and measured in the HDI index we see oil-rich Oman has a relatively low HDI of 0.589 and Costa Rica quite a high one of 0.842 - 43% higher than Oman's.

The latest annually updated Human Development Index (HDI) ranks 173 countries by a composite measure of life expectancy, education, and income per person. Norway remains at the top of the HDI, with Sweden, Canada, Iceland and Australia close behind, displacing Japan and outranking the United States. But the rankings between countries are very close: Australia, for example, had dropped from second to fourth place, but the difference between these ranks is miniscule.

Changes at the bottom of the rankings have also been very limited. Sierra Leone is still ranked last, with the bottom 24 countries on the index all in sub-Saharan Africa. However, there have been major changes in the rankings since 1990: At the top of the index, Norway has shot up six places since 1990, and Sweden and Australia have both risen nine places. The United States and France have all dropped four places over the period. Japan has fallen five and Switzerland six. In East Asia, many economies have made striking progress since 1990, despite the financial crisis that hit the region towards the end of the decade. China has risen furthest, with an increase of 14 places. Singapore and the Republic of Korea have both moved up eight places, Thailand has risen 10, and Malaysia has risen 12. (Taiwan which is not included in these UN statistics is also somewhere near the top.)

As many as nine countries in Latin America and the Caribbean have also risen five places or more since 1990, including Chile, Costa Rica and Panama.

At the same time, the pain of economic transition has taken its toll in many Eastern and Central European countries and the former Soviet Union. The Russian Federation and Ukraine have fallen by 20 places since 1990 – and Moldova and Tajikistan have fallen by 30 or more places. Only Croatia, Hungary and Poland buck the trend, moving up by five and eight ranks respectively since 1990.

Those countries with detailed internal statistics enable us to see how sharp differences are between regions. India's Punjab and Kerala states do far better than the other states of India. In fact the southern state of Kerala has health indicators on a par with that of the U.S., despite a per capita income level much, much lower and annual spending on healthcare of just $26 per person. In Turkey, of its 67 provinces 18 are in the high category of human development, 42 in the medium and 7 in the low. In the United States, with the HDIs of white, black and Hispanic populations separated, whites rank number 1 in the world (ahead of Norway), blacks ranks number 31 (next to Trinidad and Tobago) and Hispanics rank number 35 (next to Estonia). This, despite the fact that income levels are considerably discounted in the HDI calculations.

It is more difficult, given the paucity of information, to compare rural and urban areas. In Morocco, where it is possible, the rural HDI is 66% of the urban, a greater disparity than between different provinces.

Of course, it is valuable to know if countries are improving over time. It has been possible to make this calculation in 110 countries. The largest increases in HDI were for Taiwan, Brazil, Mexico, Benin, Ghana, Mauritania, Rwanda, South Korea, Peru, Bolivia, Senegal, Uganda, Barbados, Laos, Malaysia, Nepal and Thailand. Brazil's big jump was due mainly to its rapid improvement in education. Peru and Bolivia's were as a result of social policy reforms. And South Korea and Malaysia upped their investments in people, to increase productivity and accelerate economic growth.

Two-thirds of the 15 newly independent states of the former Soviet Union fall into the category of high human development, the other third into the medium. The formerly socialist countries have already made major investments in the education and health of their people – and thus have considerable human capital available for the transition ahead. The average life expectancy for these countries is 70 years, and the population per doctor is around 300, compared with 63 years and 5,000 respectively for developing countries. Sadly, since the break up of the Soviet Union most, including until very recently Russia, have seemingly lost their bearings and their Human Development ratings have plunged.

To factor in the environment, in particular the depletion and degradation of the earth's resources, is a complicated task. The best way to begin would be to "green" GNP statistics. At present GNP can give a perverse result. For example, GNP will rise if a deteriorating environment causes disease and this results in increased health expenditures.

At the end of this look at the HDI, we are left with one overriding distinct, and fairly accurate, impression – that economic growth does not invariably translate into improved human well-being. There are 26 countries whose HDI rank is 20 or more places lower than their per capita rank. This shows that if they spent their incomes better and planned their investments more wisely they could considerably improve their human development levels. Fourteen of these countries are in Africa, ten are Arab states and only two are in Asia.

It is clear that there is no automatic link between economic growth and human progress. Some countries, relatively few, have successfully married the two; many, if not most, have not. Two stunning examples of growth combined with equity are Taiwan and South Korea. (Both countries, tellingly, are ex-Japanese colonies.) But few other countries match their performance. Nevertheless, there are a number of countries which over a long period of time have made significant improvements in human development, even in the absence of high growth or good distribution, by means of well structured social expenditure – Botswana (until it was very badly hit by the AIDS epidemic), Malaysia, Brazil and Sri Lanka, in particular. There are also countries which have successfully averted the most serious effects of recession and natural disaster by carefully targeted interventions – Botswana and Chile for example.

One of the most successful is Bangladesh, a country that has moved from basket case to show case in less than 20 years. Income poverty dropped from 48% of the population in 1989 to 34% in 2000. Most of the population is now becoming literate. Population growth has been lowered and the labour force shrunk. Maternal and children's health has been advanced. And this has happened in a country of 133 million people where terrible floods are an annual hazard and which for a period of time in the 1980s was written off by outsiders as a country that could never be made to work. Much of the turnaround in spirit came from the driving success of the NGO sector, for example the Grameen Bank that successfully extended small loans to impoverished women to help start micro businesses. But there was also progress on the industrial front. Bangladesh's labour-intensive garment exports jumped from $867 in 1991 to $4.6 billion in 2002.

But there are many countries where, despite periods of rapid GNP growth, human development has not improved significantly, the distribution of income is bad and social expenditures are low – such as Pakistan and Paraguay.

The task for most countries, still unfulfilled, is to maintain the kind of economic growth that enriches human development. Human development without economic growth cannot be sustained (budget deficits get the upper hand in a moribund economy). And economic growth without human development merely stores up intractable social problems for the next generation.

Opportunity is everything. No one much cares if one is behind as long as the future beckons and the road is clear. Tragically, for too many developing countries, the disparities in the distribution of global economic opportunities appear to be widening. Whether we look at the financial markets, foreign direct investment, goods and services or the chance to emigrate, everywhere the developing countries face, at best, half-open doors. Until they open, as wide for the outsider as for the insider, there is little chance that the poor will get a fair crack at life. The essence of the problem is markets. If they were both freer and better monitored the poor would benefit.

Heated ideological discussions have often marred an objective analysis of the relative roles of markets and the state. Some believe in the benevolence of the state *and* the need for constantly correcting the ill effects of the market. Others glorify the virtues of the market-place and argue that the economy should be liberated from the dead hand of state bureaucracy. Both groups assume, to a large extent, that the state and the market are necessarily separate and even antagonistic – that one is benevolent, the other not. In practice, both state and market are often dominated by the same power structures.

This suggests a more pragmatic third option: that people should guide both the state and the market, which should work in tandem with people sufficiently empowered to exert a more effective influence over both.

If people's interests are to guide both the market and the state, action must be taken to allow people to participate fully in the operations of markets and to share equitably in their benefits. Markets should serve people – instead of people serving markets. After all, markets are only the means – people the end.

Changing markets to make them more people-friendly should start by maintaining the dynamism of markets but adding other measures that allow many more people to capitalize on the advantages that markets offer.

Free markets provide the most efficient mechanism yet devised for the exchange of goods and services – impersonally matching supply and demand, bringing together buyers and sellers, employers and workers and constantly setting and resetting prices so that the economy works at peak efficiency. Free enterprise provides a mechanism for unleashing human creativity and entrepreneurial ability.

There are three critical questions that demand attention: Are the markets really open? Are they accessible to all the people? And what is their impact on the distribution of income and other development benefits and opportunities?

Most markets are stifled by barriers – many raised by government regulations and some by powerful interest groups. And markets are not automatically or inevitably people-friendly. They make no value judgments. They reward those who have either substantial purchasing power or valuable commodities or services to sell. People enter markets as unequal participants and often leave with unequal rewards, even when markets operate neutrally. So, for all their efficiency at matching buyers and sellers, markets can also be associated with increasing inequality and poverty, as well as large-scale unemployment.

Markets may also place very little value on environmental concerns and the needs of future generations. Soil, water, fossil fuels and minerals are important inputs to the production process. But their market prices often fail to reflect their true scarcity value, leading to overexploitation and depletion. Company profit and loss accounts seldom register the true costs of pollution – which are passed on to the rest of society. Similarly, national income accounts fail to register the constant depletion of natural capital – and thus hide from policy-makers the high cost of environmental neglect. Costa Rica, during 1970-90, lost natural capital (soils, forests) amounting to more than 6% of its total GDP. And in Indonesia, during 1971-84, these losses were more than 9% of GDP. Yet in both countries national income accounts were silent on this continuing hemorrhage.

Sustainable human development demands more of markets – that they continue to offer their advantages but that they do so in a more balanced way, combining efficiency, equity and sustainability. Markets are, after all, not an end in themselves. They are a means to human development.

People-friendly markets allow people to participate fully in their operation and to share equitably in their benefits. Making markets more people-friendly will require a strategy that maintains dynamism but supplements them with other measures to allow many more people to capitalize on the advantages they offer.

Most markets suffer from three types of distortion. First, there are distortions in the workings of the markets themselves. Some may be due to monopoly power, as well as to short-term business considerations that make the markets less competitive, less efficient or less respectful of environmental concerns. Others are due to controlled prices, fiscal disincentives and constant government intervention in the market.

Second, there are distortions in the form of disparities among people who enter the market. Many people lack the education, the assets, the credit or the skills to be competitive – or are excluded on the grounds of sex, race or ethnicity.

Third, the markets often fail to reflect external costs and benefits – be it pollution (an external cost) or the prevention of communicable diseases (an external benefit). In addition, there are areas where markets are missing altogether. National income accounts do not, for example, include household work – nor do they measure the depreciation of natural capital assets over time. For both, a supplementary accounting should be made.

Traditional discussions of markets have focused more on their efficiency than on their equity aspects. But since markets are only a means towards human development, we must closely examine ways to build a bridge between markets and people – to make them more "people-friendly". The measures that would make such a radical transformation possible can be divided into four groups.

First, certain preconditions need to be met for markets to be kept free. This means investing in people so that they are healthy and educated enough to be productive. The newly industrializing, fast-growing countries of East Asia are not just highly competitive because of their low wages but because their workforce is skillful and enterprising. If people are to participate freely in markets, they need both physical and financial resources. This means land reform for agricultural societies. In the industrialized, it means progressive taxation that ensures that assets and wealth are not just concentrated among the successful. Credit needs to be made more widely available – especially to small-scale enterprises that are potentially the engine of growth.

Businesses need good infrastructure, roads, electricity, improved water and communications. And they need to be brought to the countryside where in many developing countries a majority of the people lives. In South Korea and Taiwan the non-farm income of farm families now exceeds their income directly from agriculture.

Adequate funding for research and development is also important. If R & D is left to the private sector alone there may be little research directed to subsistence farmers and small-scale industries, or alternative environment-friendly energy technologies. An enterprise culture needs a good flow of information – honest advertising, efficient labour exchanges, price information and transparency in contract making. This must be supported by the rule of law, enabling clear, open and legally enforceable transactions. Property rights, likewise, must be respected, both from illegal forced seizure by superior force or from capricious nationalization.

In too many developing countries business is corrupted by bribery. This saps initiative and distracts from the real challenge of productive investment. Discrimination can be as undermining as corruption. Women, ethnic minorities and the disabled are excluded from serious economic life. Many "low-caste" people have paid a heavy price, sometimes with their lives, when they have dared challenge the market barriers that society erected against them.

Markets also need accompanying conditions to ensure that they are people-friendly and work as efficiently and equitably as possible. This means a stable economic environment, governed by sound fiscal and monetary policies, controlling inflation and violent fluctuations in the exchange rate. The government, too, must keep many of its interventions to a minimum. Changes in excise duties, tariffs or price controls distort the market. When government does intervene to accelerate development, it should follow the discipline of both the international and domestic market and make its interventions simple, transparent and subject to rules rather than official discretion.

There are occasions when corrective action is necessary, when the market, if left alone, would not produce a desirable outcome. Anti-monopoly legislation is necessary to keep markets open. Banks and financial markets need to be regulated to keep them both open and accountable.

Standards have to be enforced – drugs must be tested and approved before they are sold; food manufacturers must meet standards of hygiene; cars of safety; workers must be protected with safe working conditions; children must be prohibited from work and the disadvantaged encouraged; trade unions must be allowed to organize, with the power to strike; the environment must be nurtured and protected so that companies do not maximize short-term profits at the expense of pollution and degradation.

The pricing of environmental resources – or more effective regulations – can ensure that everyone works under the same rules and that today's production does not pass on some of its costs to society in general or deplete resources that need to be conserved for future generations.

Social safety nets are a necessary corollary to open markets, to catch the victims of the competitive struggle, the unemployed and to protect the lowest income group, the young, the old and the disabled. In the Scandinavian countries, as much as 30% of GNP is spent on unemployment benefits, social security and health care. In the US and the UK it is around 15%. There has long been a debate over just how substantial these safety nets should be. If they are too firm and reassuring they may discourage people from working. If they are too open or flimsy they may let those in real hardship fall through.

Developing countries have weak state safety nets relying on support from families and community. They do, however, often distribute food supplements to children or provide labour-intensive public works programmes to generate income, especially in times of disaster.

For most people, the best form of market participation is through productive and remunerative work. It is not only a question of livelihood; it is a matter of self-esteem and political influence.

High unemployment is today, with the exception of East Asia, an almost universal problem. Employment is consistently lagging behind economic growth.

In the industrialized countries, productivity may be rising but it is not creating new jobs. In the developing countries it is the same although some new jobs are being created. We are witnessing a new phenomenon – jobless growth. There are four main reasons for this. First, the search for labour-saving technology was encouraged by the demographic situation in industrial countries when, in the 1960s, stagnating population growth led to growing labour shortages. Second, it was enhanced by rising labour costs, as well as an active trade union movement. Third, technological innovation in the civilian sphere, often the by-product of military research and development, has a preference for capital-intensity. Finally, the prevalent technology reflects the existing pattern of income distribution. Twenty per cent of the world's population has 83% of the world's income. Clearly technology follows purchasing power.

Taking into account the number of employed and unemployed, the total new job requirement for the next decade is around one billion. This means, in the developing countries alone, increasing total employment by 4% a year.

In sub-Saharan Africa we are likely to see a growth rate in the labour force of 3 % a year, while productive employment will increase by only 2.4%. In Latin America and South Asia the situation will not be much better.

Even when jobs are available, job security is diminishing. Employers have been reducing their reliance on a permanent labour force. Instead, they tend to engage a highly skilled core group surrounded by a periphery of temporary workers, hired on a short term or part-time basis. This problem exists in industrialized countries too, but it is more pronounced in the developing countries.

Nevertheless, we can see in Japan and East Asia an alternative. One of the essential starting points was land reform. In the Republic of Korea, between 1952 and 1954, the proportion of cultivators who were owners increased from 51% to 94%. As a result, between 1954 and 1968 the labour used per hectare increased by 4.7% a year. It was a similar story in Taiwan, leading to a sharp rise in income and purchasing power.

Besides redistributing assets these two countries simultaneously invested in the health, education and skills of their people. The workforce was ready and able to take advantage of the latest technologies and methods of production as they were introduced. These societies also established a comprehensive framework for the rapid growth of private enterprise; and they combined outward orientation of their economies and exposure to foreign competition with support for national economic capacity building. Labour productivity in these two countries has been increasing at an annual rate at 10% or more.

In some industrialized countries a few pioneering companies have begun changed methods of work to increase productivity and to cut down turnover in the workforce. In Sweden, ASEA Brown Bovery Group ended the traditional production line and introduced a system where workers moved among different tasks and took charge of many aspects of production. Labour turnover fell from 39% to nearly zero. Whereas before only 10% of production arrived on time, afterwards the level rose to 98%.

Too often human beings have had to fit into roles preordained by economic theorists, state planners and the developers of technology. A much more refreshing approach is to start with human beings, invest liberally in their education and technical skills and see how their energy and creativity can best be released.

One of the surest ways of encouraging employment is to promote small businesses. In both the industrialised world and the developing countries the number of these is increasing. In Malaysia, for example, 86% of a sample of firms were found to have been started by their owners, who were relatively young and well-educated and often had experience of working in the same field with another company. In both the industrialized and developing countries an increasing proportion of these small firms are being started by women.

To encourage this process further, nothing is more important than that governments ensure access to capital. The capital market is generally unfriendly to the small entrepreneur, particularly the poorest ones, partly because they lack collateral and partly because banks prefer to deal in large amounts. Thus banks often ignore the needs of small-scale operators in agriculture, industry and services – or between 30% and 70% of the labour force in developing countries.

Lack of credit can be a significant brake on progress. In Ghana, small enterprises report that up to 50% of their capacity is idle because of a shortage of working capital. A 1989 survey found that almost 90% of the enterprises perceived the lack of credit as a serious constraint to new investment. And if they get credit, smaller firms tend to pay interest rates around one-third higher than larger firms. A similar situation was found in Tunisia.

Three important groups find it difficult to get access to credit: small farmers, entrepreneurs in the informal sector in general and women. Bangladesh's large owners of land, who constitute 7% of rural households, received 37% of institutional credit in 1988/89. Now thanks to the work of grass roots nongovernmental organisations the situation has been transformed with astonishing results.

Women, in both the formal and the informal sectors, also have great trouble getting bank loans. Women account for about 18% of the self-employed in developing countries. But in the Philippines, only 10% of formal credit goes to women, and in Pakistan, the Agricultural Development Bank makes less than 0.1% of its loans to women.

Without access to formal credit, many poor people are forced to turn to money-lenders who charge usurious rates (in Bangladesh, 70% of total rural credit used to come from moneylenders). One common mechanism in many countries is a "five-six" arrangement, in which a borrower receives five pesos in the morning and repays six pesos in the evening – 20% interest a day.

Experience shows that the best way to support small-scale enterprise is to combine improved availability of credit with measures aimed at enhancing competitiveness. In western Guatemala, for example, the weavers of Momostenango use almost 40% of the country's wool to weave ponchos, blankets and other products. But the quality of the wool had been low, and the weavers lacked credit to expand production. In 1966, a foundation with technical and financial support from the government and international donors was set up to help the farmers, the weavers and those marketing the finished products. A year later, 14 technical assistance centres were organised to help increase wool quantity and quality. Funds of up to $20,000 were available to offer credit to weavers to increase production. As a result of these and other measures, export volumes have increased substantially – 11 weaver groups with 160 members have been formed to fill export orders.

People-friendly capital markets would address the needs of those groups who find it difficult to get credit. First, in terms of preconditions, a better distribution of assets (such as land) would increase their chances of offering collateral. Second, the corrective actions would give special access to weaker groups – either through government action or through informal credit schemes, such as cooperatives, savings groups or credit unions. These have played an important role in many industrial countries, as well as in the developing world. In Togo loans from credit unions grew by 33% over the last decade.

One of the most important forms of assistance to small enterprises is training – not just vocational training but also an introduction to management skills. One interesting example of a more comprehensive approach is the Malawian Enterprise Development Institute, targeted mainly at educated employment youths. In addition to vocational training, the programme offers training in business management and entrepreneurship. At the end of the course the graduates are rewarded with a tool-set and loans, but they are not given a trade certificate, which might encourage them to go simply into wage employment.

There is also a need for a working system of enterprises with medium-size and large firms feeding off the smaller ones. In Europe, large enterprises such as General Electric, Olivetti and Philips have all developed broad-based technological cooperation networks for manufacturing new technologies available to smaller companies.

People-friendly markets should encourage and nurture small enterprises, for the profit not only of the individual entrepreneurs but for society as a whole, through steady increases in output and employment. In the developing countries, the informal sector is growing almost everywhere. And small-scale enterprises are often part of this sector. In Latin America, whereas 25% of all non-agricultural employment was in the informal sector at the beginning of the 1980s, by the end of the decade it was 31%. Today it is nearer 40%. In some Asian countries, including India, the Philippines and Sri Lanka, wage employment in the urban informal sector has been growing faster than in the formal sector. In India, twice as many jobs have been created in the unorganised manufacturing sector as in the organised.

A profound shift is underway in the world economy – from agriculture and industry towards services, giving a comparative advantage to a country with educated people rather than plentiful natural resources as in industrial times. This rapid expansion of trade in skill-intensive services offers a tremendous opportunity to developing countries – if they can impart new knowledge and skills to their people. At present most developing countries are net importers of services, whereas in the US, which has the biggest service sector, it accounts for 72% of its GDP, 80% of its employment and a large and growing proportion of its exports.

More credit, more skills, more small businesses and more emphasis on service are all ways of dealing with the problem of growing employment. But at the same time we must consider employment safety nets for those who cannot find work. Some developing countries have designed employment guarantee schemes, offering poorly paid work through public works programmes building road and irrigation works. In Botswana and Cape Verde such programmes are estimated to have saved the lives of 60,000 to 90,000 people in each country during the 1980s.

One of the largest public works programmes in the developing world is the Employment Guarantee Scheme of Maharashtra, in India. This was started in 1972 to provide employment on request at a stipulated wage, within 15 days, no more than five kilometers away from the participant's village home. In 1990-91, the scheme provided more than 90 million person-days of work, with nearly two-thirds of the workers from households below the poverty line. As well as providing work, the scheme has helped mobilize the rural poor as a political force and acted as a check on the power of local officials. The programme pays the official minimum wage, which is somewhat higher than the market wage (around $1 a day). It is one of the most cost-effective schemes anywhere for helping the poor.

In the future, it would also be desirable to consider whether one cannot expand employment guarantee schemes beyond their traditional, primary public works-oriented fields. Certainly, they could cover many environmental tasks that need to be done. They could also focus more on provision of social services, which would be critical to improved human development. They could include proposals for national service in exchange for guaranteed education, as currently proposed by the new US administration. Too many societal activities remain undone while too many people remain unemployed. It does not take much to match unmet social needs with unemployed human resources.

When trade unions are closely in tune with their members and also with national needs they can make the whole industrial process work more smoothly. Germany and the Scandinavian countries have shown it is not impossible to achieve high wages and shorter working weeks when employers, unions and government work closely together. Nevertheless, in all these countries the cooperative system is not working as well as it used to. Trade unions in the industrialized countries have been undermined from different directions – the growing number of unemployed, tougher legal restrictions, the fragmenting of the labour force as people work in services or part-time jobs and the movement capital and enterprises to lower wage countries. In developing countries a smaller proportion of the workforce is unionized because there are fewer workers in the formal sector. In Latin America it is only 20%. In Africa it is only 1 or 2%. In Asia, in Singapore and Sri Lanka it goes up to 40%. Compare this with 81% in Sweden.

If in the years ahead trade unions are to be in the forefront of participation in the workplace, they are clearly going to have to reinvent themselves to represent a new generation of workers.

There have now been fifteen editions of the United Nations' Development Report. Together they enable us to draw a fairly accurate portrait of the progress of human society. Contrary to our often tormented images of emaciated children, economies overwhelmed by a tide of debt and mismanagement and even the weather as a hostile force whose spite seems to worsen over time, the truth for most countries and most people is that life the last 30 years has become more liveable and probably, too, more fulfilling. The World Bank has estimated that the world poverty numbers fell from 1.5 billion people in 1981 to to 1.1 billion in 2001 when judged by the frugal $1-a day standard at 1993 purchasing-power parity. Xavier Sala-i-Martin of Columbia University is even more positive. He finds that the global poverty rate fell from 13% to 7%.

The glass of human well-being may not be full but it is certainly not empty. Only in one continent – Africa – is the waterline below the proverbial half-way mark and, in too many countries, sinking. Nevertheless, even in Africa there are enough streams of hope that allow us to believe it can one day emulate the progress made in other parts of the world.

This balance sheet on human development begins optimistically, recording the remarkable steps taken by humanity in improving its condition in an historically very short span of time. But there is an immense job yet undone, and there are many complexities, economic, political and social, that have to be overcome to realize people's true potential. It is there for the unlocking. Only our world's selfish and often archaic institutions, habits and mores keep the billions of people still struggling for a decent living from being able to live in security and comfort.

The essentials of progress over the last three decades are simply put. On average life expectancy has increased from 46 years to 63. The mortality rate of children under five has been halved. Two-thirds of all one-year-olds are now immunised against major childhood diseases. Developing countries make primary health care accessible to 72% of their people, safe water available to 68% and per capita calorie supply as a percentage of requirements increased from 90% to 107%. 75% of the children of the Third World are now immunized, although it is only 50% in sub-Saharan Africa. Adult literacy rose from 46% to 65%. Although the South's average per capita income is only 6% of the North's, its social progress had been so effective that its average life expectancy is now a remarkable 80% of that of the rich industrialised world and its average literacy rate a significant 66%.

The share of the World's people living in extreme poverty is slowly but steadily declining, from 29% in 1990 to 23% in 1999. This progress was driven by the performance of 30 countries with nearly half of the world's population whose economies sustained a 3% annual growth in real income per head between 1990 and 2001.

Often the goals publicised by the UN at its mammoth conferences are derided by critics. While some of the sniping can be justified there are many cases when it misses the mark and works to understate what has been achieved. Smallpox, a World Health Organization goal, was eradicated in 1997. The immunization of 80% of infants against major childhood diseases was achieved in about 70 countries by 1990. Child deaths from diarrhoea (the number one child killer) were cut by half during the 1990s. Infant mortality was cut to less than 120 per 1000 live births in all but twelve developing countries. Polio was eliminated from 110 countries. The number of reported case of guinea-worm, a debilitating tropical disease had fallen by 97% by 2000. During the 1990s child deaths were cut by 20% in a hundred countries; in developing countries as a whole malnutrition dropped by 17%; access to safe water increased by over 4 billion people.

All this has been in half the time it took the industrialised countries to arrive at the same goals when they were developing. It is quite astonishing that this progress has been made despite inadequate resources, an often inhospitable international economic climate and, in many countries, not always the wisest or more responsive of governments. If this kind of momentum can be achieved in less than perfect conditions then it is not hard to imagine the further steps that can be made in a more democratic, socially aware and more responsibly managed world, one that, indeed, now appears to be within our grasp. The scope of the unmet needs on the balance sheet is vast.

800 million people go to bed hungry every day. Nearly 900 million adults still cannot read or write. 1.5 billion people have no access to primary health care. 1.75 billion people are without safe water. 100 million people are completely homeless. A billion people eke out the barest existence in perpetual poverty. 40 million newborn children are not properly immunised. 14 million die every year before they reach the age of five and 150 million are malnourished. Twelve times as many women in the South die in pregnancy or childbirth as in the North.

Two problems seem intractable. The first is what is called "income poverty". For a poor country to halve the proportion of people living on $1 demands a minimum growth rate of nearly 4%. But over the last decade only 24 Third World countries have grown this fast, although that does include China and India that contain well over half of the developing world's population. This leaves 127 countries, admittedly many of them with rather small populations but still containing a third of the world's people. Around thirty countries in Africa and the former Soviet Union have gone backwards the last few years and their share of their people in poverty has almost certainly increased. In Africa it is the coincidence of the onslaught of Aids and the rise in armed conflicts, combined with usually high amounts of foreign debt, that have pushed so many countries into reverse. Nevertheless, because of rapid progress in India and China, the world's two most populous countries the UN target for reducing by half the proportion of people living on less than a $1 a day is likely to be reached.

The second major problem is child mortality. Although 85 countries are making progress towards the UN's target date of reducing levels of under-five mortality rates by two thirds by 2015, these 85 contain less than a quarter of the world's people.

The poorest countries are highly concentrated in sub-Saharan Africa. Twenty three of Africa's forty-four countries are failing in both growth and achieving this elementary target of income per head and a reduction of child mortality.

It is in Africa, first and foremost, that we see most clearly the elemental fight for food. Although the world over enormous progress has been made and some 57 countries with half the world's people have halved the share of people living in hunger or are on track to do so by 2015, Africa's lack of progress pushes the average for the developing world right down. During the 1990s the number of people living in hunger fell by just six million a year. At this snail's pace it will take another 130 years to rid the world of hunger.

Nevertheless, even if poor, a careful use of resources can achieve wonders. Benin in West Africa which has a GDP per head of only $990 looks as if it will have all its primary school age children in school by 2015. During the 1990s

Ghana reduced the percentage of its people suffering from hunger from 35% to 12%. In contrast oil-rich Qatar with 20 times the income is falling far behind. It is a similar story comparing Tanzania in East Africa and Guatemala in Central America. Guatemala has more than seven times the national income of Tanzania, but it is Tanzania that is shooting ahead with its aim to give girls the same chance of going to primary school as boys. Guatemala is far behind.

There is no good reason why the essential goals of human endeavour should not be achieved for nearly everyone within half a generation. We have both the knowledge and the resources. But it does mean a different perspective, both domestically and internationally. It means cutting back on the military. It means winding down inefficient public enterprises and ensuring that government subsidies are actually aimed at the very poorest. It means emphasising personal priorities and appropriate spending patterns. It means sound and judicious governance, involving people in decisions which affect them and winning their acquiescence by demonstrating competence and fairness. Improved incomes are also important. There can be no sustained momentum over the years without a rise in income.

Any society on earth could do so much more than it does now if it paid more attention to the essential policies which are fundamental and life-giving to human development. Many societies are so distorted and so degraded by their failure to relieve poverty that their room for creative manoeuvre is almost infinite.

If we look at these criteria of progress in more detail the course of this argument becomes even more obvious. Life expectancy, as mentioned, has risen in thirty years from 46 to 63 years, but it is an average and inside the average there is a world of differences. In Latin America life spans are only two years less than that of the industrialised countries, 69 years.

But in Africa life expectancy is a short 51 years and in Ethiopia only 42 years. In Asia life expectancy is 64 years, but this average has been inflated by the performance of one country, China, which has seen a remarkable jump from 47 years to 70.

Overall life expectancy walks hand in hand with a country's income level. But there are enough exceptions to prove that if a country is intent on putting life before riches it can achieve a significant improvement even in modest circumstances. Sri Lanka with a GNP of only $400 per head has a life expectancy of 70 years, the same as the United Arab Emirates whose GNP per head is $15,830.

This contrast is even more telling when one looks at infant mortality rates. Overall, in developing countries, the infant mortality rate has fallen from 149 deaths per 1,000 births in 1960 to under 71 today. But a country like Jamaica has got it down to 15 compared with Brazil, a country with twice the capita income but nearly four times as many infant deaths per 1,000 births. In Africa, too, one can find the same contrasts. Mauritius, which has the lowest infant and child mortality rates in Africa, has pulled down its deaths of children under five from 104 deaths per thousand to 29, better than higher income countries like South Africa and oil-rich Gabon.

Improvements in the literacy rates have transformed the ability to read and write within a generation. Not only has this given people access to knowledge for improving their own immediate lives but also for shaping a more informed and shrewd opinion about the world outside. The literacy rate of men rose from 53% in 1970 to 71% in the first half of the 1980s. Women have lagged behind, a rate of only 50%, but on the other hand the number of girls going to school has been increasing more rapidly than boys. Even Africa has seen especially fast progress in adult literacy, but it has only reached 47%. Latin America, in contrast, is up to 85%. Asia is in between at 59%, an average held down by the very poor progress in Bangladesh, Pakistan, Nepal and Afghanistan. Indeed, three quarters of the 900 million illiterates are concentrated in Asia's most populous countries: India, China, Pakistan, Bangladesh and Indonesia.

The growth in per capita income has been more uneven than the rates for literacy and child mortality. Between 1965 and 1980 the average growth in the developing regions was a healthy 2.9%, to be followed by a growth rate of 2.5% during 1989-1990. But the recession in the industrialised countries in the early years of the last decade, compounded by debt, climate and management problems, particularly in Africa and Latin America, cut deeply into the rate of progress. In Africa, incomes per head declined by 2.4% a year and in Latin America by 0.7% a year. Wealth is not well distributed in most developing countries. With few exceptions, a small fraction of the population gets a disproportionate share of the national income. Land too, particularly in Asia and Latin America, is inequitably distributed.

Nevertheless, overall, the percentage of people living in absolute poverty has fallen, although at not a fast enough rate to diminish the total number of poor. And in Africa the percentage of poor has actually increased and now amounts to about half the total population. Asia has made the most progress and it is also where the most people live. Not surprisingly, this is where most of the very poor live – three quarters of a billion people. The majority of the poor live in the countryside and poverty is increasing fastest among women. So much more could be done if the perspective and priorities of governments could change, however poor their countries be.

Food, health, water, sanitation and education are the basic elements of human survival and fulfilment. Without these at a minimal satisfactory level, humankind does not fully progress. In most parts of the Third World there have been significant advances in the availability of all of these. Only in Africa progress slipped back on a wide front.

Food production has made a quite noticeable advance. The daily supply of calories in the developing world increased from 90% of total requirements in 1965 to 107% in 1985. The dark lining in the silver cloud is the fact that the countries which needed to improve most have increased food availability least. For the poorest countries the supply of calories increased from 88% to 90% of total requirements. At least sixteen African countries saw an actual decline.

Hunger today may be stunting the lives of as many as 800 million people. While Africa as a continent is the most hit, the largest concentration of numbers of hungry is in Asia.

During the 1980s and 1990s a number of developing countries came close to providing primary health care for all – South Korea, Costa Rica, Jamaica, Tunisia and Jordan in particular. But most developing countries fall far short of this target. On average only 72% of the population in developing countries had access to primary health care in 1990. The number of doctors does not necessarily correspond with good health. Latin America has proportionately more doctors and nurses than any other region, but only 86% of people have access to health services. Kuwait has more doctors per person than Switzerland, yet its infant mortality rate is four times higher.

Progress in improving water and sanitation has been much slower than in health. Yet for many countries a dollar spent on clean water and good sewers would produce a greater improvement in the quality of life than a dollar spent on doctors or hospitals. Nevertheless, by 1986 about 70% of the population in the developing world had access to safe water, up from 35% a decade earlier. During the 1980s access to safe water increased by 130% and access to sanitation by 266%, both much more than in the 1970s and the 1990s.

Just as it seemed that modern science could short-cut many of the hazards of underdevelopment, a new disease has torn many poor countries asunder, both in lives lost and broken and, cumulatively, in the loss of some of society's most educated and active members. The HIV (human immune deficiency virus) epidemic has infected around 8 to 10 million adults and half of them are likely to develop Aids sometime in the next decade. It is estimated that a further 15 million new cases of HIV infection will be added in the present decade – more than half in the developing world, with a high proportion in eastern and central Africa and the likelihood of a rapid rate of the growth of infected people in India and Thailand. Apart from the loss of usually young life, the financial implications in terms of medical costs are staggering. The costs per patient range from one-third to twice the per capita national income in Tanzania to ten times as much in Zaire.

Educational improvement, by comparison, is another success story. By the end of the 1980s an impressive 80% of all children of primary school age were enrolled. Several countries in the developing world were close to the goal of universal primary education. Even in Africa progress has been rapid; half the children now attend both primary and secondary school. In Latin America and the Caribbean the number of girls in primary school equalled the number of boys. In East and Southeast Asia in the newly industrialising countries 90% of both boys and girls attend secondary school. Elsewhere, however, female enrolment laps a distance behind that of boys.

Tertiary educational opportunities have also increased, rapidly so in the Asian newly industrialising countries and Latin America. Indeed, some Latin Americans appear to do better than the old industrialising countries, although, in practice, standards are often less rigorous. All this progress bodes well for the future economic opportunities of the South. With four times as many students in primary school and twice as many in secondary school as the North its competitive edge is in the making.

All these advances together unequivocally suggest that for most of the world's people life is steadily becoming more liveable. Sadly, however, population growth eats away at many improvements and means that a growing number of people, albeit a smaller percentage of the whole, continue to suffer from severe deprivation.

Since 1960 the population of the developing world has doubled. In Africa in particular this phenomenal rate of increase shows little sign of abating. Elsewhere, however, the rate of growth is falling.

The question for the developing countries, ever more pressing given the difficult economic environment they confront, is how to maximise the use of the resources they have. Above all, how to find productive employment for their ever-growing, albeit better educated, work force. It is not just population growth that has pushed up the number of the labour force, it is partly the sharp increase in women seeking paid work and also poorer families trying to increase the number of income earners in the family.

Many of these new entrants into the labour market are finding work in the so-called informal sector – in Africa it accounts for 75% of new jobs – where a job is nothing more than a corner stand on a pavement or the backroom of a house.

Nevertheless, education is paying dividends. Even in Africa the private returns to primary education are as high as 43%. The returns on female education are even higher, leading to reduced fertility, lower population growth, reduced child mortality, lower school dropout rates and improved family nutrition.

One study of farmers in Korea, Malaysia and Thailand showed that, using modern technology, they increased their output by 3% a year for every additional year of schooling they received. The higher level of education for the farmers of the Indian Punjab explains in part why their productivity is higher than their neighbours across the border in Pakistani Punjab.

One consequence of improved education is greater knowledge of the world outside and of the economic alternatives it offers. This, together with improved and relatively cheaper means of travel, means that it is possible to journey far afield in search of new opportunities.

There is both a "brain drain" and a "brawn drain". The developing countries have lost not only eager young workers with few skills but also many of their mostly highly educated, their "best and brightest", depriving their countries of vital skills and energy. Nevertheless, their remittances to relatives and savings accounts back home are often an important source of foreign exchange. Some countries can afford the exodus more than others, but Africa in particular has seen the upper ranks of some professions practically decimated. Altogether, within the span of a generation, some 40 to 50 million people have moved from the South to the North.

The above review of the progress of the developing world, positive as it is in terms of accomplishments for many countries, would have presented a more upbeat picture if so many countries did not succumb to such severe inequalities – between urban and rural areas, between men and women, and between rich and poor both in income levels and in their access to public services.

For a start, two-thirds of the people live in the rural areas. But in many countries they receive less than a quarter of the resources spent on education, health and sanitation and they earn 25% to 50% less than those who live in the towns and cities. Political and economic power, particularly in the early stages of development, is urban concentrated. The consequence is a very lop-sided, often self-destructive kind of development:

- Infant mortality: In several Central American countries the rate is 30% to 50% higher in rural areas than in the towns.
- Life expectancy: Rural Mexicans can only expect to live 59 years; those in the town 73.
- Nutrition: Malnutrition, despite the often easier availability of food, often runs 50% higher in the rural areas.
- Literacy: In some African and Asian countries rural illiteracy rates are twice those of the town.
- Health: Hospitals with sophisticated equipment are concentrated in the town; people in the rural areas often have to make do with simple clinics, and there are fewer health facilities per head of population than in the towns.
- Water and sanitation: Here the extremes are even greater. On the average rural people have half the services of the town-dweller. In Brazil access to sanitation services was 86 times higher in the towns.
- Income: Again the discrepancies can be as much as double. In Africa it runs much higher – in Nigeria by a factor of almost five.

Male-female differentials are another source of severe inequality in many countries. From the 1960s onwards women did share in the progress afoot in many developing societies, but in a number important respects life did not improve for them as fast as it did for men.

Women, disproportionately, carry the burden of work. Throughout the Third World women are not, as widely perceived, merely mothers and housewives but they are often a critical contributor to the family's food supply. In Africa in many cases women are expected to produce or purchase nearly all the food eaten at home. Women typically work about 25% more hours than men. In rural India it is as much as 15 hours more a week.

In many developing countries more girls than boys die young, the reverse of the situation in the industrialised countries. Girls get less to eat, receive less medical care and when pregnant do not receive the care and attention sufficient to minimise the maternal mortality rate. No other North-South gap is wider than the maternal mortality rate. In the industrialised countries it is often less than 10 per 100,000 live births. In some developing countries it is as high as 1,000.

Educational opportunities for women still lag a distance behind those of men. For the developing world as a whole the female literacy rate is three quarters that of the male; in many countries it is more than that. However slowly, the gap is beginning to narrow.

The social dividend of investing in women's education is immense. In Bangladesh child mortality is five times higher for children of mothers with no education than for those with seven or more years of schooling. Better educated women also have much smaller families.

The income gap that most tears at the fabric of society is the one between rich and poor. Many developing countries have a far worse income distribution than the United States, the most unequal of the industrialised countries. In Brazil, a relatively rich developing country, whose per capita income is eight times that of India, the expected life span of its poor is no higher than the average in India. In Mexico the top 10% live 20 years longer than the rest of the population. In Colombia infants in poor families are twice as likely to die as those of the rich. In rural Punjab in India in landless families the child mortality rate is 36% higher than among land-owners. In one Indian village in the south the literacy rate was 90% for Brahmins and 10% for the lower classes. In Zimbabwe child malnutrition is severe when average family income is $51, mild at $168 and non-existent if over $230.

Government social expenditure on public services if carefully managed – as it was in Sri Lanka during the 1960s and 1970s – can do much to even out such severe disparities. But there are many examples where – as in Egypt – free or subsidised services do not reach many of the poor. They are concentrated on the urban areas and information about them is more accessible to the better educated who then manage to pre-empt the benefits. Moreover, it is overlooked that even free services have a cost. To get to a school or a clinic takes both time and, if it's a bus ride away, money. The very poor have neither.

Too often, government expenditures are not even targeted to reach the poor. In the Philippines in the early 1980s, annual subsidies to private hospitals catering to upper-income families exceeded the total resources appropriated to primary health care and mass health programmes, including malaria and schistosomiasis eradication.

If one combines this review of urban-rural, male-female and rich-poor disparities, it is obvious that those most severely affected by inequality are poor, rural women. There are around one billion of them and their numbers are growing. Many are illiterate. Their incomes have not increased and in many countries have fallen. They receive no medical attention at child bearing and their children are bereft of health care.

All this reminds us of the tremendous task still before us, despite the giant steps the world has taken over the last thirty years. Sadly, the opportunities realized during the 1960s and 1970s began to disappear in the 1980s, particularly in Africa and Latin America, rather less so in Asia. A growing mountain of debt compelled a large number of developing countries to take their foot off the economic and social accelerator. Indeed, for a number of them it meant going into reverse. The total external debt of developing countries multiplied thirteen-fold over the last two decades from $100 billion in 1970 to $1,350 billion in 1990. The debt became so huge and new lending so small that the net flow was actually reversed – towards the richer countries. Between 1983 and 1989 rich-country creditors received a staggering $242 billion in net transfers. The debt was highly concentrated. Over half was held by just 20 countries, with Brazil, Mexico and Argentina holding the most. Overall, the two continents that have truly suffered massive economic setbacks because of their debt burden are Latin America and (sub-Saharan) Africa. The debt of sub-Saharan Africa is 100% of its GNP. In Latin America it is 50%.

Even today, after two decades of retrenchment and adjustment, followed by some significant debt relief for the poorest countries, only some of these countries are back to where they were twenty years ago. In seventeen Latin American and Caribbean countries per capita income fell during the 1980s. In Africa income per head fell by more than a quarter. In Asia, however, only a few countries were severely hurt by recession. China and Southeast Asia made rapid strides and South Asia also improved its per capita income considerably.

Although we only have piecemeal data, there are enough bits and pieces of evidence to suggest that for many countries the decline in infant mortality rates was slowed or even reduced. Many households lost income and had to cut expenditure on essentials such as food and medicine. In Ghana in 1984 even upper-level civil servants could only afford two-thirds of the least-cost diet to meet nutritional needs. In Dar-es-Salaam, Tanzania, over half the women in low-income households reported that they'd been forced to cut down from three to two meals a day. In Jamaica in 1986 a family of four needed two to three times the minimum wage to be able to afford even a minimal diet.

Wage earners bore the brunt of the crisis. In Africa and Latin America wage cuts of a third to a half were not exceptional. In Latin America unemployment grew by 6% a year and in Africa by 10%. Rapid food price rises added to the squeeze. The removal of food subsidies, together with devaluation and decontrol, pushed the rate of increase up faster than other prices.

Governments felt forced to cut back on social services – Senegal by nearly a half in the first five years of the decade. Bolivia's health expenditure was cut by 70%. Some countries by carefully budgeting, controlling military expenditure, together with specially tuned employment and nutrition schemes, did manage to protect the most vulnerable groups from the worst of the downward pressure – Zimbabwe, Botswana, Costa Rica, Chile and South Korea. Some countries, like Jamaica, which started well by redirecting resources towards priority areas, were finally overwhelmed by the scale of the retrenchment they had to make. It was absolutely impossible to maintain social spending at the accustomed level.

In the 1990s when there should have been another surge in progress if the prophets of globalisation were right the true story was rather different. For many countries, building on the setbacks of the 1980s, the 1990s were a decade of despair. In Latin America and the Caribbean, the Arab states, central and Eastern Europe and sub-Saharan Africa the number of people trying to survive on less than a $1 a day increased. Some 54 countries are poorer now than they were in 1990. In 21 a larger proportion of their people is going hungry. In 14 more children died before the age of five. In 12 primary school enrolments shrank. In 34 life expectancy fell. In 21 countries the HDI decreased. Such reversals in previous decades were rare.

In the 1990s average per capita income growth was less than 3% in 125 developing and transition (i.e. ex Soviet) countries and in 54 of them average per capita income fell. Of the 54 countries with declining incomes 20 are from sub-Saharan Africa, 17 from Eastern Europe and the Commonwealth of Independent States, 6 from Latin America and the Caribbean, 6 from East Asia and the Pacific and 5 from the Arab states. These failing countries fall into two main groups- the ex communists of the old Soviet Union who could quickly recover and the permanent group dominated by sub-Saharan Africa. In the latter case it was the spread of Aids more than any other single factor that was responsible for the appalling setbacks.

These enormous and widespread setbacks occurred even though there was almost continuous boom in the western world during the 1990s and many politicians, especially in America argued that increased globalisation would lift all boats on this great tide of prosperity. It didn't appear to. Or rather, it was limited to the 30 successful countries which admittedly, containing India and China, were nearly half the world's population.

One awful thing is clear: rapid economic change, even in slow-moving economies, all too quickly overturns traditional norms and values and it also can produce sharp economic and social inequity. It can make people feel insecure and vulnerable, depriving them of both dignity and optimism.

In April 2000 two researchers at the Inter-American Development Bank, Mayra Buvinic and Andrew Morrison published in *Foreign Policy* an alarming essay. They showed that homicide rates around the world increased by more than 50% between 1980-84 and 1990-94. In the industrialised world the increase was 15%. It was up by 80% in Latin America and 112% in the Arab world. However, both Asia and the Pacific, where the social controls of the family are arguably the strongest, had declining rates, although in China, with its fast industrialisation and intense inward migration, there was a sharp increase too. More up to date figures, although not available for every part of the globe, show that the rate of homicides has accelerated, particularly in Latin America and Africa.

Universally, emotional negligence or physical abuse in early childhood is obviously a crucible for the development of violence in the next generation. By the 1980s, after two decades of fast growth in population growth, in many parts of the Third World more than one fifth of the population was aged 18-24. Despite this tide peaking nearly two decades ago, homicide rates have not ebbed. Once aggressive behaviour is embedded it becomes difficult to quickly root it out. It both transmits itself to the next generation and stays ingrained in the present generation, even as they age. Moreover, often society starts to tolerate more violence than it used to. One can see one vivid example of this with British football violence. Society took it on the chin for too long; it took the authorities the best part of a decade to move to try and control and suppress it.

Cities, especially the new upstart parts of them, have few built-in social controls. It is in these mushrooming cities that the number of children born out of wedlock has increased most rapidly, particularly in Africa and Latin America. An unwanted child is an extremely vulnerable creature; the explosion in the number of street children in many parts of the world means that growing up right now are hundreds of thousands who owe little loyalty to the normal constraints of society. In Africa, according to UNICEF estimates, there are more than 40,000 children and adolescents fighting in the wars of the eastern Congo. Altogether it is estimated that there 300,000 children under 18 serving as regular or guerrilla soldiers, porters, spies, sexual slaves and even suicide commandos in over 50 countries. Carol Bellamy, UNICEF's executive director, has said that 540 million children, or one in four children in the world, live with violence that might erupt at any time, or with displacement in their own countries.

A recent US study argued that increases in abortion rates are associated with declining murder rates. Despite its controversial conclusion, it has the ring of truth. Anything that cuts the number of unwanted children may have a benign affect.

Of all the faults of globalization, nothing is worse than the export of violent and prurient images by cinema, video, the web and television to friable societies who have neither the background nor the "sophistication" to separate fact from fiction. Second is the drug trade, and no one is more to blame than the main consuming nations who have criminalised the buying and selling of drugs to the point of counter-productiveness. A free market would pull the rug from underneath the black marketers and allow resources to be switched to educating and helping abusers out of their habit.

Organised crime is a highly profitable billion-dollar business. Meanwhile, the costs of policing and insurance are mushrooming, siphoning off resources that could be put to better use elsewhere. The drug trade is probably the most profitable criminal activity of all. Drugs can destroy people's health. But the vast amount of money going into the pockets of the drug barons and their marketing forces is criminalising and corrupting whole societies, exacerbating political violence and discrediting or undermining both the police and the judiciary. It is estimated that over 50 million people imbibe drugs. Two million people earn their living from drug production and trade. The value of this trade exceeds that of oil and is only surpassed by that in arms.

Drug abuse takes its toll on its users. They are a third less productive then non-users, three times more likely to be involved in accidents at work and twice as likely to be absent from work. Drug abuse leads to miscarriages and infant deaths. Intravenous drug takers also risk and promote the spread of Aids. Despite all the attempts at control, the incentives for producers are enormous and the number of consumers is expanding. The US alone spends $2.5 billion in a single year on law enforcement against drug production and trafficking, with not much to show for the effort.

In summing up this discourse on human development one thing is more than clear: each of the Third World's continents has its own story. Asia with 70% of the world's population has seen phenomenal progress economically, socially and politically over the last three decades. Life expectancy has increased from 46 to 64 years and the number of children in school has increased from 57% to 71%. Nevertheless, the differences between regions are so large. We can see the picture more clearly if we look at Southeast Asia and East Asia first and South Asia second.

Some countries in East and Southeast Asia have achieved fairly rapid reductions in infant mortality – around 5% a year, in particular, China, Singapore, Taiwan and Hong Kong. Around 85% of the region's children are immunized – a higher proportion than the average for the industrialised countries.

In several countries people can now expect to live beyond 70. At the same time contraceptive practice is commonplace – 66% of all couples use it, compared with 70% in the industrialised countries. Not surprisingly, population growth is much lower than the average for developing countries.

One important reason for this general state of rising well-being were the decisions made years ago to redistribute land more equitably and to emphasise employment-intensive economic growth.

Now many of those countries, like the industrialised countries which they are close to emulating, are building future growth on the foundations of high levels of health and education and advanced diversified, production structures. South Korea, Taiwan, Singapore and Hong Kong are the four countries most advanced in this way. But Thailand and Malaysia are not too far behind.

South Asia, while not exhibiting such spectacular success, has also made measurable progress the last 30 years. Bangladesh raised its average life expectancy from 40 to 53 years but, nevertheless, this is still ten years lower than the average for developing countries. But immunization coverage of one-year-old children has shot up from 1% to 60%. In Sri Lanka it is now 89%. In comparison, Pakistan, which has about the same GNP per capita as Sri Lanka, has a life expectancy 13 years less.

Inequality remains severe throughout the region, between rich and poor, male and female and between different ethnic groups and regions. In the rural Punjab landless families have an infant mortality rate 36% higher than those of landowning families.

Latin America and the Caribbean have been the site of impressive achievements in human development, despite the rather dramatic slow-down in the rise of well being during the difficult 1980s. Between 1960 and 1980 the less than five mortality rate dropped from 157 to 72 per 1,000 live births. Average life expectancy is now only seven years short of the industrialised countries. In Barbados, Costa Rica and Cuba people actually live longer than they do in the industrialised countries.

The region has the highest education levels of the developing world. Some countries, Argentina, Barbados, Guyana, Jamaica, Uruguay, Trinidad and Tobago, have literacy rates of over 95%. With 40 scientists and technicians per 1,000 people the region is well above the developing world average of ten.

The economic collapse of the 1980s resulted in an immense set-back. In some countries child malnutrition and infant mortality started to rise again. Moreover, in good times and in bad, the fruits of life in a number of countries are shared badly. The top one-fifth of the population in Brazil earns 26 times more than the bottom fifth. In Peru the bottom 40% gets only 13% of the national income. (In Morocco it is 21%, in India 20% and Indonesia 23%).

Some countries, too, still have a long way to go, even to match the regional average. Only just over half Nicaragua's population has access to safe water and in Bolivia, Haiti, El Salvador and Paraguay it is much less than even half. Likewise, Bolivia, Paraguay and El Salvador have very low rates of school enrolment.

Despite appearances to the contrary the region does not spend much on its military; its ration of military to health and education expenditures is less than one-third the average for the developing world. But money is wasted in loss-making public enterprises, which tend to benefit the wealthy.

The revolution in oil prices has given many of the states of the Middle East and North Africa some of the developing world's fastest income increases. At the same time there has been a remarkable improvement in human development. Life expectancy has jumped from 47 to 62 years, mortality rates for children under five have been reduced by almost two-thirds, and access to health services is the highest in the developing world and access to safe water second only to Latin America. Nevertheless, there still remain 60 million adults who are illiterate and there are 40 million people living below the poverty line.

The countries that have oil shot far ahead of those without. GNP per capita varies from $480 in Sudan to $15,770 in the United Arab Emirates. But even those oil-rich countries that now have reasonably good human development have index rankings that lag far behind other countries with a similar GNP.

Interestingly, some of the non-oil-rich Arab countries, Tunisia, Lebanon, Syria and Jordan, although they have relatively modest levels of GNP, have a better income distribution than their oil-rich neighbours and levels of human development higher than average for the region.

Political instability and big military expenditures threaten the region's future and the chance of upgrading health and education in line with the region's wealth.

Inequities in the region have led to large numbers of migrant workers, both skilled and unskilled, leaving the poorer Arab countries for the richer. While their remittances are an important source of hard currency for their home country, the migrants drain from their homeland much needed skills and vitality.

Before the arrival of Aids sub-Saharan Africa had taken important strides forward in its human development. Infant mortality rates had fallen and life expectancy had increased. Adult literacy had increased by two-thirds. But ravaged by Aids life expectancy has gone into reverse. Botswana, once the fastest developing country in Africa, is now the most Aids-affected country where more than a third of adults have HIV/Aids, and a child born today can only expect to live 36 years – about half as long as they would if the disease did not exist.

For most of the 1980s economic growth in Africa was less than population growth, although there are now many signs that the trend is reversing. More than half the population has no access to public health services; two-thirds lack safe water; eighteen million people suffer from sleeping sickness; malaria kills hundreds of thousands of children every year; Aids is spreading fast, devastating many families; and in the poorest countries a quarter or more of the children die before the age of five.

We should learn from our mistakes – and there have been enough mistakes for everyone to take some share of the blame. "Trickle down economics" which simply depended on the creation of wealth as fast as possible has not worked. Sometimes growth helps poor people, but sometimes it does not. And despite all the talk of the marvels of globalization we can say with some assurance that sometimes it helps poor people and sometimes it does not. It all depends on how globalization is managed. As the Nobel Laureate in Economics, Joseph Stiglitz, has put it, "in some cases it is not even to liberalize or not to liberalize. There is considerable evidence that while speculative capital flows increase economic growth they increase economic instability. And at what pace to liberalize trade and what policies should accompany it? A World Bank study showed that Africa was worse off after the Uruguay Round. We always must ask: Are there pro-poor growth strategies that do more to reduce poverty as they promote growth? And are there growth strategies that increase poverty as they promote growth … [as happened] in Latin America in the 1990s."

There are many reasons that explain why economic development continues to bypass many of the world's poorest peoples and places. Poor governance arguably has to head the list. Whilst in the early stages of growth a country may get away with a benign dictatorship (but for every one benign there have been a dozen malign), by the time economies become more sophisticated democratic governance appears to produce the best results. Economic success is correlated with democratic institutions.

Next in importance is the lack of a more level playing field in the international trading system. Rich countries block the agricultural exports from poorer countries and then compound the problem by subsidizing the exports of their own farmers. The simpler industrial exports – textiles in particular – suffer similar problems.

Many poor countries, now attempting to introduce more sensitive policies, find they are hamstrung by the debts run up by previous regimes. Debt relief is invariably too little or too late.

Size also is important. A small, landlocked country, with high population growth is of little interest to potential foreign investors. This is why so many African countries face a dismal future, for even with the best will in the world their development is going to be slow.

Tropical countries in particular carry the heavy burden of depleted soils and degraded ecosystems. Endemic tropical diseases regularly take a toll that countries in more temperate climes rarely have experienced. Malaria and tuberculosis are particularly widespread and vicious diseases and now has been added to these, particularly in Africa, the pandemic of HIV/Aids.

Nevertheless, even the poorest countries can make a great amount of progress if they introduce good governance and concentrate their own investment wisely, whilst receiving carefully directed and well-managed assistance from richer countries. Half a dozen issues need to be concentrated on. First and foremost is the need to invest in human development – in nutrition, health, education, water and sanitation. Only in this way can there be a productive and healthy labour force able to stand up to the rigours of the world economy. Second, priority needs to be given to small farmers, the backbone of most poor countries. Third, countries need to invest in infrastructure, power, roads, ports and communications that will attract new investment. Fourth, countries must encourage the private sector, especially small and medium-sized enterprises. Fifth, they must never overlook, as development accelerates, the need to protect the biodiversity and ecosystems that support life. Sixth and most important is the need for people to feel involved in the destiny of their country. This means democracy and free expression, which includes allowing girls and women the same rights as boys and men so that society can work on all cylinders, rather than half. Indeed, if one wanted to single out from a complex, interlocking list of what is most needed one would say the two priorities for most poor people are a supply of clear, pure, running water and the education of their young girls. Between them these two items can do more for development in its early stages that any other single policy.

We should also be more conscious than economists usually are of what makes for human happiness. One illuminating analysis was made by Robert Wright in *Prospect* magazine where he compared happiness in the Third World with that of the rich world. "Indonesian workers", he writes, "want to raise their income by moving from farm fields to Nike factories. Nike customers want a shoe that has not just a generic "air sole" (old hat) but a "tuned air unit" in the heel and "zoom air" in the forefoot."

The main part of his thesis is more seriously straightforward: "Once a nation achieves a fairly comfortable standard of living, more income brings little if any additional happiness". The point where wealth ceases to imply more happiness is, he argues, around $10,000 per caput annually – roughly where Greece, Portugal and South Korea are today. So in terms of psychological pay-offs, the benefits of globalization go overwhelmingly to the world's lower classes, nations with a per capita income of under $10,000.

Still, he concedes, even if in wealthy societies the really affluent are a bit happier there is a per capita income level beyond which money brings "declining utilitarian bang per buck". People adjust quickly to changing living standards. Fifty years ago in many western societies central heating was considered a luxury; today it is viewed as an essential. Even so, it raises the question if making more money improves happiness, even a bit, why doesn't the US collectively get happier as it gets richer? According to polls Americans are less happy than they were in 1973. The answer seems to be that what gratifies people at this level is not their absolute income but their ability to point to an improved relative position – I'm better off than Mr Jones. One result of this is that developed societies may tend to work too hard in order to consume more material goods and so consume too little leisure and thus enjoy life less

So in this situation one man's gain is another man's loss. A zero-sum game. Compare this with developing countries where as people become more educated and healthier, have better nutrition and build, as is usual with economic progress, a more democratic society more disposed to respecting human rights, they increase their happiness without reducing anyone else's. However, in this mad world, fast economic progress for the poorer nations can at an early stage in development throw up problems that neutralise some of the happiness achieved – pollution, crime, abandoned children and so on.

But, as I have argued above, if societies are sensible they can with good human development policies reap the harvest of development without paying so many of its costs.

Human development, we can see, does not necessarily mean uniform human progress. The infant mortality rate may fall but human confidence and security may diminish as other changes alter the bonds and bindings of traditional life. Economic progress itself is neither a straightforward matter nor an uninterrupted push forward. Its uncertainties, upheavals and setbacks can create more misery than its momentum creates happiness. And the wide discrepancies between North and South and between regions within the South are also sources of potential tension.

If our goal is the betterment of human life we are compelled to work at many levels. Economic growth certainly, but at the same time ensuring a fair and reasonable distribution of its fruits. We need to be aware of all the other elements in society that need to go forward at the same pace as national income, if not faster. We have to realize that even the poorest country can do much by a better use of its scarce resources. We also have to watch carefully and attentively for the harmful side-effects and pitfalls that are the inevitable corollary of forward momentum. Only if all this is done can we be sure that humanity as a whole advances and development is not just for the benefit of a privileged minority.

# 10 Does Africa Have a Future?

The African famine of 1985 that engulfed almost half the continent was one of the handful of great watershed events since the Second World War. It was the most severe famine since the Bengal famine of 1943. But more significant than that, it was the first time that public opinion the world over – East and West, North and South – had ever been quite so roused and so forthcoming about a common issue. Those who, five years before, at the time of the Cambodian famine, had spoken of "famine fatigue" were proved incredibly wrong. It was as if nobody remembered the confusion and chaos of that event, the siphoning off of the food by the fighting forces and the cynical use of it to rebuild the strength of Pol Pot and the Vietnamese to fight another day.

No matter that the surface evidence suggested that history might repeat itself – there was civil war in Ethiopia and in Sudan, Angola and Mozambique there were Russians arming one side, and the CIA or the South Africans often arming the other, and governments run by cynical tough-minded men who had little compunction about using food as a weapon of war – public opinion was not put off. Never has the wave of human generosity in the wake of a famine been so enormous. Never had there been so many extraordinary fundraising events. From great pop concerts with half the musicians playing in Philadelphia and half in London to mass races with 20 million runners starting simultaneously in 78 countries. For once the public pushed the media to report more than it planned to. People wanted to know and they wanted to give.

There are probably a dozen reasons for this, but one stands out above all the others. The outside world realized that the African continent was in a deep crisis that would not go away even if civil war ended tomorrow. Africa was a continent on a downward slide and had been for some time. This famine was the culmination of years of political upheavals, misrule, false starts and false practices and policies that were ill thought out and poorly applied.

Few men and women in the street knew the details of this, but they appeared to instinctively to know that this hunger was not just because of one more war or one more season without rain. It was a profound and revealing manifestation of the disturbance of Africa's inner equilibrium. It was, perhaps, unless something dramatic were done, the beginning of the end.

People gave and governments were pushed to give. Long-standing cynicism about the value of international cooperation gave way to the need for effective coordination. The Secretary General of the United Nations established a special emergency office to pull sense and direction out of the multiplicity of contributions. For the first time in many a year the UN was everyone's first choice.

Africa's predicament is peculiarly severe – of that there can be little doubt. Every other Third World continent has broken through the sound barrier of economic growth. China, India and Indonesia, the despairing basket cases of yesteryear, between them carrying two thirds of the developing world's population, are pushing ahead fast with growth rates that make the progress of the now industrialized world look pitifully slow at the time they engaged in industrial and agricultural take-off in the nineteenth century. Even more dramatic is the pace of economic advance of the smaller Asian countries – South Korea, Pakistan, Sri Lanka, Taiwan, Singapore and Hong Kong. In Latin American, despite immense political and economic upheavals, progress also has been rapid. Latin America as a whole has doubled its income in twenty years.

Both Asia and Latin America have grown well ahead of their population explosion. The number of very poor are falling, not only proportionately but absolutely too.

In Africa it was the reverse. In the seven years since the oil price hike of 1979, following the Iranian revolution, only a handful of countries experienced economic growth. The vast majority had population growth rates that were outstripping their food production and half were experiencing the ravages of famine.

Yet for most of Africa's recent history it had not been always like this. Since the days of independence, in the 1960's, Africa for the most part moved forward. Whilst there were no "miracles", as in Asia or South America, there was discernable progress. Some countries, in particular Ivory Coast, Malawi, Cameroon and Botswana, did exceedingly well. The majority moved forward more slowly. Even so they kept their heads above the rising tide of population growth and were strong enough, much to the outside world's surprise, to weather the first oil hike rise in 1973 when prices quadrupled almost over night and the western world went into recession, reducing its demand for African raw materials.

Nevertheless, beneath the appearance of progress much was crumbling, unnoticed by both African governments and outside observers.

Investment was being concentrated in the urban areas. The rural areas in some countries were ignored and in others milked lopsidedly. Too many African countries thought their future lay in industrialization and this they attempted to do, creating inefficient, expensive projects behind high tariff walls. For the most part their products were shoddy and the overheads enormous.

More often than not they were state enterprises, dependent on subsidies from the central government. Because someone had to pay for these, farmers were encouraged, but in a narrow and exploitative way, to produce crops for export, not food for home consumption. An emphasis on earning hard foreign exchange was encouraged – the growing of coffee, tea, rubber, cocoa etc. – but often the farmers saw as little as half the selling price. The balance went into the government exchequer.

Investment in food production was minimal. Food was relatively cheap to import and indeed food aid from Europe and North America was plentiful and available. Consequently, the price paid to African farmers for food was miserably low and the investment in facilities to take their produce to market was minimal.

Whatever the political system – socialist, capitalist, democratic or dictatorial – the urban populations carried most weight with the politicians. What scarce investment resources there were heavily skewed towards the town. Even in Tanzania, where the political leadership argued that the future of the country lay in the rural areas, this was so, as were pricing policies that continued to provide cheap food for urban workers at the expense of the farmers who grew it.

Meanwhile, the pressures steadily mounted. Population was growing and most countries did little about it, often arguing that their problem was Africa's wide-open spaces and too little population to fill it. In theory they were right, but in practice the most fertile areas that had adequate supplies of water, roads, schools and marketing facilities were usually overpopulated in relation to their immediate productivity. Over the long run it should be possible to develop Africa's less populated areas, but it will require investment in quantities that will not be available in the foreseeable future.

If development could not keep up with population growth it could not keep up with itself. In the heady days of independence most African countries invested in dramatic programmes to increase the number of schools and hospitals, to move from being predominantly agricultural economies to starting an industrial base, to building airports with runways large enough to take "747" jets and sports stadiums attractive enough to hold international games. It was nation building, necessary at a psychological level for countries that had existed before as peripheral members of a metropolitan power, but who now needed the elementary perquisites of a self-contained country.

There was nothing wrong with all this in itself. The trouble was not in the politics nor the psychology, but in the economics and the management. To pay for this was demanding. In the past the new burgeoning foreign aid programmes – not just from the metropolitan powers but also from new givers like the superpowers and would-be philanthropists such as Scandinavia and Holland – made it possible. However, it still cost the African countries money they had to find themselves. The aid donors provided the capital costs but Africa had usually to pay the running costs. The temptation was to tax the farmers, using as a device marketing boards that are compulsory buyers of all export crops and which keep back up to half the selling price for the government coffers.

Even then the sacrifice might have seemed justified if the projects had worked, but too often they did not. What Africa has suffered from most is the lack of management skills. Africa has not yet produced a solid cadre of experienced administrators who can run, effectively and profitably, concentrations of economic power – industrial complexes, public works projects and agricultural estates.

Added to this has been the lack of funds to continue the level of maintenance and the care and attention to projects that were envisaged by the planners and builders. Whatever the project, village water pumps, a nation-wide phone system or a massive dam supplying irrigation channels and power, when it comes to maintenance, supervision and the supply of spare parts it is often the same story, a slow slide to disrepair and misuse and, often, eventual disintegration of effective service.

It is easy to criticise Africa. Whilst all these points are true it also cannot be denied that most African countries are trying to develop in a continent that is extremely hostile to man.

Africa has the poorest soils and the most severe climate of any of the inhabited continents. Glaciers that left fertile mineral belts across Europe and North America never reached Africa. Intense volcanic activity that produced highly enriched soils throughout South America and the Caribbean was intermittent in Africa. Only the soils of the Kenyan Highlands,Burundi/Rwanda and parts of Tanzania and Ethiopia are of volcanic origin. Also there are the silt soils of high fertility around Lake Chad and in the Nile valley.

Most of the soils of Africa are easily leached of their minerals. Heavy seasonal rains wash the nutrients below the reach of the plants' roots. Metal oxides are also washed downwards and the soils, exposed to the sun, become "hard pans" – impervious layers that make the water flow slow and cropping difficult.

The Green Revolution in Asia was made possible because of the plentiful supply of water, both river and groundwater. But in Africa the rivers are expensive to dam and the water table is much lower than in Asia, making tube wells more costly and complicated.

Moreover, human activity may be prolonging and intensifying the dry spells natural to the climate. Over-cultivation, overgrazing and deforestation have taken their toll. Denuded soil and rock reflects solar radiation back into the atmosphere, warming it and dispersing the cloud cover. More recently there have been the uncertain effects of global warming.

Inevitably, this accumulation of pressures, malfunctionings and setbacks has created an enormous potential for political rupture. Whilst wealth is no guarantee of political harmony nor poverty no excuse for violence the fact is that in a situation where change is so fast and so precarious the normal everyday tensions between ethnic groups, tribes and countries are exacerbated to the breaking point.

Colonial policy, which arbitrarily drew territorial dividing lines across the map of Africa, was a recipe for disaster. Once the metropolitan powers withdrew in the 1960's, conflicts which had been artificially constrained by empire rule were free to burst forth, but more severely than in pre-colonial times. By 1985 the 51 independent African nations had experienced at least 60 coups. By 1989 almost all African countries were either dictatorships or one party states.

But the big drought clearly exacerbated conflicts. In Ethiopia the dissident provinces of Tigre and Eritrea, long at war with the central government, became even more uncompromising about a negotiated solution. In Angola and Mozambique anti-government movements, long in existence, strengthened their position in the face of the deteriorating economic performance of the central government. In the Sudan the government was overthrown and a war of succession by a dissatisfied population in the south flared into renewed activity.

War, which already had been ravaging the African continent from time to time over the previous twenty years, seemed with the drought to be consuming it at both ends. Never have there been so many refugees – some 4 million, a disproportionately large percentage of the world's 10 million.

The drought, which consolidated its devastating hold in the course of 1984, had been in the making for many years. There had been 17 consecutive years of below average rainfall in the area called the Sahelian zone that lies between the Sahara and the equatorial forest.

For the five years since 1980 the drought had been particularly severe and in 1983 and 1984 rainfall was more than 40% below the average.

The African emergency which ensued was a human tragedy of the proportions of world war. Indeed before the massive famine relief operation began in late 1984 it looked as if more people might die than died in the whole of World War II.

As it happened, the most mammoth relief operation ever mounted averted wholesale disaster. Still, probably more than a million died and the 30 million who were affected but who survived went through a pain and suffering that would be beyond the capacity of most of us to endure. 10 million had to abandon their homes and lands in search of food, water and pasture for the animals.

The modern story of the famine began in Ethiopia when a BBC camera crew in October 1984, searching for a famine story to beat a documentary on hunger scheduled by the rival commercial channel, stumbled on a situation of appalling horror. Children were dying in droves in their mothers' arms. A stunning piece of photography by Mohammed Amin, combined with a moving commentary by Michael Buerk, struck through the nerve ends of viewers and led to an unprecedented surge of anger, compassion, political activity and donations. NBC relayed the film 24 hours later in the US with the same effect.

Voluntary agencies, governments and the United Nations moved into high gear. Reporters and personnel poured into Ethiopia and then into Sudan, the rest of the Sahelian zone and further south.

After a long and painful period of decline Africa had reached its nadir. It is almost true to say it could go no further down. It seemed as if Africa at last, out of extreme adversity, had developed the will to save itself. Economic development began to be taken forward in more rational steps. Democracy began to spread. Needless to say, Africa is a very large and diverse continent and this process was not universal. In Zimbabwe governance was in nosedive position since the early 1990's and remained so in 2006. In Nigeria, the continent's most populated country, with half of the West African population, decline was only reversed when its evil dictator, General Abacha, died of a heart attack whilst in bed with three prostitutes.

In June 1994, shortly after the advent of democracy in South Africa, Nelson Mandela, its first president, spoke at a summit meeting of the Organisation of African States: "We must face squarely that there is something wrong in how we govern ourselves. It must be said that the fault is not in our stars but in ourselves."

One by one throughout the 1990s governing elites began to come to their senses. Twenty-five states established multi-party democracies.

Two stories which I have researched myself give some indication of the kind of progress African countries can make. They are the Tanzania of former President Ben Mkapa and the Nigeria of President Olusegun Obasanjo.

I shook Tanzania's dust off my feet 20 years ago and looked back only in anguish. I first arrived in this former colony – a place the British never put their heart into – in 1964, just after independence. I was one of the first contingent of volunteers who lived out in the bush and happily did what we could for the new African socialism of President Julius Nyerere. Later, I interviewed Nyerere many times, both for television documentaries and the *International Herald Tribune*. The last time I saw him in 1979, we had sat outside his house on the Indian Ocean, both of us exhausted after a four-hour interview on Rhodesia and South Africa – he was playing an important role as an intermediary between the guerrillas and London and Washington. As the sun went down we sipped our wine and watched the dhows gliding in from a day's fishing or trading trip to Zanzibar.

Last April, 41 years later, as I walked away from the presidential office in Dar es Salaam after my first interview with the current president, Benjamin Mkapa, I headed down to the ocean and reflected on why I had stayed away so long. Again, it was evening time. The women were cleaning the fresh fish on the white sand. The dhows were flitting landward. Nothing had changed, but everything had changed. Nyerere had steered the country into an economic hole, as he himself recognised before his death in 1999. It seemed likely then that most Tanzanians would live on a dollar a day as far into the future as anyone could see. Now my hopes were recharged. Tanzania, during Mkapa's ten years of office, has become a relative success story, albeit from a low base. Although still one of the poorest countries in Africa, with a national income per head of $290 compared to the African average of $490, Tanzania has been growing at an annual rate of almost 6 percent over the past five years, and inflation seems to have been conquered on Mkapa's watch.

Mkapa stepped down after two terms in the general election of last November, but in an orderly, democratic transition. The opposition parties have a presence, but despite an increase in their vote were not be able to stop the ruling Chama cha Mapinduzi (CCM) party's candidate, foreign minister Jakaya Kikwete, cruising to victory.

I first knew Mkapa when he was Nyerere's press secretary. When I asked him why he abandoned Nyerere's legacy to create a rather successful, if still budding, capitalist economy, he gave two reasons. First, he had watched Deng Xiaoping unleash capitalism in China and saw the country climb from rags to comparative riches. Second, it was the end of the Cold War and the western aid donors, in particular the Americans, the British and even the Scandinavians, were no longer interested in propping up a declining country just because it was pro-Western.

Joseph Mungai, Tanzania's Minister for Education, whom Mkapa rates as the most dynamic member of his cabinet (he has been struggling to transform education despite losing nearly 3,000 teachers to Aids every year), recalls a story about Nyerere that rings true. On becoming Tanzania's leader, Nyerere called on Mao Zedong. Mao told him: "I give you one piece of advice: don't create a middle class." And Nyerere never did. Indeed, when I asked what Nyerere would say to him if he returned to earth, Mkapa replied: "He'd say I'd given away too much of what was in public ownership. And he would be upset that I had built up such a prosperous capitalist class."

Since coming to power in 1995, Mkapa has left his reformist mark on everything from tax policy to privatisation, from the bureaucracy to human rights, from political freedom to a free press. Of Nyerere's well-meaning but autocratic Christian socialism there is hardly a sign left. As deputy foreign minister Abdul-Kader Shareef put it to me, as we sailed across to his birthplace in Zanzibar, "Nyerere was redistributing poverty... We are not anti-socialism. But before distributing wealth we must create it."

Nyerere was a Catholic idealist, never a Marxist. He aspired not just to replace white rule with black rule, but to build a society based on *ujamaa,* a Swahili word meaning "togetherness." Nyerere had a vision of village socialism, where tractors and fertilisers could be managed by village teams and used in communal fields, with the village selling and buying in from the outside world on a co-operative basis.

His ideas fell on deaf ears, for Tanzanian peasants were used to living on scattered family holdings and leading fairly independent lives. But Nyerere brushed aside opposition and tradition. He ordered the relocation of people whose families had farmed the same plots for hundreds of years. Some moved voluntarily, beguiled by Nyerere's rhetoric. Others had to be cajoled. Villagers were herded together and told: "This is your village site," yet often found no running water, decent land or roads. Later Nyerere admitted that even in his home village, Butiama, *ujamma* had not taken hold, and it was gradually abandoned.

All the while Nyerere kept most of his critics at bay. His manner was disarming. He was often the first to articulate what had gone wrong. Despite his own western education (at Edinburgh University) he believed that Westminster democracy was alien to a people who had long sorted out their problems under the shade of a baobab tree. He brought in one-party government, although softened by competing candidates in each constituency. And he was tough with anyone he thought was blocking Tanzania's socialist path, unsettling Zanzibar or troubling the liberation movements like the ANC, with their bases in Tanzania. The jails filled up.

Nyerere was most compromised by his Zanzibar policy. Even today, that tail of two small islands can wag the mainland dog, as Mkapa discovered. It is the one issue that could upset Tanzania's progress in attracting foreign investment ($260m last year).

In 1964, just after Tanganyika was granted independence, Zanzibar, also recently released from British rule, was caught up in an unexpected revolution. The African half of the population overthrew its Arab and Indian rulers. Nyerere, worried about their communist rhetoric, persuaded the revolutionaries to merge Zanzibar with the mainland. Tanzania was born.

It was a stormy marriage. The new Zanzibari leader, Sheik Abeid Karume, was a constant embarrassment. All attempts Nyerere made to moderate the regime failed. In 1972, unsurprisingly, Karume was murdered. But Zanzibar's unsettled politics rumbles on. The African Zanzibaris still feel that they are not properly consulted and the Arabs are unhappy because they are no longer top dogs. The 1996 election was rigged. The election in 2000 was never fully completed. In early 2001 there was a serious uprising in Pemba, the smaller of Zanzibar's two islands. The 2006 election, although more transparent, was still marked by irregularities and some violence.

Nyerere's legacy is, however, generally a benign one. Zanzibar aside, he developed a civil consciousness that knitted the country's diverse tribes into one people and built a political culture that was essentially non-violent. It made Mkapa's job much easier. The fast economic development pursued under his stewardship, albeit capitalist rather than Nyerere's socialism, had good foundations on which to build.

For now, the Tanzanian economy continues on course. Emulating its neighbour Uganda, where the economy has been transformed over the last 19 years under the stern tutelage of Yoweri Museveni, Tanzania has many of the ingredients for take-off.

Most impediments in Africa are man-made, as they were in Ivory Coast, which grew for decades at 7 per cent until its benign dictator, Felix Houphouet Boigny, died in 1993. Then, because there was no deal on his successor, factionalism tore the country apart. The same could befall Uganda, where Museveni rewrote the constitution so that he could run for reelection a third time. Only the democracies with firm term limits look promising for the longer term: Senegal, Mali and Ghana, with their steady 5 per cent growth rates; Madagascar (6 per cent); Mozambique (7-9 per cent); Botswana (7-10 per cent – the world's fastest growing economy during the 1990s); Nigeria 6%, and Tanzania. Tanzania's faster growth can almost be measured from the day that President Ali Hassan Mwinyi returned the country to multi-party rule, three years before Mkapa's election victory in 1995, and took the clamps off the media and parliamentary debate. Growth gradually picked up – averaging 4 per cent during 1996-1999 and rising to an average of 5.8 per cent during 2000-2006 – and inflation slowed down.

When at university I studied tropical agriculture the basic text was Pierre Gourou's *Le Monde Tropique*. It was a sympathetic account of the difficulties of tropical life – leached soils, uncontrollable disease for humans and animals, either too much forest as in the Congo or too little as in the Sahel. Moreover, Africa's rivers did not have the fertile flood plains of the big Asian rivers, hospitable to paddy. It was a tale of woe that I used to explain to anyone who would listen why Africa would have the devil's own job of ever making it. But the progress of the countries listed above – and there are another 17 in sub-Saharan Africa which attained 5 per cent growth in 2003 – shows how inadequate this explanation is. For a start, growth does not depend solely on the land. These countries have shot ahead because, as in Tanzania, a combination of mining, tourism, small manufacturing and non-traditional exports such as flowers, timber, fish and precious stones have got them going. Agriculture, of course, has to come next – two thirds of Tanzanians still live on the land – if the growth rate is to reach 7 per cent or higher and stay there, but the signs I saw are propitious. Already, according to a recent IMF working paper there has been a steady reduction in poverty in Tanzania over the last five years.

Extensive privatisation of the large but moribund state sector has released commercial energy. For the most part it has been successful. There were a few cases of insiders getting control of productive assets at knock down prices. And, as with the recent row over the privatisation of the household water supplies of Dar es Salaam, where a British and German-run company had its contract terminated by the government, it is difficult where necessities are concerned for public opinion to understand the needs of the capitalist to make a profit, or for the capitalist to understand the real needs of poor people.

I am returning to Iringa – eight hours by road from Dar es Salaam – where I worked 40 years ago. An hour or so before we arrive, the scenery begins to change from the endless, empty, dry savannah to the bold outcrops and massive boulders of outsize granite that characterise much of Tanzania's southern highlands. Seemingly wedged between the rocks are the small, brown, mud-built houses of what was, when I was last here, an impoverished peasant class. But now I can see that the green of the maize fields is broken up by a new crop, the waving, yellow heads of sunflowers. Each house has a small press for making oil and the vendors beside the road are selling not just little heaps of vegetables, as in the past, but massive baskets of tomatoes. Finally the road winds up to Iringa, once a flourishing colonial outpost but now a bit tatty despite the fetching sight of purple jacaranda trees, a legacy, along with the rustic, stone-built local government buildings, from pre-first world war days when Germany was the ruling master. (Germany controlled Tanganyika and parts of Zanzibar in the late 19th century, and held on to the mainland until 1919. Both Tanganyika and Zanzibar were then ruled by Britain until the early 1960s.)

The state-run factories established by Nyerere are falling into ruin. But in the town's market new life is sprouting. Where before there were a few women selling a pile of potatoes or a handful of onions, there are now mountains of every vegetable and fruit: courgettes and guavas, cabbages and mangoes. There are beans and lentils, and fish from as far away as lakes Tanganyika and Victoria. And everywhere those great baskets of tomatoes whose surplus pours into a new factory, making sauce. I found a new jam factory processing local fruit, and a cigarette factory using the tobacco that I used to encourage my dozen peasants to grow. What does it matter that the towering silos for corn are now empty? With their mobile phones, which cover 90 per cent of the villages in the district, and with selling restrictions removed, traders are finding their own immediate markets elsewhere in the country, or even in Zambia and Zimbabwe.

If diet has been transformed, so has health. There are 40 new dispensaries scattered around the district, with a couple of nurses for each, and half a dozen health centres with a doctor in attendance. The dispensaries help with childbirth and inoculations (which are up all over Tanzania) and a free supply of condoms. The country folk in Tanzania are still wary of birth control, but attitudes are changing – fertility rates have begun a slow decline and the health clinic I visited had run out of its quota of condoms. If Tanzania can get its birth rate down, the fruits of its agricultural revolution in the making will begin to show. But in a country where sex begins for most in their early teens and virginity at marriage is a concept known to only a handful of tribes, progress is going to be slow while Aids, already frighteningly prevalent, can only gather speed. Around 7 per cent of adults are infected with HIV, and this is expected to rise rapidly over the next few years. Still, neighbouring Uganda has turned the tide on Aids dramatically – why shouldn't Tanzania?

What is remarkable is that the Iringa peasants have done so much, so fast on their own initiative, mainly just because price controls were lifted and the market became their incentive. And in half a dozen other regional centres a similar story can be told. But Mkapa says he has neglected agriculture and that whoever takes over from him must make it a priority. As the economy grows,

Tanzania has to feed its growing urban population. They will certainly have the buying power to give the farmers the incentives they need. But it is also a question of know-how and services. The peasants need decent roads, a lighter tax burden for the agricultural sector, micro-credit and subsidized fertiliser (the IMF has at last allowed Tanzania to subsidise the transport of fertiliser). And they need improved seed – the sooner Europe withdraws its opposition to genetically modified seeds, which makes it impossible for a country that wants to be a major agriculture exporter to start using them, the better.

At the same time, Tanzania must continue its policy of attracting expatriate, professional farmers. There used to be small colonies of those – in the southern highlands and in the north around Arusha. Over the years, many gave up because the socialist tax and marketing policies hemmed them in. Now those that remained are getting a second wind – like the big dairy farmer near Iringa and the coffee farmers who is selling specialty coffee to Starbucks. Tanzania should, like Nigeria, welcome white Zimbabwean farmers. Land is still plentiful. Why not encourage European, Australian and American farmers to set up businesses, as long as they establish outlying subsidiaries among local peasant farmers?

What else does Tanzania have to do? Historically, its political stability led to it receiving more aid than most other African countries – $16.6bn from 1970-96. Its debt burden was effectively halved in 2001 under the so-called "enhanced highly indebted poor countries' debt relief initiative," a move which would have saved the country around $3bn over 20 years. But this was superseded in June 2005 when Tanzania became one of the 18 countries to benefit from the G7 finance ministers' agreement to completely write off multilateral debt – saving the country over $100m in repayments a year.

Does the country need a lot more aid? Has the debt relief removed a millstone from its neck? Is the much talked-about corruption really as bad as outsiders say? I posed these questions to Dar es Salaam's elite – to the dazzling but shrewd German woman who represents the IMF, to the well-informed Kenyan adviser to the World Bank, to discreet diplomats, to ebullient Tanzanian economists, careful bankers, proud businessmen and reflective ministry of finance officials. Along the way I had a number of opportunities to bounce questions off an undefensive president and Joseph Mungai, Minister of Education, who once attended an evening class on current affairs I taught in Iringa. There was a strong consensus in the replies, even though the Tanzanians flushed with their success so far, perhaps make the mistake of thinking that progress will get easier, not harder.

The future, in part, has to be more of the same – continuing macroeconomic discipline, more mining and more up-market tourism. Tanzania is one of the most beautiful countries in the world, with wildlife parks, some in the south rarely visited, the 18,000 year-old rock paintings of Kondoa-Irangi, thousands of miles of safe Indian ocean coastline and, on its coast and in Zanzibar, a rich historical legacy including the remains of Kilwa Kisiwani, an African city of the 9th century and various Arab settlements from the 10th century onwards including the mosques and houses of the Omani colonization in the 18th century. Dar es Salaam itself, despite some ugly skyscrapers, is full of tree-lined streets and pretty old German-era colonial buildings, and the mayor recently announced a plan to restrict traffic in the city centre. In tourism it should go for style and taste and, in a country where Muslims dominate the coast and Zanzibar, decorous behaviour. That, instead of mass-market tourism, is the way to maximize long-term revenues.

Tanzania is belatedly giving priority to secondary and tertiary education so that its woefully undereducated workforce can be prepared for the challenges ahead. Its policy of a primary school in every village and better trained teachers has already produced results: the primary school-leavers' national exams have a pass rate of 49 per cent against the previous 20 per cent. The country could move twice as fast if secondary education had not been neglected for so long and if Aids were not killing so many teachers.

And then there is corruption. Ten years ago Mkapa made corruption a central issue in his election platform. The diplomats still complain about it. The Americans refuse to give Tanzania aid under their millennium challenge account because they say there is too much corruption. But this can be exaggerated. While corruption should not be excused, it needs, especially in Tanzania, to be put into perspective. First, unlike many African countries, the rot never started at the top. The state is not being bled dry by competing rent-seeking factions of the elite: all Tanzanian presidents have been clean and the country is relatively homogenous (it is made up of a number of different tribes, but, unlike neighbouring Kenya, none is big enough to dominate). Second, when one presses a diplomat to name names, the offences do not seem that serious – a minister fiddling with wildlife hunting licenses here and, despite a modest salary, buying an expensive farm there. Third, tax reform and more vigorous monitoring have done away with a lot of evasion, and tax revenues have increased fourfold over the last eight years. At local level, freeing markets and improving social services has helped. No longer does one have to bribe to get a child into school or a license to sell something. Still, corruption remains a problem in the bureaucracy and, despite all the promises, there have been no successful prosecutions. Even more disturbing, parliament has failed to discuss audited government budgets for several years now. Is the shadow of the majority CCM party too overbearing after 40 years in power?

And what is the role of the outside world? The argument about western agricultural subsidies raging in the columns of the *Financial Times* and the *Economist,* and more recently in the Africa Commission report, is too esoteric. Any deal made during this Doha round of trade talks in which poor nations make concessions on agricultural access in exchange for cuts in European, American and Japanese tariffs and subsidies would probably help, but would also be weighted in favour of the richer world and the richer developing countries. A better idea would be for Tanzania and likeminded countries to call the bluff of Western countries and demand an absolutely level playing field, in which both sides dismantle all subsidies and tariffs over the next decade or so. Such an approach, cutting through the labyrinthine complexities of Doha, would radically shorten the time frame of negotiations. It would also open up internal African trade, currently frozen by protectionism. In the last 40 years, Tanzania has weathered the demolition of its sisal industry as artificial fibers replaced its principal export crop. Like all developing countries, it has also survived 40 years of declining prices for agricultural commodities. If trade barriers to agricultural produce were removed, it could do even better.

Tanzanian farmers, under-resourced though they are, have managed to feed a population that has grown from 12m to 37m over the last 38 years. Rarely in recent years has the country needed to import food. If farmers had access to an unsubsidized world marketplace, they could start to meet its demands too, especially in the age of mobile phones. And the same goes for most food-importing countries: show me a peaceful African country with functioning markets that cannot meet its own food needs most years. Of course, famine does strike when the rains fail, as happens from time to time in Tanzania. But, as in Tanzania, if there is reasonable transport and the markets are unrestricted, food will go from areas of surplus to those suffering.

Does Tanzania need more aid? Should it be doubled, as the Africa Commission and Jeffrey Sachs suggest? There is no doubt that aid works. The proof of that can be seen in both Tanzania and Uganda from the times when they were given little or no aid. Nothing moved. Look at both countries now and you can see aid projects delivering. Even the Asian tigers, with their undemocratic but capable "development" states, could not have got going without aid. The Americans put South Korea and Taiwan on the road to success.

But aid only works if the macroeconomic conditions are right and governance and management are effective. A good example is the TanZam railway built in the 1970s by the Chinese – their most ambitious foreign aid project ever. At a time when the war in white-ruled Rhodesia had cut off Zambia's lifelines to the south, this aid project was a godsend, giving Zambia access to an Indian Ocean port. But look at it now: decrepit engines, ill-maintained rolling stock, it takes three days to travel what used to take one. Now the Tanzanians are trying to do what they should have done decades ago: letting railway routes out on a long lease. Only with sophisticated management of the sort Tanzania does not yet possess can they be made to work as they did. The Chinese and the Indians have agreed to step in.

Aid today is arriving at healthy levels – around $1bn a year. The British are giving the most and no longer demand it to be earmarked for specific projects. Instead, most money goes straight to the treasury, so that the government itself has the responsibility of making sure it works. The Nordic donors, the third largest, are doing the same, but the Americans, the second largest, still insist on direct project lending.

Last year's decision on debt forgiveness will be a boon to a country that was struggling under the burden of repayments. The permanent secretary at the ministry of finance told me that if the country had 100 per cent debt relief from all its creditors it would not need more aid. But Tanzania is not being held back by lack of aid or debt relief: What it needs is not lots more aid (although some could be well spent on infrastructure) but more *surety* of aid. I have seen too many aid projects in Africa that start well but then collapse after a few years when the donor pulls out, leaving the maintenance costs to be paid by the country itself, which has neither the money nor the management skills to keep it going. Gordon Brown's idea of borrowing from future aid budgets for a big bang of aid now seems the wrong emphasis.

And, more than aid, Tanzania needs more foreign investment for industry, agricultural processing and infrastructure. Investment is increasing at a steady rate – up from $151m in 1995 to $260m now, although limited to mining and tourism. Diplomats claim that corruption is a deterrent, but businessmen dismiss the argument because investors know how to factor that into their costs. Only foreign investment brings with it the knowledge and skills to facilitate the kind of export-led growth that the country's planners pray for. The door is wide open.

If the new president can be as dynamic as Ben Mkapa, if aid donors hold steady, if rich countries open up their agricultural markets and, of course, if the world economy continues to grow, then Tanzania has a reasonably bright future. This generation of Tanzanians has learnt from the mistakes of Julius Nyerere (and his accomplices in the World Bank, the Swedish international development agency, the British ministry of overseas development and journalists like myself). I think the Tanzanians now know how to keep their ship pointing forward.

I shared a plane journey with Olusegun Obasanjo in 1999, just after he had been elected to his first term as a civilian Nigerian president. On that occasion he threatened to throw me out at 35,000 feet after I had asked him some hard questions. Fortunately, I have known Obasanjo for over 20 years and he was only joking – on occasion he loves to play the African "big man", which he is certainly not despite his gruff and intimidating manner. Still, I am never sure if we are buddies. I am a journalist. He is a politician trying to build consensus in a bitterly fragmented society emerging from 20 years of military dictatorship, where corruption, poverty and criminality seethe in great urban agglomerations. This is still a country where ethnic or religious differences can turn a minor quarrel in the marketplace about ownership of a palm nut tree into an all-out pogrom, requiring the poorly trained army to impose order in its ham-fisted, sometimes brutal and biased way.

On that plane journey shortly after his first election victory, he told me that he was "going to crack the whip." I knew what he meant. After he stepped down as military president 24 years ago, he bought a farm and attempted to persuade his countrymen that the future lay in the soil, not in oil. I had witnessed an incident on the farm in which he turned on one of his workers who had started to argue with him. Obasanjo picked up a piece of thick steel wire and made as if to whip him. The man immediately begged for mercy and changed his tune. It was over in a second, but I understood how he had risen so quickly to the top of the military hierarchy during the civil war.

My next flight with Obasanjo was to Liberia in 2004, in his Nigerian air force 727 jet with its double bed, walnut paneling and comfortable chairs for the inner circle of a dozen aides. I decided this time I was not going to let him off the hook on army atrocities. Sure enough, after a while, he said angrily, "I'm not going to sit here and take any more of this." I said, "so you ARE going to throw me out at 35,000 feet!" He calmed down

I had asked him about the 2002 Amnesty International report on Nigerian army brutality. In November 1999, soldiers killed over 250 people in Odi in retaliation for the deaths of 12 policemen. Then, in October 2001, over 200 people in Benue state were killed after 19 soldiers had died. "On many occasions," concluded Amnesty in its damning report, "this violence appears to have been unleashed with government ... complicity." That tough conclusion is partly the consequence of Obasanjo's meeting with Amnesty Secretary General, Pierre Sane, three years ago. Obasanjo was uncompromising in his defence of the army, appearing to rationalise its abuses on account of the provocation the soldiers endured. He hadn't changed.

"It's lies. Amnesty tells lies," replied Obasanjo. "What is the army supposed to do when it and the police are viciously attacked?" Obasanjo has a love-hate relationship with Amnesty. Following his 1998 release after three years in a Nigerian jail, he met Amnesty in London to thank them for their agitation on his behalf. He is a 100% convinced democrat.

When it comes to the army, however, the former general feels he must defend it. Many of the thuggish senior officers who served the dictator Sani Abacha in power from 1993 until his death in 1998 are long removed. Still, roll Obasanjo a question on the army's propensity to rape and loot and the reply comes back: "Tell me any commander who can stop his men raping after victory arrives when they've been two years in a hole in the ground." He was drawing on his own experience as a young commander during the 1960s Biafran war, which claimed over a million lives after the province of the Ibo people tried to secede. My question had been prompted by a UN report about the army's behaviour during a peacekeeping operation in Sierra Leone three years ago and the reports that came out of Liberia 13 years ago when, as now, Nigerian troops were deployed to try to end a war.

Well here we are in Liberia again. The plane has landed. Unbelievably for a country wracked by 23 years of intermittent war, there is still a red carpet to be rolled out. The remnants of Charles Taylor's scarlet-bereted army salute Obasanjo and lead us on to the streets of Monrovia.

It's 30 years since I have been in this godforsaken country. I was covering one of Africa's many wars on that occasion in neighbouring Guinea for the *New York Times*. Even then, slumbering peacefully under the relatively benign if autocratic rule of the descendants of liberated American slaves, Liberia was a third rate place compared with the British and French ex-colonies next door. Today, conditions are appalling. Even the UN's special representative, Jacques

Klein, talked about filling his bath with buckets of water and eating by candle-light. How much worse must it be for those lining the road as we drive into town. The power and telephone lines are down along the highway. Until the peace agreement in June negotiated by Obasanjo and his colleagues in Ecowas (the 16-member union of west African states) the rubbish was piled high, the markets were empty, the water supply was a trickle and cholera was rampant in the slums.

Today it looks a little better. The markets are open, rubbish is being collected, Red Cross Land Rovers – fighting the cholera epidemic and bringing in food and medicine – are ubiquitous, and the UN agencies are grinding away on numerous fronts in their usual understated, under-reported way. And Charles Taylor is languishing in a luxurious government guesthouse in Calabar on the Nigerian coast. The peace deal which spirited him away on in the same jet in which we arrived was sealed by Obasanjo – a *quid pro quo* for Taylor abandoning Liberian politics and also the politics and wars of Sierra Leone and Ivory Coast in which he was the chief gunrunner, diamond smuggler and stirrer-up of mayhem.

Obasanjo is the crowd's hero. Every few hundred metres he is forced to stop. He wades into the people. Somewhere in his entourage is the Nigerian force commander, Festus Okonkwo. After rigorous training by American advisors two years ago, he has moulded his peacekeeping force into an apparently disciplined, professional army, of which everyone, from the UN to the American ambassador to US officers I met on attachment to it, speaks highly. This, at least, is no longer an army to embarrass Obasanjo.

Nine years ago, Bill Clinton pulled the US out of Somalia after the death of 18 US rangers and falsely blamed the UN for the incompetence of its pacification effort (the rangers were under US command at all times, not the UN as was implied). Thus began another period of US alienation from the UN. In Liberia, by contrast, George W. Bush put a naval task force with 2,000 marines offshore and 200 soldiers on the ground. These troops, combined with the Nigerian force, have turned the tide of violence and with it, perhaps, the future of African peacekeeping. As Obasanjo told me five years ago, the world "looked the other way" when the Rwandan genocide began. It could have been stopped, he argued, and now he is proving his point in Liberia.

Back in Nigeria after our one-day visit to Liberia, the country is losing oil revenue and once again living up to its international reputation for ethnic conflict. I am eavesdropping on a dinner conversation between Obasanjo and an ex foreign minister. It is clear that the president is preoccupied with the continuing violence in the area around the oil town of Warri. The roots of the conflict lie in the arbitrary military rule of previous regimes, but the Obasanjo government is not innocent either. As the governor of the region, James Ibori, said recently, "the process of local council reforms was carried out by a central government that has little knowledge of the area. As a consequence, the balance the British colonial administration and subsequent governments used to stabilise relationships among the three ethnic groups was destroyed."

The system under which the locals give up the land and provide the labour, and the federal government then rakes in the revenues, was imposed on the peoples of the Niger delta region – the Ijaws, the Itsekiris and the Urhobos – who, as one Nigerian observer remarked, "quarrel in the afternoon and make up at night, producing children they dare not call bastards," It has also been applied to the nearby Ogonis who, inspired by the execution of writer Ken Saro-Wiwa (ordered by Abacha), led the most effective campaign against the authorities.

Despite Obasanjo's pledge early in his first term to give the locals a bigger slice of the oil revenues and despite his attempts to mediate, the delta area remains very tense. While I was in Abuja, the capital of Nigeria, Obasanjo was host to five hours of talks with the Itsekiris and was scheduled to talk to the representatives of the other two tribes as well. He wanted to go and negotiate on the spot – a sort of Dayton-fest in the delta swamps. The previous week he had told a delegation of women from the delta, as the local *Guardian* newspaper reported, "that the overdependence on oil as the main revenue of Nigeria" was one of the factors responsible for this crisis. "Oil and gas have blinded us ... Oil and gas have taken us away from the values that we used to know. Oil and gas have brutalised us. We are no longer our brothers' keepers". The trouble with this "goose that lays the golden egg," he continued, is "getting other forms of development to go forward ... The delta is by nature difficult terrain, difficult to live in."

Reforming Nigeria's police has perhaps been easier than sorting out the delta. The police are ubiquitous, unlike the soldiers who stay in their barracks until they are whisked to trouble. Everyone has a story of their rough behaviour, their constant demands for bribes, their inability to get on top of the crime that has grown since democracy arrived. Newspapers reflect the widespread anger and disillusionment. At the end of August 2004, Obasanjo announced that most of the 10,000 policemen assigned to official bodyguard duties would be withdrawn. Just days later, the bodyguards of the vice-president beat unconscious a photographer whose crime had apparently been to get too close during a ceremony. After a policeman took two students he had detained to a graveyard and shot them dead, Obasanjo let it be known he was going to shake up the capital's police force. Slowly, the police are shaping up, shying away from pestering motorists for bribes at their impromptu roadblocks and from dealing out rough and violent justice on their own whim and whistle.

The courts are finding their stride too. The tension between the secular courts and the Shari'a courts that some northern Islamic governors are said to be promoting – partly as a tool for undermining Obasanjo, a pro-American, Christian, ethnic Yoruba from southwest Nigeria – simmers on. The case of Amina Lawal, accused of adultery and threatened with death by stoning, is just the tip of the iceberg. But the higher secular courts have shown daring and maturity, and on occasion have waded into issues of daunting complexity. Two years ago, the Supreme Court, exhibiting a new sense of independence and self-confidence, ruled on the sensitive issue of the offshore/onshore oil revenue allocation between the states and the federal government. The courts have also been given new powers to combat high-level corruption. Last December, Obasanjo had to drag congress by its hair into passing the Economic and Financial Crimes Act (the newly elected congress seems less resistant). Several western countries, alarmed by the ease of money laundering in Nigeria, had threatened sanctions if the law was not passed. However, as Nenadi Usman, the Minister of Finance, told me, it is hard to win prosecutions when the few people who have hard evidence are not prepared to go into the witness box and the police are not as sophisticated as the criminals. One thing the various scams show is how adept the Nigerians are at financial improvisation. If only this could be channeled into legal activities, more Nigerians might end up like Bayo Ogunlesi, head of global investment banking at Credit Suisse First Boston, the first African to head a major western bank.

Obasanjo has also struck a blow for the rule of law by taking to the International Court of Justice the charged dispute over who owns the oil-rich Bakassi peninsula, Cameroon or Nigeria. Although Obasanjo was pressured by his minister of defense to threaten Cameroon with military action, and popular opinion was nationalistic, Obasanjo did not budge. When Cameroon won the case, he gave the nation a gentle lecture on the need to be law-abiding.

Even the long moribund economy is beginning to grow. Since 1999, income per head has increased and foreign debt, after an initial rise, is falling again. Yet judging from the scale of the rollout of mobile phone networks (a Dutch telecommunications adviser told me Nigerians had achieved in three years what had taken Europe 20) the foundations are being laid for an upsurge in business activity. Even the street vendors wave their phones and in a city like overcrowded Lagos, where lengthy waits in traffic jams and petrol queues are common, the mobile phone is heaven-sent. Landline use has also been transformed – over 2m homes and offices are now connected and Nigeria's network is said to be the fastest growing in the world.

Privatisation of state industries is proceeding at full throttle. This is something of a turnaround for the non-economics minded Obasanjo, who at first exhibited qualms about selling off the family silver. But Nigerian Airways, once a bottomless pit for billions of lost naira, has been disbanded. British Airways and Virgin Atlantic now compete with full loads on the highly profitable Lagos to London routes, and at home competition between a growing number of private airlines keeps prices down and flights plentiful. According to the newly appointed privatisation chief, who trained for years in Japan's privatisation authority, the railways are one of the next big targets. In theory Nigeria has an enviable rail network, but its revenues are far less than its income and wage and pension liabilities. "Before it's saleable," he said, "we have to put a lot of money into it, but we'll get it and we will do it and model it on the successful Japanese rail privatisation scheme."

Nigeria's state steelworks on the banks of the immense Niger River must count as one of the industrial wonders of the world. Out in the bush, in the midst of undulating, iron-rich mountains, sits this giant white elephant, built over 20 years ago, a cathedral to Nigeria's high industrial hopes. It has lost more money than the treasuries of most African countries would see in a decade. Now it, too, is being privatized. The early dream of Nigeria becoming an industrial nation may be realizable after all.

Still, five years after Obasanjo came into office, the state clings too tenaciously to its omnipotent, omnipresent role. According to the *Financial Times,* a startling 82 per cent of state expenditure goes on funding the machinery of government. Budget monitoring is still in its infancy.

I had lunch with a village headmaster, five hours' drive from Abuja, in what he described apologetically but accurately as "his hovel." His English was excellent, his reading wide and his commitment to education passionate, and yet he was eking out a living on a pittance that was invariably paid late. Meanwhile, Abuja has seen the construction of a world-class football stadium and sports complex in rapid time.

Obasanjo gets angry when I take him to task on his priorities, and suggest that with the money spent on the stadium he could have given every village clean water. "Do you know what it would cost to install pure water just in the homes of Abeokuta?" he asks, referring to his medium-sized home town (where nearly 20 years ago I stayed with him and his wife). I found out he was right – the cost would be prohibitive – and that, moreover, the government has dug more wells in villages in the last four years than in the previous 20. Likewise, the immunisation of children has taken enormous strides forward. The bottom rungs of society, where most people still live, are not being neglected.

We outside observers may have to adjust our thinking. Rather surprisingly, Nigeria is, according to the world values survey, the happiest country in the world. But it is no longer a simple, village-based African country. Its space engineers are clever enough to have worked on a (British) satellite that a Russian rocket has recently launched. Why shouldn't Nigeria have a modern football stadium now that it has entered the top ranks of international competition? Football tourism could help develop the under-exploited tourist industry in this magnificent country. Crime is clearly a problem but it also seems to me to be exaggerated by fearful expatriates stuck behind barbed wire.

No one in Nigeria – and very few in Britain or America for that matter – can write more evocatively than Ben Okri. But he no longer gets it quite right; or perhaps Nigeria has changed since the civil war period in which he set his 1991 Booker-winning novel *The Famished Road:*

"Everywhere there was the crudity of wounds, the stark huts, the rusted zinc abodes, and the rubbish in the streets, children in rags, and the little girls naked on the sand playing with crushed tin-cans ... The sun bared the reality of our lives and everything was so harsh it was a mystery that we could understand and care for one another or for anything at all."

Of course this is still part of it. Reforming the country may in many respects be impossible, at least during the remainder of Obasanjo's second and final term as president, which ends in 2007. Under the surface Nigeria is not a nation state at all, and tensions between the four main ethnic groups-Hausa,

Fulani, Yoruba and Ibo-and many smaller ones, still threaten to explode. Yet something is moving. Okri's country is a Nigeria Nigerians no longer want it to be. And so too is much of the rest of Africa. The great famine of 1985 is now, for most Africans, a distant memory.

# 11 Will China Dominate the Century?

When in 1964 China first tested a nuclear weapon, the West had every reason to be worried. Here was a country that had recently fought the United States in Korea, had threatened countries as far afield as India and Indonesia and had supported revolutionary movements all over the Third World.

But today, the threat of Chinese military domination should worry the West very little. Its nuclear arsenal is rather small: a mere 24 intercontinental nuclear missiles that are able to reach the United States; no aircraft carrier battle groups for projecting its power; and very few destroyers. China is constructing no long-range bombers and has no military bases abroad. Its 70 submarines rarely venture outside Chinese territorial waters. Even vis-à-vis Taiwan, against which it has deployed 750 short-range missiles, China does not have the makings of an invasion force that could overwhelm Taiwan's defenses.

Nevertheless, both the White House and a majority in the US Congress continue to act as if the United States must contain China militarily, even while professing engagement.

John Mearsheimer, professor of political science at the University of Chicago, argues, "China cannot rise peacefully" and there is "considerable potential for war". In Tokyo early last year, Secretary of State Condoleezza Rice, when asked to defend the presence of such a large number of US troops in Okinawa, replied that they were there to balance the rise of China. Later in the year, during a visit to Indonesia, she said that the US had an "interest in building up [Indonesia] as a major commercial and military power ... to help counter the growing influence of China". (Yet three years ago in a speech to the International Institute for Strategic Studies she condemned "balance of power" politics as outmoded and dangerous. She said," We tried this before; it led to the Great War.")

The assumption seems to be that the economic juggernaut will in the long run turn into a military threat. But it does not follow that an increase in China's regional power and influence will translate into a reciprocal decrease in American power nor wealth. The cake can grow for both. It is not a zero-sum game.

Why Washington feels that the United States' longtime presence is East Asia is threatened by China owes more to paranoia than good sense.

Often overlooked is what Foreign Minister Tang Jiaxuan of China told former US Secretary of State Colin Powell, that China "welcomes the America's presence in the Asia-Pacific region as a stabilizing factor."

China's success has been grossly over hyped. China still accounts for only a small proportion of world trade, and even in its region the latest figures show that China is a long way from dominating East Asian trade. Total regional imports from China are about 9 percent compared with Japan's 17 percent and America's 18 percent. Although Germany is Europe's biggest exporter to China, its exports there are only 7 percent of its total; Britain's are 2%.

The apparent high flow of foreign investment into China is used to trumpet China as the wave of the future. But most of that flow comes from ethnic Chinese. And much of the so-called investment from East Asia originates in China and makes a trip via places like Hong Kong only to come back as foreign investment to attract tax concessions.

China, unlike India, still does not yet have enough ingredients for long-term success. It does not have any world-class companies of its own. Its legal framework is rickety, and there is no guarantee that a dictatorial political system will have the flexibility to contain the stresses and strains of economic expansion pursued at the current rate.

In terms of literature, films or the arts in general, China is overshadowed by much smaller Chinese communities – in Hong Kong, Taiwan and Singapore.

It is probably only a matter of time before the faddish fascination with China switches to booming India. Once it does, it is unlikely ever to switch back, as investors realize what it is like to have a haven where the law works, albeit too slowly, and democratically elected politicians are not just accountable, but persuadable and approachable.

I was becoming impatient. I had sent both Sonia Gandhi and Manmohan Singh messages by all sorts of different routes but, once the astonishing election results were known in mid-May (2004), Indian politics was a 20 hours a day affair – the principals barely had time to sleep, much less grant an interview to a foreign reporter. For the first few days the question was, would the communists, who had won 7 per cent of the vote, surpassing their own best expectations, join the Congress party in forming a government of the left? Despite arguments in favour by communist heavyweights such as the new speaker of the Lok Sabha (lower house), Somnath Chatterjee, the communists decided against. They would support a Congress government, but from the outside.

Following the announcement that they were staying out – and therefore perhaps making mischief – the Indian stock market had its worst day in its 129-year history. Congress realized that to stop the rot it had to take over the reins of government. To calm the markets, Manmohan Singh, author of India's post-1991 economic revolution, was wheeled out as the likely new finance minister. Five days after the election results came in, APJ Abdul Kalam, the president of India, received Sonia Gandhi to discuss forming a new government and the Congress leadership made it clear, as did the communists, that they expected her to become prime minister. Then the real storm broke. The Bharatiya Janata party (BJP), the party of the outgoing Hindu nationalist government, announced that it would boycott her swearing-in. As an Italian, they said, Gandhi was unacceptable.

Sonia Gandhi stunned her party and the world when she acquiesced in this BJP veto. She had many reasons. It was clear that her political opponents would continue to use her Italian origins to undermine her government. In such an atmosphere another family assassination could not be discounted. Besides, her ambition if any was to clear the way for the future ascendancy of one of her two children, and her incredible victory had already secured that. Late into another night of debate, it was announced that Manmohan Singh would be prime minister, while Sonia Gandhi remained president of Congress.

I had just flown back from Calcutta, the capital of Indian communist rule, to New Delhi. The next morning the city was quiet for the first time in days. My Indian journalist friends assured me that my messages to my old friend Manmohan were getting through and I would be called in soon. At breakfast the next day, a bit de-hyped, I realized that I did not really share their confidence. I cancelled my appointments and took a taxi to Singh's residence in a quiet leafy street where I had spent the morning with him just over a year before. The house was blocked off by a street-long barrier. I circumnavigated it on foot, walked past an Indian soldier who saluted me, and on through an unmanned metal detector and into a makeshift hut inhabited by a man with a phone. I gave my name and five minutes later I was ushered into the garden. Gursharan, the prime minister's wife, was standing there and she whisked me straight into Manmohan's study.

The house, although large and surrounded by a big garden, is modest inside. Manmohan's study is furnished only with a couple of old chairs, a wicker settee, a desk and bookshelves. Manmohan was sitting there alone, hands resting together. He seemed to be lost in contemplation. "I am so tired", were his first words. "Only two and a half hours' sleep last night." I could see he was overwhelmed by a situation he could scarcely have foreseen.

During the 14 years I have known him, Manmohan has been a man whose heart beat on the left.

Although widely known for his term as governor of the central bank and then the finance minister who introduced deregulated capitalism and globalization to India with stunning results, I remember him first as the secretary-general of the South commission, presided over by Julius Nyerere, the very socialist former president of Tanzania. They wrote a report in 1990, mainly the work of Manmohan, that tore into western capitalism and its exploitative relationship with the Third World. I wrote a column in the *International Herald Tribune* saying his criticism seemed overdone, even for an (adopted) Swedish social democrat like me, and the Singhs responded by inviting me out for dinner in Geneva, where they then lived.

As we talked now, I became even more aware than before that this brilliant economist had beaten Clinton and Blair to the "third way" back in 1991, and that he is determined to use capitalism's energy to improve the prospects of India's poor. "We are centre left," he said. "But we are stealing the clothes of the centre right. Our economic reforms are half incomplete. We have to take them to their logical end. The BJP government was not able to get its act together. It was incoherent, faction-ridden and unable to be effective with its privatization policies. When we left office in 1996 the growth rate was 7.5 per cent. Under the BJP it slowed to 5.5 per cent." I asked him if he could raise it to 8 per cent, high enough to give China a run for its money. "Eight per cent would require a Herculean effort," he replied. "We have an investment rate of 25 per cent of GDP and a savings rate of 23 per cent. We need to increase our savings rate and have an investment rate of 28-30 per cent, combined with increased efficiency. This is too ambitious for now. But over five years we can do it. If foreign inflows can rise from the present 0.7 per cent to 3 per cent of GDP, it can be done. China has 3.5 per cent. We have to change the mentality of foreign investors. And this we can do if we have stable politics. For now, if we can grow at 6.5 per cent in a sustained manner we can make an impact on poverty and unemployment."

What is the most important single issue, I asked. "Mass poverty," he replied instantly. "Seventy per cent of our population live in the rural areas and we have to give them good water, primary healthcare, elementary education and good roads." "What about land reform?" I said, knowing that this was the sacred cow of the communists. "We can't have it. It would cause a revolution. Anyway, we are not like the Latin American countries. We don't have the scope for it here. What is important is for sharecroppers to get rights established so they can invest in their land with security. We need to be like the communist government in West Bengal. But we must have fast industrialization too so that we can draw people off the land."

Although India's spending on its vast conventional forces, nuclear bombs and missiles amount to a fairly small percentage of GDP, India's perpetual confrontation with Pakistan over Kashmir unnerves investors. Indian public opinion seems rather insouciant about nuclear war – 80 per cent of Indians were not born at the time of the Cuban missile crisis, much less Hiroshima. Manmohan does not share this attitude. For him, peace in Kashmir is urgent business. When I had last seen him in 2002, he and Sonia Gandhi had been up all night finalizing an agreement whereby Congress, after Kashmir's first free election in decades, would enter the coalition government together with a local moderate Muslim party, an initiative backed by the then prime minister, Atal Behari Vajpayee of the BJP. The move has worked to diminish violence, improve the local human rights situation and prove to Kashmiris that New Delhi is serious about them running their own show. "The talk of war," Manmohan continued, "is stopping us realizing our economic potential. We have an obligation to ourselves to solve this problem... Short of secession, short of redrawing the boundaries, the Indian establishment can live with anything. The constitution of India has a built-in flexibility for legitimate aspirations. In Tamil Nadu in the 1960s we had a problem of would-be secession. Secessionists in the end were elected to government and that ended the situation." This seems to offer Pakistan quite a lot of leeway, although its Kashmiri, al Qaeda-trained, ideologues and fighters might not appreciate it.

Then he added an interesting afterthought: "People on both sides of the border should be able to move more freely. We need soft borders – then borders are not so important." "But surely," I said, "whatever you do, the Kashmiris have not forgotten that Nehru promised them a plebiscite?" "A plebiscite," he replied, "would take place on a religious basis. It would unsettle everything. No government of India could survive that. Autonomy we are prepared to consider. All these things are negotiable. But an independent Kashmir would become a hotbed of fundamentalism."

Manmohan was visibly overcome by weariness. His private secretary appeared, clearly a little put out by my unannounced presence at this early hour and the new prime minister ushered me, a cup of tea in hand, into the old kitchen to chat with his wife. (I couldn't help thinking, as I said goodbye, that this homely scene with a journalist and a premier could never take place in China.) I repeated to Gursharan what Manmohan had said to me about Sonia Gandhi: that she "is a person who likes to be told things straight – not in the Indian roundabout way. It helps having a European mind." "Yes, that's right," she replied, "It's a good balance they have." "So they are going to run this government together?" I ventured. "They will go on working closely. They always have."

I returned to West Bengal. I wanted to get out into the villages and see what Indian communism was all about, to understand what Manmohan meant when he talked of emulating what the communists had done in India's most densely populated state. Two hours' drive out of Calcutta, I am in the village of Daura, in Howrah district, accompanied by Tirthankar Mitra, a journalist from the *Statesman* newspaper. The temperature is C47° in the shade and we are out in the broiling sun. I enviously watch the women being towed along by their furiously pedaling husbands as they lounge, gorgeously sari-clad, parasols aloft, on carts attached to bicycles. I have never seen so many bicycles, even in China. I envy too the children splashing in the village ponds, I can't help thinking of Bengal's drought of 1943 and the subsequent terrible famine, one of the worst ever recorded anywhere in the world, in which 3m people died. "Whatever happened to famines?" I ask my guide. "The last one was 17 years ago. Now we have dams and wells everywhere and where we grew one crop a year we now grow three." Bengal has the highest rice production of any state in India.

Everywhere we go, on almost every house and shop, hangs the red flag emblazoned with the hammer and sickle in bright yellow. Next to it I often see a row of Hindu gods or a shrine. I am taken to meet Balaram Khanra, a sharecropper, who grows mainly rice. Back in 1967 he was jailed during the early communist struggle with the feudal landlords. Today he proudly tells me that he is in "peaceful possession" of the land. Before, sharecropping meant giving 75 per cent of his produce to the landlord; now it is reduced to 25 per cent. He shows me around his brick house – a septic tank was installed in 1986, electricity arrived in 1992 and in 1998 he added a black and white television and an electric fan.

In all the villages, infant mortality, the birth rate and illiteracy are falling rapidly (all indices are much better than the Indian average), and yields are increasing. For 20 years now agricultural production has been growing state-wide at well over 4 percent a year. The proportion of West Bengal's population below the poverty line has dropped from 50 per cent in the 1970s to around a third today.

This peasant revolution began in 1967 when the communists first came to power in coalition with other left-wing and centrist parties. There was resistance from the landlords and, independent of the party, a group of students and peasants in Naxalbari began a guerrilla movement, modeled on Mao and, indeed, financially supported from Beijing. The so-called Naxalites were ruthless, burning title deeds and beheading landowners, The communist authorities eventually put down the uprising, but from then on their task was easier – the landlords were now cowed enough to co-operate with the communist government's land reform plans. As Buddhadeb Bhattacharjee, the chief minister of West Bengal, explained to me in his office in the Writers' Building in Calcutta, "We did three things: we took some land away from the landlords, we gave rights to sharecroppers and for farm workers we imposed a minimum wage of 58 rupees (about one euro) a day."

Land reform, he argued, "should not be a question of capitalism or communism. Look at South Korea, Taiwan and Japan – in all of them, land reform was the key that unlocked rapid economic expansion and industrialization." The president of the West Bengal chamber of commerce, Biswadeep Gupta, a big industrialist, agrees with him. "There is now an enormous economic savings surplus in our rural areas. In rural India this state has the highest. This is going to drive growth for investors. Now we are selling things that once were considered unnecessary for living, everything from soap to motorbikes,"

Will Manmohan Singh push for such land reform elsewhere in India?" I asked Somnath Chatterjee, the communist Lok Sabha speaker. "We are giving Singh unconditional support. And we know that he is putting a lot of emphasis on the rural poor. About 700 farmers have committed suicide this year because of indebtedness. There is no alternative to land reform. Of course, it will depend on the political make-up of each state. We don't expect to see it in BJP states. But Congress must make an adjustment to coalition policies."

The communists might have achieved more of their objectives if they had entered the government. Promising to vote with it gives them some influence but not as much as if they had taken the risk of losing some of their identity, and thus votes, in the next state elections. But the bottom line is that if the communists don't give Congress the support it needs to rule effectively, mid-term elections brought on by the fall of the government would let the BJP come roaring back. Indeed, if the communists prove difficult, Congress can always threaten to play its trump card – to call a new election to ask for a stronger mandate. Given Sonia and Manmohan's popularity, they would probably win it.

Judging from what Manmohan told me, he will take steps towards the communists: giving sharecroppers greater security and possibly even the minimum wage for farm labourers. But he won't move to strip titles from big landlords, as they are one of Congress's important constituents. This is similar to the policy advocated by Professor Roy Prosterman of the Rural Development Institute at the University of Seattle, one of the world's greatest authorities on land reform. West Bengal's reform, he tells me, has been a stunning success, but he recognizes the political and financial difficulties of spreading similar legislation to the rest of India. For him the worst problem is the landless, who make up about 11 per cent of rural families. He believes it is possible to give these people "homestead plots," a fraction of a hectare sufficient for a garden, trees and a few animals. "This would require less than one third of 1 per cent of India's arable land, transforming our assumptions about the affordability of land reform."

How far will the communists bend in supporting Congress? Over the last ten years, they have changed from a party of absolutist dogma to one of surprising pragmatism. "We are globalisers now," says Bhattacharjee. He is very critical of the old communist policy of supporting militant unionism, which regularly closed down whole businesses, often violently. "Now we say labour productivity is not just the responsibility of management. The unions must co-operate too." He is determined to woo the multinationals and especially the information technology sector where he is convinced Calcutta can overtake Hyderabad, given its large numbers of well-educated people (bequeathed by the educational institutions of the Raj) and the lowest crime rate of any major city in India. West Bengal's fiscal deficit is large and interest payments on debt the highest in India, but it now has one of the highest rates of growth of the Indian states. Moreover, relations between Muslim and Hindu are harmonious. The BJP does not do well here.

Still, Calcutta has a population of 6m, of whom 1.6m live in slums. If no longer as badly off as described by Dominique LaPierre in his best selling book, *The City of Joy,* their conditions are still wretched. When I visited Calcutta 25 years ago, I thought I had entered the inferno. I will never forget watching one man whose job was to rescue used toilet paper and tear off the unsoiled bits for further use. The gutters were crammed with the homeless.

Today, the number sleeping on the pavements is down to a few thousand. The streets are reasonably clean, yellow taxis have replaced rickshaws and the city exudes economic activity. The communist party swept the board in Calcutta, a city in which they usually struggle. Despite its popularity, it cannot resist the temptation to intimidate opponents. Bhattacharjee still hangs a portrait of Lenin in his office, explaining, "I believe in class. I don't think capitalism is the last chapter of civilisation."

So this is Congress's coalition partner. Like Ravindra Kumar, the editor of the liberal *Statesman* – the one local mouthpiece that is consistently critical of the communist fiefdom – I cannot help wonder if the communists will keep Congress in power for a full five-year term. He blames them for the big stock market crash and says that they should have "explained their position more articulately." After all, only a few days before the election Bhattacharjee had called Singh "the torchbearer and lackey of the World Bank and IMF."

Singh will have to deal with the communists' ambiguities. He told a post-election press conference: "Life is never free from contradictions." He added: "Our friends on the left have a different perception of past economic policies, but they are also great patriots and that patriotism and burning desire to make this century the Indian century is something I see common to all Indians."

There is room for manoeuvre, as Kumar argues. "The fact that Congress has already watered down its privatization policy to please the communists shows that Singh is flexible. But this is not an imperative for economic reform. Reform is about opening up competition, cutting down controls and the Marxists these days won't object to that."

The big question is whether Singh can set India on the path to overtake China in a decade or two. India has a lot going for it that China does not. Apart from its thriving democracy and free press, it has world-class companies, especially in information technology, biotechnology and pharmaceuticals. It has the intellectual capital of its emigrés returning from Silicon Valley. Its banking system has relatively few under-performing assets. Its capital markets operate with greater efficiency than China's. Above all, it has the rule of law. As one western banker said to me, "China progressed so fast because it had no law. But now India will overtake China because it has law."

India has changed profoundly in the last 30 years. The number of poor has been halved. The middle class is as big as the population of "old Europe," and is growing fast.

Two years after my early Sunday morning meeting with the new prime minister my optimistic hopes have been exceeded. The growth rate is now well over 8%, many solid economists see it soon reaching nearer 10%, new extensive anti-poverty programnes have been enacted and, not least, the western world belatedly appears to be waking up to the coming power and prosperity of India.

The Chinese dream is always oversold, observes Chris Patten, the former EU Commissioner for Foreign Affairs, in his most recent book *Not Quite the Diplomat*.

He argues that there is a "mindless China frenzy". Many of the big Western companies who have rushed to invest in China have lost their investments.

Deals are announced but then go sour. According to Joe Studwell, editor of the *China Economic Quarterly* "it is unlikely that a quarter of the $40 billion of deals signed on government-to government trade missions in the mid 1990s ever went ahead." On his first "showbiz" trip to China the US Secretary of Commerce Ron Brown claimed he had netted $6 billion worth of business. The US embassy later said the figure was more like $10 million.

Despite the Chinese proven propensity for linking political concessions with trade deals China represents less than 2% of all Western exports added together. A useful market yes. But not one where threats to abort a deal because of a tough stance on human rights should ever have had the leverage they sometimes have had.

China, since the days in 1793 of the mission of Earl McCartney, emissary of King George III, has kept its distance from the West, preferring to be as "self-contained as a billiard ball", to quote the great historian, Alain Peyrefitte. It was Peyrefitte who argues in *The Collision of Civilizations* that McCartney's decision not to kowtow to the emperor gave the Chinese the impression that their civilization was not respected. They withdrew into their bunkers and have remained for the last two hundred years prickly, ultra sensitive, quick to take offence and too ready to assume the worst of the West's motives.

Thus, among Sinologists, there has developed a strong school of thought that there is only one way of dealing with China – a sort of delayed reversed, kowtow, always leaning over backwards neither to provoke nor to annoy China, even allowing China to rewrite whatever language it is negotiating in. This is combined with projecting the economic growth rates of the Deng Xiaoping era into the far future. But China does not possess the institutional framework (unlike its rival, India) to contain such endeavour. Reasoning of this kind, as the last British governor of Hong Kong, Chris Patten, has written in his provocative book *East and West*, has encouraged China "to think it can become part of the modern world entirely on its own terms. Were that to happen it would make the world a more dangerous and less prosperous place. China remains a classic case of hope over experience, reminiscent of de Gaulle's famous comment about Brazil: 'It has great potential and always will.'"

When will the outside world begin to put China into some sort of perspective? Despite its immense size, a fifth of the world's population, and the longevity of its great civilization, its possession of nuclear weapons and its permanent seat on the Security Council of the United Nations, it is not a budding superpower.

In the 1970s it was Brazil that was going to be the superstar of the decade – and perhaps for evermore. In the 1980s the talk was of Japan. In the 1990s China, Brazil and Japan came unstuck in different ways – Brazil, after decades of being the century's fastest growing economy (along with Taiwan), because it overspent and over-borrowed and, in its massive state and social sectors, chronically under performed; Japan because its quasi-feudal company and ministerial structures protected too well the dross as well as the gold in a system that could never bring itself to embrace capitalist meritocracy in all its parts. Now, as unemployment, inequality and crime rise, the indications are increasing that China might be looked back on as the third big falling star of the latter half of the twentieth century. China perhaps, after all, is not "a miracle about to be performed". In China the veneer of end-of-the-century technology and know-how is eggshell thin.

China's economy today is just one-seventh the size of America's and one-third the size of Japan's, despite its huge population. According to China's own central planners it will take another forty-five years – until mid century – before it will be a modernized, medium-level developed country, say like Brazil or Mexico today. And this assumes a benign political and legal environment in the coming years which, given the reality of China's institutions, is a bold premise.

Unless China can make a smooth transition away from central control by a Communist dictatorship to a sophisticated, multi-layered, defuse and flexible democracy and one in which the rule of law and respect for human rights prevails it will never even achieve this target, much less dominate the century.

Democracy as a concept it not as alien to China as is often assumed.

In late 1912, following the abdication of China's last emperor, the country, led by the founder of modern China, Sun Yat-sen, held an election, albeit one limited to males over twenty-one who paid tax, owned property, or held at least an elementary education. It was considered to be fair and well run. If that election had been followed through and not aborted by the Nationalist Party of General Chiang Kai shek, China today would have been another Japan.

Later, after the Communists came to power in 1949, there was talk once again of democracy. A liberal constitution was enacted. Thousands of overseas Chinese returned, lured by the promise of a free society. In 1954 there were popular elections for local legislatures. Only in the mid 1950s did Mao Zedong assert the full powers of his dictatorship plunging the country, according to Bruce Gitteng in his book, "into a twenty year nightmare that killed between forty and fifty million people". (In a new book *Mao – The Unknown Story* by Jung Chang and Jon Halliday this estimate rises to 70 million.)

In the spring of 1989 large-scale anti-government uprisings spread to over 300 cities. Democracy and human rights were the rallying cries. Until Deng Xiaoping overruled president Zhao Ziyang, who appeared ready to countenance reforms, and sent the tanks in to mow down the students gathered in Beijing's Tiananmen Square, it seemed as if a new era of political reform was about to begin. Ten years later in a remarkable interview on CNN, Bao Tong, the former chief of staff to Zhao Ziyang, who spent several years in prison after the crackdown, said that Zhao had wanted negotiations with the students "based on democratic principles and the use of law".

He went on to say: "I continue to believe that most of the senior leaders did not want to see a crackdown on the students and on academic and company leaders who supported the students and recoiled at the thought of sending in troops". But these senior party people soon lost their jobs and now live in quiet retirement.

"What the public didn't know", continued Bao, "was that Zhao's policy had obtained support of a majority at both the Politburo meetings of 8 May and 10 May." (The Tiananmen Square massacre was on 4 June.) "But Deng tragically overruled Zhao."

If such divisions went right to the top of the Communist Party eighteen years ago, one can be sure that they exist in today's China too. China is being tugged towards democracy and human rights by powerful forces within as well as without. It is also now obvious that the Chinese people themselves care very much about open politics and civil liberties – this is not just a Western concoction or imposition. Where has there been more political struggle? Where have there been more dramatic eruptions of outrage about civil liberties?

Does outside pressure add to or distract from this? Wei Jingsheng who was, until his release at the end of 1997, Amnesty's longest serving political prisoner in China, is very clear about that. His own treatment and conditions in prison, he told me, bore a direct relationship to the amount of fuss made about him. The louder the noise, the better he was treated. Yet even Wei's release had a double edge, or rather a quid pro quo. The Americans in 1997 hatched a deal with Beijing: if he and fellow dissident Wang Dan were released, the Americans – and their European allies – would also withhold their support from moves to condemn China's human rights record at the UN.

Thus, America's latter day turn-around on the UN's annual vote on China's abuse of human rights is of great significance. In early 2000, Washington announced that it would itself introduce a resolution at the UN Human Rights Commission to condemn China for what it said was a deteriorating human rights situation. Trade, the sale of technology, exchanges of experts and other foreign relations will be treated on their own merits, said Washington. Human rights apparently is now going to be treated on its. The two will no longer be mixed, which has meant for the best part of thirty years the West has diluted often beyond taste its efforts on behalf of China's dissidents. As Wei Jingsheng has shrewdly observed: "The Chinese government's concept of human rights has not moved towards the universal standard of human rights. On the contrary, the human rights values of Western politicians have moved closer to those of communist China."

It is Marxist-Leninist communism that holds China back. Discarded in the economic arena, it holds sway in the political. The Confucian heritage is no impediment to democracy, as countries as diverse as Taiwan, Japan and South Korea attest. After all Confucianism stressed that an individual's duty in society was to seek a just or moral outcome. Religious toleration, inherited from

Buddhism and Taoism, which have long been important influences, existed in China before it did in the West.

The Chinese dictatorship justifies itself by pointing to its superior efficiency and vision. Certainly, compared with India, policies can be pushed through with lightening speed. But one of its greatest policy mistakes, the vast $25 billion Three Gorges Dam project, would probably never have happened in a more questioning society.

Democracy is not just a question of more freedom and more human rights. "It excels at allowing capital, ideas and labour to be freely organised and reorganised as technology and entrepreneurship develop and interests change." (Gitteng, *ibid*)

Democracy tends to work in favour of widening education, alleviating poverty, introducing effective regulation and, most important, spreading the rule of law.

China says that it wants to create a legal system that is regarded as fair and predictable by foreign investors and companies, but this is extraordinarily difficult as long as the Communist Party regards the law as one of its principal instruments of control.

It is difficult at the moment to be sure which way the leadership is moving. In his first few years as president Hu Jintao has cracked down on the media, the Internet, religion and all forms of dissent. Yet premier Wen Jiabao, visiting two years' ago Qinghua University in Beijing on the anniversary of China's pro-democracy May 4th movement of 1919, is reported to have said, à la Gorbachev's glasnost, "Our first step should be to open the flow of information. Only then can we enable the public to supervise the government and prevent social instability."

When Jang Zemin was party chief in 2001, one of his top advisors admitted that there existed a "freedom faction" within the Party that believed in initiating democratic reforms. There are avowed liberals in the ruling circle, albeit now retired, like Li Ruihan, Wan Li, Tian Jiyun and Qiao Shi. Most important among the group of young liberals in senior positions is Jiang protégé Zeng Qinghong, appointed to the Politburo in 2002 when Hu became president. He is the author of the Party's moves to embrace pluralism in the 2000s and whose speeches often refer to the need for direct elections at all levels and the introduction of new political parties.

But democracy and human rights in China will not arrive until the Chinese people themselves push. Civil society in China is still weak. Karl Marx explained that the stagnation of imperial China owed much to the lack of a strong bourgeoisie.

There is nothing like the Catholic Church of Poland which was the prime force in catalyzing the overthrow of communism in Eastern Europe. Nor is there anything resembling the old democratic parties of Hungary, or the large dissident intellectual circles of Czechoslovakia.

China does have a revolutionary heritage rooted in its intellectual class, dating back at least to Sun Yat-sen, founder of the post-imperial Chinese republic, but that class still has to find a way to spread their message. The lesson of Tiananmen Square, which becomes clearer with the passing of time, was that the students failed, not so much because of the ruthlessness of Deng's repression, but because they refused to make alliances with other social groups.

During their protest the students linked arms to prevent outsiders joining the demonstrations. Even after 40 years of communism, the old Confucian values rating mental labour above manual remained intact. Not until the final week in May did the students, aware that the army was likely to be brought in, seek support in the factories.

Despite the airs and graces of the students, sections of the working class did mobilize. The official newspaper, *Workers' Daily*, reported that "so-called 'workers organisations' sprouted up everywhere in various disguises".

More surprisingly, entrepreneurial groups also mobilized, able to engage in action without fear of losing jobs and grants. They even bought the students fax machines. They too were given the brush off by the students who, doubtlessly unconsciously, fused Confucian prejudice against business people with communist claptrap on capitalist exploitation.

Taiwan, where democracy has advanced so successfully the last two decades, shows that the Confucian heritage does not have to be a barrier to modern cross-class alliances. But Tianamen Square showed us what a lot of hard work lies ahead to develop China's civil society in a similar way. It has certainly not got to the point where, as Wei Jinsheng, optimistically told me, "every ordinary Chinese now recognizes the need for a complete change in the dictatorship inside China".

The danger today, as the extraordinary economic growth of China continues and with it the rapid growth of a materially-focused bourgeois, is that the cause of democracy, free speech and human rights will not be given the focused energy that is needed to push them along. It is a telling indictment of China's top-heavy system that reform is more talked about by people who hold, or who have held, high positions than the students and young educated professionals themselves.

Nevertheless, important steps forward are in the works. Although technically illegal, direct election of governments in the country's townships are now gathering pace, the consequence of village-level elections initiated at the end of the last century – complete with elected village heads who confront party chiefs on TV and even campaign from the back of trucks fitted with loudspeakers. Democracy is putting down roots.

Similarly, local peoples' Party Congresses are taking off in major urban areas as well as in the provinces. In 2001 the Congress of the north-eastern city of Shenjang rejected the report of the local court, accusing it of corruption. In the city of Wuxi, Congress stripped the local government of its environmental protection powers for its failure to implement them. As Gitteng observes, "The pageantry of democracy created by the Party to legitimize its rule is transforming into democracy itself. Since the Congresses have both the constitutional and the moral high ground, the Party finds it cannot control its own creations."

Still, it is always one step forward and a half step back. After initially tolerating them, the Party clamped down in the late 1990s on nascent opposition groups such as the China Development Union and the China Democracy Party. Activists are still vigorously prosecuted under the State Security Act and the press has been compelled to rein in its freewheeling ways. The Internet is increasingly controlled. Nevertheless, mobile phones with their text messaging are more difficult to control.

Deng Xiaoping once promised that China would be a democracy by 2035. It would be ironic if Deng's timetable is about right and we have to sit and wait for the passion of a new generation to push the democracy battle to completion. Like second-generation middle classes the world over China needs their priorities of political and humanistic concern rather than material to come to the fore. Meanwhile, as China struggles with its paradoxes and dilemmas, India with its secure democracy will pull ahead. The impediments before India – less state interference in licensing, deregulation and liberalization in the economic sector – are much easier for India to solve than it is to bring a nation the size of China to drink at the trough of democracy. Political stability and legal security are India's trump cards in this race between the tortoise and the hare.

Those questions and doubts over economic progress and the evolution of democracy are all very well, say many observers of China, but the fact is there is enough economic growth and astute political leadership to make sure that China does become a great power. Just look at its burgeoning military strength that leaves all other Asian powers in the shadows.

In July 2005 the US Pentagon released a report to Congress on China's military power, arguing that China has been raising its defense budget and modernizing its military.

But this is quite wrong. In recent decades China's relative military power has actually declined. Its military effort peaked in 1971 at the end of the Cold War. From then on until rather recently deep cuts in military expenditure were the order of the day. The People's Liberation Army has been cut from five million to nearer two. As for modernizing, it is procuring new weapons at a far slower rate than the old ones wear out.

Cui Tanka, the director general of the Foreign Ministry's Asian Affairs Department, speaking at a conference in Hong Kong last year, said that although he believes US naval influence is expanding in the crucial sea lane of the Strait of Malacca, he expressed no concern about it. He hoped that China, South Korea and Japan could work together to ensure the flow of energy to North East Asia.

For many decades China's air force was the world's largest. But today it has shrunk and more than a thousand (nearly half) of its combat aircraft are types long considered obsolete by other major air forces. Even Taiwan outnumbers China two to one in fourth generation fighters. As for China's navy, it is remarkably small.

The press, together with the Pentagon, often highlight China's missile threat to Taiwan, reporting that it now has 750 missiles pointing at the offshore island. But it has so few launchers it could only launch 100 at a time. Moreover, they are relatively inaccurate, easy to intercept and only a threat to cities not to military targets. Taiwan, with its superior attack aircraft, could easily win an air war, even if some small parts of its major cities were destroyed by a missile attack.

China would have to divert vast sums from economic development to defense if it wanted to begin to catch up with the US. And the US would see it coming, giving it ample time to match it. Neither is going to happen. China is increasingly tied to the American economy- two fifths of its exports go to the US. Its vast overhang of savings are invested in the US bond market. As for Taiwan, China is Taiwan's leading trade partner and the recipient of most of the rich island's foreign investment and high tech expertise. It would not make sense to China's present leadership to push for a rapid increase in defense spending when the need is not apparent, the opportunities for military play so few and far between and the calls on government spending for both development purposes so intense, not to mention its economic dependence on Taiwan. It is most unlikely that a country that is embarking on a programme to add 10,000 kilometers of railway passenger lines, including 2,000 kilometers capable of taking the 300 kilometers per hour trains it has recently ordered from Germany, is much interested in the unsettling and economic debilitating prospects of war. It should come as no surprise that Wang Tisi, the Director of the Institute of International Strategic Studies at the Central Party School, Beijing, should write recently in *Foreign Affairs*, " It would be foolhardy for Beijing to challenge directly the international order and the institutions favored by the Western world – and, indeed, such a challenge is unlikely. Deng Xiaoping's prediction that 'things will be all right when Sino-US relations eventually improve' was a cool judgment based on China's long-term interests."

Beware of extrapolation, a British Chancellor of the Exchequer once remarked: it can make you go blind. There are many signs that China is not going to continue growing at its present rate of knots. Indeed, many observers are doubtful about the official GDP statistics. Jim Walker, an economist with CLSA, a brokerage firm in Hong Kong, recently concluded that the official GDP statistics were a "fantasy world". Most outside experts see a much greater degree of volatility than the official statistics suggest. Provincial statistics are notoriously unreliable, as local officials are known to inflate them to avoid being punished for poor management of the economy. The central statistical office calculates GDP through counting increases in value-added production even though much of its statistical input comes from state-owned enterprises which provide poor data. Walker routinely deducts 2% from official Chinese growth statistics.

Even if we use Chinese statistics, the overall rate of progress between 1978 and 2003 is not overwhelming. In that period China's per capita GDP grew at a compound rate of 6.1%. This gives a total increase of 337% over a quarter of a century. Compare this with Japan's which increased by 490% between 1950 and 1973. Both South Korea and Taiwan have done even better – the former with 7.6% compound growth a year between 1962 and 1990 and Taiwan with 6.3% between 1958 and 1990, the years when they were bursting through the industrialization sound barrier.

The statistics we do have show up some near insuperable problems. One is that 40% of China's bank loans are considered "bad", a gigantic missallocation of capital. Japan, South Korea and India have never had this problem. Another is that China could grow old before it grows rich. Not very long ago China was one of the world's most youthful countries. But the one-child policy has had an enormous impact. As early as 2015 China's working age population will begin to fall. By 2040, just a decade before China hopes to be a middle-income country, it will have 100 million citizens over 80. That is more than the current worldwide total.

In a world where radical innovation comes from young people, China will be far "older" than both the UK and the US, and far "older" than India. Arnoud de Meyer, deputy dean of Insead, the European business school, author of a recent study of Asian innovation, writes that in relation to its huge development needs China may already have too little skilled manpower. McKinsey, the management consultancy, reports that only 10% of China's graduating engineers are good enough to work for foreign companies. It is not surprising that China's software industry lags behind India's because of its fragmented structure and poor management.

India is far ahead in this regard. India has "an enviable pool of high quality, talented professionals" and the largest population of English speakers outside the US, reports a study by Mercer Human Resource Consulting. Moreover, wages among professionals are much lower in India than China.

Living costs in Chinese cities are much higher than in India's. It is not surprising that foreign direct investment is now falling in China, albeit from very high levels (and at the same time capital flight is on a fast rise), while India's is increasing and is likely to increase further once the constraints on foreign investment are further loosened. If one looks at the non-ethnic Chinese component of foreign investment China does less well than booming Brazil.

US companies earned something over $8 billion from their business and investments in China in 2003. But they earned around $7 billion from Australia, a market of only 19 million people and over $9 billion from Taiwan and South Korea with a combined population of 70 million. From Mexico, with approximately the same population, they earned well over $14 billion. Moreover, American companies which have made big money from China are those like Wal-Mart, the retailer. They are the ones who buy from it rather than the ones who invest in it.

Within China inequalities, in particular rural-urban, have been increasing rapidly, whilst in India they appear to be closing. With massive layoffs in the rust-belt areas, arbitrary local levies on farmers, pervasive corruption and toxic industrial dumping, many inhabitants of the countryside have become militantly agitated. Chinese police records measure over the last decade a sevenfold increase in the number of incidents of social unrest. In the past decade the incidence of riots, demonstrations and strikes has increased by about 60% a year.

India has its fair share of unrest but regular ballots act as a safety valve that gives the country stability and balance. China's leaders are obviously very concerned about rural unrest and new laws aim to tackle the issue of insecure tenure of the land.

Soon farmers will be given 30-year rights over their land, providing them with a longer time horizon for investment. This will have the benefit of reducing China's astronomical savings rate which leads to an overvalued currency.

In 1800 China accounted for 33% of world manufacturing output, far greater than Europe's 28% and America's 0.8%. Today China makes around 12% of world GNP. According to the UN Human Development Index China is 107<sup>th</sup> in the world pecking order, alongside Albania and Namibia. Shanghai and Beijing may have the same average income levels as Greece or Singapore but vast areas of China are like Haiti at worst and Bolivia at best.

Guy de Jonquieres, *The Financial Times* expert on China, signed off a recent column wondering "whether China's future is as a high-tech powerhouse in its own right or as the world's biggest branch-plant economy." It is "an open question", he concluded. No observer that I know of expresses this kind of doubt about India's place in the century.

It is not going to be China's century. Indeed no country will dominate it. India certainly will be one of the big six, along with the US, the EU, Japan, and probably Brazil and Russia. China will be lucky if it finds itself in seventh place.

# Index

# The Raoul Wallenberg Institute Human Rights Library

1.  Göran Melander (ed.): The Raoul Wallenberg Institute Compilation of Human Rights Instruments
    ISBN 0 79233 646 1
2.  U. Oji Umozurike: The African Charter on Human and Peoples' Rights
    ISBN 90 41 10291 4
3.  Bertrand G. Ramcharan (ed.): The Principle of Legality in International Human Rights Institutions; Selected Legal Opinions
    ISBN 90 41 10299 X
4.  Zelim Skurbaty: As If Peoples Mattered; Critical Appraisal of 'Peoples' and 'Minorities' from the International Human Rights Perspective and Beyond
    ISBN 90 41 11342 8
5.  Gudmundur Alfredsson and Rolf Ring (d.): The Inspection Panel of the World Bank, A Different Complaints Procedure
    ISBN 90 41 11390 8
6.  Gregor Noll (ed.): Negotiating Asylum; The EU Acquis, Extraterritorial Protection and the Common Market of Deflection
    ISBN 90 41 11431 9
7.  Gudmundur Alfredsson, Jonas Grimheden, Bertrand G. Ramcharan and Alfred de Zayas (eds.): International Human Rights Monitoring Mechanisms; Essays in Honour of Jakob Th. Möller
    ISBN 90 41 11445 9
8.  Gudmundur Alfredsson and Peter Macalister-Smith (eds.): The Land Beyond; Collected Essays on Refugee Law and Policy
    ISBN 90 41 11493 9
9.  Hans-Otto Sano, Gudmundur Alfredsson and Robin Clapp (eds.): Human Rights and Good Governance; Building Bridges
    ISBN 90 41 11776 8
10. Gudmundur Alfredsson and Maria Stavropoulou (eds.): Justice Pending: Indigenous Peoples and Other Good Causes; Essays in Honour of Erica-Irene A. Daes
    ISBN 90 41 11876 4
11. Göran Bexell and Dan-Erik Andersson (eds.): Universal Ethics; Perspectives and Proposals from Scandinavian Scholars
    ISBN 90 41 11933 7
12. Hans Göran Franck, Revised and edited by William Schabas: The Barbaric Punishment; Abolishing the Death Penalty
    ISBN 90 41 12151 X
13. Radu Mares (ed.): Business and Human Rights; A Compilation of Documents
    ISBN 90 04 13656 8
14. Manfred Nowak: Introduction to the International Human Rights Regime
    ISBN 90 04 13658 4 (Hb)
    ISBN 90 04 13672 X (Pb)

15. Göran Melander, Gudmundur Alfredsson and Leif Holmström (eds.): The Raoul Wallenberg Institute Compilation of Human Rights Instruments; Second Revised Edition
    ISBN 90 04 13857 9
16. Gregor Noll (ed.): Proof, Evidentiary Assessment and Credibility in Asylum Procedures
    ISBN 90 04 14065 4
17. Ineta Ziemele (ed.): Reservations to Human Rights Treaties and the Vienna Convention Regime; Conflict, Harmony or Reconciliation
    ISBN 90 04 14064 6
18. Nisuke Ando (ed.), on behalf of the Committee: Towards Implementing Universal Human Rights; Festschrift for the Twenty-Fifth Anniversary of the Human Rights Committee
    ISBN 90 04 14078 6
19. Zelim A. Skurbaty (ed.): Beyond a One-Dimensional State: An Emerging Right to Autonomy?
    ISBN 90 04 14204 5
20. Joshua Castellino and Niamh Walsh (eds.): International Law and Indigenous Peoples
    ISBN 90 04 14336 X
21. Herdis Thorgeirsdóttir: Journalism worthy of the Name Freedom within the Press under Article 10 of the European Convention on Human Rights
    ISBN 90 04 14528 1
22. Bertrand G.Ramcharan (ed.): Judicial Protection of Economic, Social and Cultural Rights: Cases and Materials
    ISBN 90 04 14562 1
23. Gro Nystuen: Achieving Peace or Protecting Human Rights? Conflicts between Norms Regarding Ethnic Discrimination in the Dayton Peace Agreement
    ISBN 90 04 14652 0
24. Maria Deanna Santos: Human Rights and Migrant Domestic Work – A Comparative Analysis of the Socio-Legal Status of Filipina Migrant Domestic Workers in Canada and Hong Kong
    ISBN 90 04 14527 3
25. Ragnhildur Helgadóttir: The Influence of American Theories of Judicial Review on Nordic Constitutional Law
    ISBN 90 04 15002 1
26. Jonas Grimheden and Rolf Ring (eds.): Human Rights Law: From Dissemination to Application Essays in Honour of Göran Melander
    ISBN 90 04 15181 8
27. Brian Burdekin, assisted by Jason Naum: National Human Rights Institutions in the Asia-Pacific Region
    ISBN 978 90 04 15336 3
28. Jonathan Power: Conundrums of Humanity: The Quest for Global Justice
    ISBN 978 9004 15513 8